W9-AUE-014

MIKE BLOOMBERG

MIKE BLOOMBERG

MONEY, POWER, POLITICS

JOYCE PURNICK

PUBLICAFFAIRS
New York

Copyright © 2009 by Joyce Purnick

Published in the United States by PublicAffairs™,
a member of the Perseus Books Group.
All rights reserved.
Printed in the United States of America.

No part of this book may be reproduced in any manner whatsoever without written permission except in the case of brief quotations embodied in critical articles and reviews. For information, address PublicAffairs, 250 West 57th Street, Suite 1321, New York, NY 10107.

PublicAffairs books are available at special discounts for bulk purchases in the U.S. by corporations, institutions, and other organizations. For more information, please contact the Special Markets Department at the Perseus Books Group, 2300 Chestnut Street, Suite 200, Philadelphia, PA 19103, call (800) 810-4145, ext. 5000, or e-mail special.markets@perseusbooks.com.

Library of Congress Cataloging-in-Publication Data
Purnick, Joyce.
Mike Bloomberg / Joyce Purnick.
p. cm.
Includes index.
ISBN 978-1-58648-577-1 (hardcover)
1. Bloomberg, Michael. 2. Businesspeople—United States—Biography.
3. Mayors—United States—Biography. I. Title.
HC102.5.B56P87 2009
974.7'1044092—dc22
[B]
2009023604

Editorial production by *Marra*thon Production Services, www.marrathon.net
DESIGN BY JANE RAESE
Text set in 12.5 point Bembo

FIRST EDITION
2 4 6 8 10 9 7 5 3 1

TO MAX

MY LOVE AND MY LIFE

CONTENTS

ONE Never Enough 1

TWO Escape from Medford 7

THREE First Millions 25

FOUR Terminal Man 39

FIVE Crashing the A-list 55

SIX Enter the High Roller 73

SEVEN Tragedy Trumps Politics 91

EIGHT Money, Money on the Wall 105

NINE Managing City Hall 121

TEN Olympian Dreams 137

ELEVEN Yes for Mayor, Not for Dinner 153

TWELVE See Mike Not Run 163

THIRTEEN Finding Act III 175

FOURTEEN Money, Money from City Hall 191

FIFTEEN Footprints 203

SIXTEEN Many a Difference 219

Acknowledgments 229

A Note about Attribution 233

Index 235

CHAPTER 1

NEVER ENOUGH

THE FIRST TIME I met Mike Bloomberg was in the late 1990s at a dinner party in his Manhattan town house. It was a typical New York gathering of the moneyed and the prominent, thrown together for an evening of polite conversation that goes in one ear and out the other.

I recall that Dan Rather was there, and Peter Jennings, and that the five-story home was an overdone tribute to marble, formal British furniture and attention-grabbing works of art.

Bloomberg himself barely made an impression. He sat at the head of the table and said little, looking bored. Later, as rumors grew that he wanted to run for mayor, I was astonished—and I was not the only one. *That* guy, the dull, quiet one whose home looks like a museum?

I'd seen mayors come and go and Bloomberg did not fit the mold any which way. The slight, self-made billionaire was the opposite of the boisterous characters New Yorkers enjoy. He had created an improbably successful company, a financial information giant that grew from a sophisticated computer terminal he developed. Few beyond Wall Street and the City of London understood much about that or knew that Bloomberg was a generous philanthropist, but the elaborate ad campaign he could bankroll would fill in the blanks. Recognition wasn't the problem. The problem was, it sure seemed, Mike Bloomberg.

He didn't have the experience or the temperament, he didn't know much about the city, and the city knew less about him. Success in business was supposed to make him a good mayor?

He was "trying to buy City Hall like it's a cup of coffee," growled Jimmy Breslin. He was spending "tens of millions of dollars of his own money to lip-sync the lyrics of politics," wrote Bob Herbert. By my reckoning, he was a rich guy on an ego trip, who should not have gotten anywhere near City Hall, no matter how many millions of his own dollars he spent in pursuit of victory.

After he won in a fluke, many New Yorkers remained skeptical, figuring he would be a caretaker mayor, serving one four-year term and moving on out. New York is hard enough for a seasoned politician to run, let alone a billionaire stiff. Bloomberg was nothing like one of those naturally expansive rich men like Nelson Rockefeller or the open, good-humored Warren Buffet.

He couldn't make a speech, couldn't—or wouldn't—answer a question persuasively and projected a solemnity that approached sourness. A small, graying man with a few too many slightly bucked teeth that discouraged broad smiles, he looked like the businessman he was in his uniforms of expensive dark suits and loafers.

He did not pretend to have patience for small talk or even a modicum of introspection. He did not feel your pain and would not admit to any of his own. Curt, profane, cranky and willful, Bloomberg said and did what he wanted, hated to admit error and was insistently private to the point of paranoia.

Even after his many well-compensated handlers burnished a vanity version of the Bloomberg story, selling it in campaign literature and ads that filled TV screens like electronic wallpaper, New Yorkers did not get to know Bloomberg the way they got to know his predecessors.

That never fully changed. Years into his mayoralty, otherwise well-informed people who learned I was writing his biography revealed a basic ignorance about him, asking whether he inherited his wealth, wondering how many times he was married, if he had any children and—despite nasal evidence to the contrary—if he was a native New Yorker.

A public that dines out on stories about its political celebrities—about Barack Obama's childhood, Bill Clinton's appetites, Joe Biden's gaffes—was starved by Mike Bloomberg. Diffidence is not supposed to succeed with a public that wants politicians to feel its pain. Neither is aloof elitism.

Yet the diffident, elite Bloomberg would become one of the most effective mayors in the city's history, holding on to high approval ratings for an unusually long time in punishing New York, earning the public's respect if not its warmth.

It is the paradox of Michael Bloomberg that his great power and wealth were never matched by the power of his personality. But, most notably in his early, most difficult days as mayor, he succeeded anyway in a tough political environment, guiding the city through both bad economic times and good ones.

In more than thirty years of covering New York, I certainly

had never encountered a leader like Bloomberg, the city's first, and no doubt last, prideful plutocrat.

Like all hugely successful people, he was lucky as well as smart. His mayoralty benefited greatly from the national prosperity that fueled the city's recovery from the terrorist attacks of 9/11. But more than timing worked for Bloomberg; Bloomberg worked for Bloomberg.

In his first term, he led the city out of recession, smoothly managing the city's finances and services, keeping the central promise of his self-financed campaign to steer clear of influence peddlers and favor-seekers.

Despite his bland persona, Bloomberg pursued bold projects full of political risk. He shook up the city's dysfunctional school system, tried to attack traffic gridlock, broadened a city ban on smoking, revived the public hospitals. He doggedly challenged dealers of illegal guns, kept crime rates down, and becalmed race relations despite aggressive police strategies that offended minority communities and civil libertarians.

And in every rundown corner of the city he aggressively cleared the way for renovation and real estate development, to the chagrin of serious city planners and devotees of city landmarks, to the delight of builders, construction unions and pragmatists who share his preference for imperfect development over neglect.

More than once, Bloomberg's ambitions outran his political skills and led to highly visible defeats. He failed to lure the Olympics to New York or build a grand stadium in a dilapidated stretch of Manhattan. He lost a campaign to force private cars out of midtown, and while his overhaul of the city schools is in itself an achievement, whether it will produce a better-educated generation is a matter of protracted debate.

He let politics seduce him, indulging a Walter Mitty dream

of running for president of the United States, and when that pursuit collapsed, he turned crudely political back home. Ignoring the advice of his staff and offending some of his warmest supporters, he reversed himself on a law he had supported and rammed the changed statute through the city's weak legislature—all so he could stay in office for a third term.

Redefining himself once again with his blatant political grab, he would write yet another chapter in the improbable life of Mike Bloomberg, a purely American story of drive and wealth, celebrity, self-discipline and restless ego.

By 2007, he was considered to be the richest man in New York, the founder and owner of a communications behemoth that plastered his name across the globe. He was one of the most generous philanthropists in the country. He owned many luxury homes, flew wherever and whenever he wanted in his own private jets, enjoyed the companionship of a handsome woman.

Notwithstanding his suddenly ruthless politicking, he remained unusually popular for an incumbent mayor. New Yorkers, a pragmatic people, tolerated his churlish manner and naked ambition for what they got in exchange: an honest, independent broker with common sense who seemed to think nothing was impossible. If he didn't mess it up, he could join the very small club of New York City's best mayors.

But Bloomberg's successes seemed unable to gratify an insatiable appetite for achievement and acclaim. He was leading a life of triumph but was as restless as ever. He was world renowned, yet not much better understood than he had been that night years earlier when prominent New Yorkers, invited to dine at his table, came away shaking their heads that this enigmatic man would even dream of harboring such grand plans.

They couldn't know that Bloomberg and grand plans were synonymous. Growing up restless in a small suburban city that could not contain him, he set the pattern early. He wanted more and better. He always would. If his capacity for soul-searching matched his drive—it does not, nowhere near—even Mike Bloomberg would have to admit that when he got what he craved, he wanted more. It was never enough.

CHAPTER 2

ESCAPE FROM MEDFORD

THE BOY WAS AS IMPATIENT as the man he would become.

Mike Bloomberg grew up in Medford, Massachusetts, a suburban city not far from Boston, and that was part of the problem—or maybe part of the solution. Medford was quiet and dull and Mike was bored. The place could not contain him. He wanted up and out and since that was not about to happen for a while, he turned into a mini-maverick, a restless loner.

He was not a great athlete. He was not a great student. But he was willful, serious and competitive in his own way, reaching the lofty rank of Eagle Scout even before he was old enough to qualify, planning his escape from his drab suburban town as soon as possible, confident in his self-assigned role as a contrarian who followed his own agenda.

"He could do everything from his point of view, you know?" his mother recalled, smiling at the thought when she was ninety-eight years old. Sharp of memory and gracious in manner as she sat in the living room of the modest New England home where she and her husband had raised two children, Charlotte Bloomberg evoked Mike's childhood as at once unremarkable and distinctive.

She described a rambunctious boy who trailed dirt into the house despite her constant warnings, scared his sister with snakes, impressed friends with the ham radio set in his room and acted out at school—"just a regular kid."

If there was one trait that stood out in Mike's childhood, foreshadowing the adult he would become, it was his stubborn insistence on taking charge. "Anything that came along, he wanted to do it!" Mrs. Bloomberg said. "He wanted to be the boss of whatever we were working on. He wanted to run everything."

There just wasn't all that much to run in his quiet hometown with its manicured streets, modest homes and squares of grass flanking parallel driveways.

Medford was a mostly Irish and Italian blue-collar city not too far from Boston, but an isolating hour away in the postwar years, before the interstate.

"It was not a bad place, but a place you want to leave, to escape from," recalled the author Paul Theroux, a Medford native and casual Bloomberg friend. "I thought it would be death to stay there, that I would just be swallowed up. It was all right to grow up there, but to stay there? Fatal."

Stable thanks to its major tenant, Tufts University, Medford boasted of an energetic past and its share of homegrown celebrities, of a thriving tradition of ship building and rum production, of playing a cameo role in the American Revolution. Fannie Farmer and Amelia Earhart had lived there. The destructive gypsy moth was mistakenly bred and released there. "Jingle

Bells" was written there. History had not exactly passed Medford by, but it had not lingered long.

By the time the Bloombergs moved in, Medford was an uninspiring suburban city with a conventional Main Street that featured Brigham's Ice Cream Parlor, a funeral home, an armory, a gracious library and two movie theaters, each with a single screen.

The town's enduring sentiment was patriotism. As all Medford schoolchildren learned before they could read, Paul Revere famously galloped through the town's High Street in 1775, warning of the coming British. To this day, Mike Bloomberg can accurately recite Longfellow's "Midnight Ride of Paul Revere" from beginning to end.

Nice. Not riveting. By the time he was in high school, he knew he wanted out. "Michael knew he always wanted to be in New York, not even Boston. New York was the place to be," recalls a high school girlfriend, Dorothy Sherman Berman. "I remember him telling me that it was very important to be successful, that he was going to be successful because once you had a lot of money you could do things to improve the world. I never forgot that."

She never quite figured out where her boyfriend's drive came from, but she offers the same guess as do others who knew the Bloombergs. They cite his strong mother, a resolute, college-educated woman who focused her energies and aspirations on her firstborn, her son. The adult Mike Bloomberg frequently mentions his mother, invoking her advice, her observations, her wisdom. Rarely does he mention his father, a good man and loyal company accountant whose diligence brought him little reward.

Charlotte and William Bloomberg bought their home on Ronaele Road ("Eleanor spelled backwards," Mrs. Bloomberg once noted) in the optimistic year of 1945, when the war was ending and a middle-class couple could afford a simple house in the country's growing suburban towns and cities.

William Bloomberg, son of Russian immigrants, was born and reared in nearby Chelsea, Massachusetts, where his father taught Hebrew; Charlotte Rubens's father, born in present-day Belarus, emigrated to England before coming with his family to New Jersey. Her mother, a child of immigrants from Lithuania, was born on Mott Street in lower Manhattan.

Charlotte—Lottie to her family—grew up in West Hoboken, Woodcliff and Jersey City, where her parents ran a wholesale grocery business. A night student at New York University, she worked during the day and earned a business degree in 1929 and got herself a job, unusual for women of that era.

Lottie worked as assistant auditor in the New York office of the National Dairy (later Breakstone's), where she was soon introduced by her boss to another employee, William Bloomberg, her future husband. The couple married and moved to Boston, living first in Allston, where Mike was born. They moved when he was two to Brookline, renting a two-family home until their landlord sold the house from under them. It was then that they decided to buy their own home in Medford, close to the dairy's offices in Somerville, where William Bloomberg kept the books.

The move, when Mike was three and his sister, Marjorie, one, was logical, but not easy. Parts of Medford were still restricted: no Jews were allowed, at least not overtly.

"My uncle wouldn't dare sell to a Jew," says a childhood friend of Mike, Thomas Buckley, about his relative, the realtor who sold the stone-and-clapboard houses in the newly built community that attracted the Bloombergs. "If he did, he would have been out of business. He knew they were buying it. He just didn't say anything."

No Jews lived in the immediate neighborhood, very few anywhere in Medford. But everyone assumed that would change, including the Bloombergs, who resolved not to let residual anti-Semitism block their path. "They weren't very happy," Mrs. Bloomberg said of some neighbors. "Our lawyer, George McLaughlin, who was Irish, bought the house and sold it to us. But nobody on the street was unpleasant to us." And so they moved into the two-story, three-bedroom house—the slightly more expensive model because it came with a finished attic and basement.

The indirect purchase became family legend, a reminder to the Bloombergs that merely to buy their own home, they'd had to devise a strategy.

"It was a significant part of the family lore, it happened, everybody was clear that it happened," said the mayor's sister, Marjorie Bloomberg Tiven. "Medford was not a Jewish city. Was it the same as growing up in a majority Jewish community? It couldn't possibly have been. It was just a fact of life. There were not many Jews. You were aware of it."

Few of Mike's Jewish classmates say they felt hostility. It was more a matter of self-consciousness about their minority status. Only about 25 of his 683 high school classmates were Jews, and they tended to stick together, by choice. "There was still some of the old stuff there, the old separation," said the Reverend Richard Black, a retired Methodist minister who knew Bloomberg at Medford High. "The Jewish kids tended to hang together, mostly."

Not, however, Mike Bloomberg. Those who remember him—and some do not—say he was there, but not there. Margie Glou, a classmate in junior and senior high, recalls him as "very bright, but not in our crowd. I don't know who he was friendly with, who he hung out with, but it wasn't us. We never felt any anti-Semitism, but we were really a minority, and we just all stayed together. I don't know where he was. He obviously did his own thing."

Michael Stadlen, another member of Medford High's class of 1960, had a similar memory of the future mogul. "He was almost a non-person," he recalled. "He was in his own little world, on his own trip."

Bloomberg is quick to confess that he was antsy—bored by his unchallenging schools and by Medford itself. Fact is, he was something of a nerd with a rebellious streak. While other kids were playuing football or grinding away at their studies, Bloomberg was off on his own earning merit badges, building a ham radio set in his room, and dragging his friend Tom Buckley to Boston with him whenever he could get away.

"He was a science nut, went to the science museum, was into wild animals, electrical things," recalls Buckley. "He rode horses, I remember—there was a trail behind the house."

Bloomberg describes a standard childhood for the era. "We were like everyone else in the neighborhood, you know? We had one car, the women didn't work, the men did, you went to public schools, it was blue collar."

His Judaism was a non-issue for him. "I never experienced any anti-Semitism. In the context that you would ask about, did you feel discriminated against, did you feel like you couldn't do anything or something because—well no, I never felt that."

Didn't he feel himself a member of a minority group, somewhat apart from the majority? "Absolutely not, absolutely not," he said with undisguised impatience. "I mean, you're a girl, I'm a boy, do I feel there's a difference? Yeah, okay, so what?"

Family life was comfortable but frugal. Vacations were family visits to the Jersey shore, to visit Mrs. Bloomberg's sister and to swim at her beach club. Pennies were neither pinched nor wasted.

Once, his father invited one of his business associates visiting from New York to join the family for a home-cooked meal. "My mother served lamb chops, which we didn't have that often. And he said, 'Oh, I can't eat this, it's Friday night.' He was Catholic. And I remember thinking, this son of a bitch!" Lamb chops were expensive. "God would have said eat the lamb chops. I think my mother opened a can of tuna fish or something."

The billionaire bristled when asked if money per se was ever an issue when he was growing up. "It's funny you mention it. Why would you do that?"

Life in the Bloomberg home was Norman Rockwell with a Jewish twist: Mrs. Bloomberg kept a kosher kitchen. Every spring the family took the blue glass dishes out of basement storage for Passover. Every night the family ate together and the kids would clean up. Mrs. Bloomberg bent the rules now and again. She kept one knife, one fork and one glass plate separate, for her rebellious son to use with the takeout Chinese food he craved when he got a little older.

"Let me tell you about my mother," her son said. "I'd go up the street to Johnny Corrado's house, and I'd eat dinner there every once in a while. Their silverware was always laid out on the sideboard, but when you'd eat, they'd have stainless steel. And I'll never forget this, I asked my mother—she was a smart woman—I said, 'Why do we use the silver and not have the stainless steel?' thinking maybe I was deprived of something. And she said, 'Because every family has a different idea of who is important. They use their silver for their guests, and that's who they think is important. I think that the family is important, and we should be using it.' So we never had stainless."

Charlotte and William Bloomberg encouraged their son without browbeating him, though they certainly could have. He nearly failed French and, his sister relates, bewildered his parents when he took two math courses one year and drew an A in one, a D in another. Turns out that on one final exam he did all the work in his head, so the teacher thought he'd cheated. His parents did demand an explanation for that one but, "They didn't push in the sense of overbearing parents," says Bloomberg. "We were a normal adjusted family, not all this craziness of today, of you have to get into Harvard, Yale or Princeton."

Both of her children describe Charlotte Bloomberg as a quiet, determined woman, above all unsentimental. "None of the stereotypes of Jewish mothers, no Yiddishkeit," said Marjorie Bloomberg Tiven.

Practical and organized, Charlotte Bloomberg made a big chart for her son to take to college and hang in his dorm-room closet. It listed which shirt to wear with which tie and pants.

Even at age ninety-eight, the pragmatic Mrs. Bloomberg did not let maternal pride cloud her judgment about her son. When he was thinking of running for president, she confessed to concern about his chances. "In some ways I would not like to see it. In some ways I think would be a wonderful thing, it would be great. But I rather doubt that it is going to happen. I don't think this country is ready for a Jewish president. In the big cities there would be no problem because you have Jewish populations. But you get out in the middle of country, where they have very few Jewish people, I'm afraid that is where you would see a lot of anti-Semitism."

It fell to Charlotte Bloomberg to keep the restless young Mike in line. "His father thought that Michael was the most wonderful person on earth and anything he did was okay." William Bloomberg doted on his son, and fretted about him.

Mrs. Bloomberg once recalled that her husband worried when his son took the car and stayed out late. "I remember lying in bed around midnight, and then you could hear when he drove in the garage, you could hear a certain noise. I would say, 'All right, he is home.' His father wouldn't go to sleep until Michael was home."

Charlotte Bloomberg became the disciplinarian. "I was a strict mother. I had to be."

There was, for instance, the matter of Mike's Hebrew training. The small but growing Jewish community of Medford established a shul in an old Victorian house on Water Street, and Mike took instruction there, but not after Mrs. Bloomberg found him horsing around there with friends. She arranged a transfer to a larger, more established synagogue forty-five minutes away, in Brookline, where Mike would benefit from more structure.

Mike's paternal grandfather did not approve because the Brookline temple, Ohabei Shalom, practiced reform Judaism. But Mrs. Bloomberg told friends she would not send her son to a place that could not control him, and that was that.

The discipline took. The Jewishness did not. Bloomberg never changed his name, never denied his heritage, but his religion found no place in his family or romantic life.

Serious and unathletic as a kid, Mike Bloomberg inherited his mother's countenance and her reserve.

"I think I'm much more like my mother," he said. "My father in many senses was the excitable one, but do I remember him ranting and raving or jumping up and down and cheering? No. My mother was much more reserved." Bloomberg says his younger daughter, Georgina, is a lot like he is—self-contained, reluctant to confide in anyone. She inherited those traits from him and he, Bloomberg is certain, got them from his mother.

"Charlotte is independent and strong, not at all neurotic; she always knows where she is going," says Ruth Mofenson Dimond, a friend of Mrs. Bloomberg's. "She is very caring, but cut and dried and matter-of-fact."

The day he got accepted by Harvard's Business School, Mike called his mother thinking she would be pleased. "'Don't let it go to your head,'" he quotes her. "That's how she reacts to everything."

By example, both parents taught their children to persevere in the face of adversity, to find a way around barriers, as they had when they decided to settle in a restricted community. Move on, they counseled, get over it.

"'Get over it'—omigod, is that Michael!" says Dorothy Sherman Berman, his high school girlfriend. Michael used to share his "ideal of womanhood" with her. That perfect woman was pregnant and riding a camel somewhere in Asia when her time came. She dismounted the camel, gave birth and then, as Michael described the imagined scene to Dotty, "wrapped up the baby and kept on going."

The sentiment, if not the anecdote, was learned at home. "My mother and my father both, you know, the term would be, 'suck it up and just get on with it'; 'don't let bad things that happen to you stop you'; 'you're in control of your life,'" recalls Bloomberg. That advice is one of his sharpest childhood memories.

William and Charlotte Bloomberg may have had a special reason to teach their children perseverance. State records show that a Bloomberg male was stillborn in Boston in 1944, the year of Marjorie's birth. The details of the records are sealed to all but immediate family. It is possible that loss was another Boston woman's, also named Bloomberg, but it was probably Marjorie's twin, a brother she and Mike Bloomberg never knew.

When I asked Bloomberg about it, he look startled. He had never heard the story. He said he wanted to think about how to handle the surprising news, wondered if it was better left alone or if he should raise it with his mother.

"Should I ask her?"

"If you want to know," I said.

The mayor wasn't sure: "Why would I care?"

If Bloomberg had a deeper reaction, he was, typically, not going to show it. More likely, unsentimental and always looking ahead, he truly did not see why he should pry into the details of a sadness his parents might have experienced so many years ago. If they had lost a child, they had clearly followed their own counsel and put it behind them, so he would, too. He never raised the matter with me again.

Bloomberg not only takes pride in fortitude but actively preaches it. He once described his approach, as mayor, to telling family survivors about the deaths of firefighters, police officers and rescue workers. "The doctors don't tell them the truth; the police officials say your son or daughter or husband 'is in the hospital.' I tell them, 'He died.' How else are you going to get over it and move on with your life?"

He continued to offer this advice even after offending survivors of 9/11. He passed it on to his daughter, Georgina, who, talking about her father one day, repeated the mantra without prompting, as if she had memorized a private script: "One of the most important lessons I learned from my father, when things happen to you that are bad, when people put you down or tell you you can't do something, you rise up stronger and you fight—you don't let it get to you."

Bloomberg's disciplined tenet threads through every phase and facet of his life, personal and professional. When he lost his job he founded a company. When his marriage broke up he became a tireless figure on the New York social scene. When he couldn't build one sports stadium, he built another. When he realized he could not run for president, he barreled his way into running for another term as mayor. Every setback became a platform for some new initiative, a springboard to a new adventure.

Bloomberg is by nature a problem solver, a puzzle decoder, who sees his journey through life as a passage through a maze. He hits one wall, he backs off and tries another route and then another until he gets where he wants to go and if he cannot, he goes somewhere else. That takes self-control, coolness, a refusal to indulge emotions or denounce the obstacles, and no vindictiveness or grudge-holding, either: they could block a necessary path.

The Bloomberg doctrine requires some tunnel vision and some callousness, too, because to get where he's going—to serve the greater good, as he would put it—he won't necessarily stop to help those who fall by the wayside. It doesn't allow for introspection or empathy either: they slow things down.

Where did Bloomberg get those qualities? Maybe from growing up as part of a very small minority, despite his insistence that his Judaism made no difference; from being a bright nerd, too smart for his uninspired schools; and surely from, as he says so often, his mother.

Although Bloomberg attributes his stoicism to both parents, he does not speak much about his father, who died of complications from a childhood bout of rheumatic fever in 1963, when Mike was in college. His relationship with his father has always been difficult to penetrate. Asked about him, Bloomberg said, "He was a nice person. He was a nice young guy and a nice old guy who just had been a bookkeeper all his life."

The son is respectful of his father's memory. He has named a medical facility after him in Israel and has honored him in other ways. But he is not sure he can still summon up the sound of William Bloomberg's voice and is not certain where his father was educated—at Babson in Massachusetts, he believes, but there is no record of his enrollment there.

Bloomberg's main recollections of his father are impressionistic: His dad sitting in a yellow leather chair, sucking on a pipe that was rarely lit. His dad's white helmet sitting in a box in the attic, the helmet he wore as the town's air-raid warden during World War II. His dad taking him to work on Saturdays, stopping at a greasy spoon on Rutherford Avenue in Medford to treat Mike to a decidedly unkosher breakfast of bacon and eggs—the inspiration for his son's favorite adult concoction of peanut butter and burnt bacon.

He does remember his father talking at the dinner table about buying tankers of milk to make cheese at the dairy. "He would be proud if he bought it cheap and the next day the price was higher." And never forgotten is William Bloomberg's response when his son asked him why he gave donations to the National Association for the Advancement of Colored People. "He said, 'Because if there's discrimination against blacks there'll be discrimination against Jews, and everyone else. We're all in this together.'" Mike was ten or twelve years old but the message resonated.

Politics was not a big subject at home or of particular interest to Mike when he was young. Bloomberg, when asked, does recall that when he was six, his parents took him to Malden, Massachusetts, to see President Harry Truman speak from the back of a train. A family hero? "We didn't have household icons."

About the time Mike was finishing high school, his father quit or was fired from the dairy, and bought a small company that sold mutual funds. It did not take off, and a few years later, when he was only fifty-seven, William Bloomberg's heart gave out.

Mike, a junior at Hopkins, kept his loss to himself. "He had external bravado, didn't want to talk about his father," recalls Dr. Jack Galotto, a fraternity brother. "He said he'd be back in a couple of days, didn't say his father died until later."

Only once, to Galotto's future wife, Mary Kay Shartle, did he confide that his father's death shook him more than he had let on.

Even decades later, Bloomberg does not talk much about his father's death, except to say it was a shock that traumatized the family. "I never had a bad day other than the day my father died." He had never known about his father's heart problems, had never questioned his parents when they said that William Bloomberg was Medford's air-raid warden instead of serving in the armed forces because he was the wrong age. He wasn't. "I didn't do the math," says his son.

The family coped after William Bloomberg's death. They had some savings; Mrs. Bloomberg got a job as an executive secretary to a Boston businessman. Mike continued to work part time at Hopkins and got through school with the help of student loans.

Mike Bloomberg's friends have always wondered if he was especially intent on succeeding because his father never did. William Bloomberg worked six- and seven-day weeks in an uninspiring job to support his family and died just as he was trying to make it on his own. Maybe his son, seeing how things hadn't worked out better for his father, resolved to make sure they did for him.

Mike Bloomberg was one difficult kid in school, his performance lackluster, his conduct minor-league disruptive. "I had discipline problems," he acknowledges. "I threw erasers. I dipped pigtails into inkwells—I was totally bored. In the sixth grade I went to Mrs. Kelly—this old battle ax who I'm sure has since gone on to meet her maker—and I had to get her to sign a paper that said I was a good student, for my Boy Scout merit badge. And I remember she looked at me and started laughing. We made a deal: that if I stayed out of the principal's office for a month, she'd sign it."

Many who knew him in high school were stunned to learn that their unremarkable classmate, a nerdy president of the Slide Rule Club, member of the Debating Club, the "home room dues agent" who hadn't even made the honors society, had grown up to be *the* Mike Bloomberg. "When I heard about the great success he had in adult life, it was like—*Michael Bloomberg?*" said fellow Medford High classmate Michael Stadlen. "If anyone would have asked who would be the most successful person to come out of this high school, I don't know how many would have said Stadlen but nobody would have said Bloomberg."

Yet Bloomberg's adult traits were emerging, evident, at least, in retrospect.

Restless in schools that did not challenge, he fixated on scouting, not a pursuit of most Jewish boys in Medford. He enrolled in a troop at the Congregational church and reached Eagle, the highest rank, almost a year before he was old enough to formally claim the honor.

A photograph of Bloomberg at twelve with fellow scouts shows a crowd of boys grinning broadly, except for one intense kid, who looked as though he had the weight of the world on his shoulders—Mike Bloomberg.

"He was serious, modest, quietly confident, seemed to know what he wanted. Most of us were punks," recalls Paul Theroux, a fellow Medford scout. "If you weren't tough, if you were basically cerebral and a nerd or a geek or didn't run with a bunch, scouting was an option. I'm sure Mike's interest in Boy Scouts arose from two impulses—one was curiosity, the other was being somewhat marginal: he wasn't a jock, I wasn't either. The Scouts made you self-sufficient without relying on other kids."

He liked, even then, being his own boss. "He didn't do organized sports, but not because he didn't have the ability," says his sister. "He didn't do youth groups, or join organized teams where you are told what to do."

Mike the Eagle Scout also played the bad boy, hanging out at the local stables with the townies, to smoke and gamble. "He told me one time that he won a lot of money, and he reached into his pocket and pulled out a pile of bills," said Susan Carley Davis, another classmate. He wound up smoking until he was in his early thirties, and only much later becoming the anti-tobacco proselytizer New Yorkers know well.

In the 1950s, with the nation focused on science to catch up with Soviet space adventures, Mike Bloomberg figured he'd become an engineer. While most Medford students did not go on to college, he knew he would and took honors courses when they were introduced in his senior year. He earned a sprinkling of As, but his transcript was riddled with Cs and Ds.

In the class "Dictionary," which characterized each senior with a single word, Mike Bloomberg's was "argumentative."

"That," says his sister, "is not a big surprise to me."

"He was an iconoclast and it was not the time to be an iconoclast," recalls another classmate, Dorothy Rubin Schepps. "It was the time to be conventional. I think Mike was smarter than the system could accommodate. His kind of intelligence did not register on the radar screen in a school like Medford High in the late fifties."

His iconoclasm was not always admired. His senior thesis, for a combined English-history honors class, caused quite a stir. Mike wrote a paper contending that the widely admired President Franklin Delano Roosevelt knew in advance that the Japanese would attack Pearl Harbor and let it happen to win support for entering World War II. Susan Carley Davis remembers the reaction of the English teacher, an intimidating woman named Kathleen Sharkey. "She had an incredible Boston accent. I can remember her taking that paper and saying in her very nasal way, 'Bloomberg, I refuse to read this *payhpa,* this is like treason toward a wonderful president." She threw the paper on the floor but Mike shrugged it off. He gave it to his history teacher, and got an A.

Still, the offended Miss Sharkey introduced him to literature, and the history teacher who appreciated his paper on Roosevelt, Mr. Lalley, engaged his curiosity. Mike was riveted by Lalley's lectures about the controversial convictions of Sacco and Vanzetti, the immigrant anarchists tried and executed for murders they probably did not commit, and the 1914 assassination of Archduke Franz Ferdinand, which sparked World War I. The disengaged student woke up.

Despite his middling grades, he recalls getting high SAT scores, and applied to several colleges, including, on the recommendation of the owner of an electronics firm where he worked part time, Johns Hopkins. Admissions standards at Hopkins, especially for non-premeds, were not as rigorous as they later became and Bloomberg got in—to the university's enduring good fortune. Making contributions that eventually totaled more than a half-billion dollars and counting, Bloomberg would become one of Hopkins's greatest benefactors, the driving force behind the university's renowned Bloomberg School of Public Health and an ambitiously thorough campus renovation.

"You know," says the famous alum, "there's a joke at Johns Hopkins: They're going to put up three statues—one of Johns Hopkins, one of me—and one of the admissions officer."

And so at eighteen, Mike left Medford and, except for visits to his mother, he never looked back.

CHAPTER 3

FIRST MILLIONS

IT WAS AT JOHNS HOPKINS that Mike Bloomberg came into his own, channeling his boyhood impatience into more productive endeavors than presiding over his high school's slide rule club.

In his memoir, Bloomberg wrote of his college years as if he was a wild and crazy guy: "Fraternities at Hopkins weren't much different from those in the classic John Belushi movie, *Animal House.* Though Hopkins was a serious place, and very competitive scholastically, we did drink and party a lot together."

Bloomberg's bravado, say Hopkins friends, was typical, reflecting the apparent need of the short kid from Medford who was never going to be a quarterback, to fit the image of big man on the then all-male campus. "That book—to me it is not really an accurate portrayal," said a fraternity brother and good friend, Dr. Jack Galotto. "He was not someone who, like, hung out in bars."

Another fraternity brother, Matthew Crenson, remembers Mike as tough, highly competitive, ambitious—and serious. That does not sound like the character Bloomberg describes in his book. "Did he exaggerate? We had a lot of parties and he was at all of them but I never saw him drunk and saw a lot of others drunk. He was very disciplined. He seemed very determined, the way he would work."

Crenson, a future associate dean of Arts and Sciences at Hopkins, said Bloomberg organized everything he could get his hands on—his fraternity, his senior class, the council that ran all the fraternities on campus, even meals at his frat house. "Guys would cook their own meals there and it was a mess. He put together a plan, hired a cook and then everyone had dinner at the frat house. We all paid a certain amount of money per month, per week. It was his idea."

If Bloomberg ever had a touch of college bad-boy in him, it disappeared the day his father died. "I remember him saying, 'Now I am the man of my family,'" says Mary Kay Shartle-Galotto, who dated and later married his fraternity brother. "He changed. He went from doing what he wanted to do in school to deciding he would go to Harvard Business School. He decided he would be president of his senior class, of his fraternity and of the Inter-Fraternity Council. He said it, and he did it." And there was one more pledge: "He said he was going to be the first Jewish president."

A mediocre engineering student specializing in Cs, Bloomberg did not get any As until he had to confront graduate school applications, but fellow students said they always saw him work hard in the lab, and at his part-time job, managing the faculty club parking lot.

The year he ran his fraternity's annual dinner—usually a festive frolic—Bloomberg arranged for a speech by Owen Lattimore, a distinguished Far East scholar and Hopkins lecturer who had been persecuted by Senator Joseph McCarthy, the red-baiter of the 1950s. Asked by bemused fraternity brothers why he turned their annual bash into a lecture forum, he said simply that he thought he'd elevate the occasion.

The assertiveness of his childhood became even more pronounced in his college years. One night when a movie line stretched down the block, he was having none of it. "We started to get in the line, he said, 'Screw this,'" recalls his frat brother's date, Mary Kay. "He goes to the first person in line, pushes twenty dollars at him, and said, 'Get us four tickets.' He got us four tickets and we walked in. That is the kind of chutzpah I'm talking about."

Bloomberg continued quietly and determinedly to defy convention. Most Jewish students joined Jewish fraternities and dated Jewish girls. Mike dated non-Jewish girls almost exclusively, going out seriously for a while with a coed from Notre Dame, and, recruited by Jack Galotto, becoming the only Jewish member of Phi Kappa Psi, the fraternity's first. The fraternity accepted him entirely, except on one occasion, when a fraternity brother called him a "bandy-legged little Jew" after Bloomberg told him to clean up the mess he'd left in the living room. Jack Galotto describes what happened next: "In seconds Mike was up the stairs and had this guy pinned on the landing. If I hadn't broken it up I'm not sure he wouldn't have taken his ice skates and hit the guy."

Following the example of classmates, Bloomberg thought he'd go to graduate school after Hopkins and chose the Harvard Business School, perhaps because Harvard's Ivy renown had always impressed his father. It turned out that once he got there, the Harvard "B School" impressed him, too, though not for its academics.

"I remember being more impressed by whom I was matriculating with than by their abilities. As a kid from working-class Medford, never before had I met people as close to the limelight. Many were the sons of famous business leaders I'd read about in the newspapers." Most, he wrote with ill-disguised satisfaction, did not succeed despite their pedigrees.

A few months before graduation from Harvard, with his college and grad school military deferments about to expire, Bloomberg thought he would survive Vietnam as an officer, then get a management job with an engineering or real estate firm. But he had no Plan B when flat feet barred him from military service. Suddenly he needed a job and hadn't set up any interviews.

A Harvard friend who had worked at Morgan Stanley one summer thought Bloomberg would do well selling stocks. New York sounded interesting. Wall Street even more so.

He applied to several Wall Street firms; one was Goldman Sachs, but the place struck him as starchy and the interviewer as distant. He moved on to "a little bond trading firm" then called Salomon Brothers & Hutzler at 60 Wall. The company hired him in 1966 and it would become his springboard to success—through a typically unorthodox route.

Mike Bloomberg had no thoughts of specializing in computer technology when he first arrived on Wall Street.

Most money-struck Ivy League graduates did not knock on Salomon's door in those days. They wanted to be investment bankers or research analysts at the white shoe, Waspy firms where pedigree mattered. Selling and trading securities was not for the genteel, the "swells" as Bloomberg called them. Just a decade earlier, Jews not descended from "Our Crowd" German families knew they should not bother applying.

Salomon was always different and while Bloomberg didn't

quite know the history, he sensed that "as someone who hadn't exactly hobnobbed with Rockefellers during his wonder years or had a mogul for a father," he was in the right place. Salomon had a reputation as a meritocracy, a place where anyone with enough energy and smarts could make it.

Even the look of the scrappy firm, located when Bloomberg joined it in an old bank building with a grand marble staircase in the lobby, set it apart. Other firms had modest-sized trading rooms, but traders sat in standard offices. Salomon had its own trading floor, a large room where everyone, from the bosses to the clerks, sat side by side at serviceable desks, in an open, democratic atmosphere that Bloomberg has favored and later recreated in all his settings.

Salomon's trading room was a scene of barely controlled chaos. Every man on the floor—they were all men except their secretaries—was smoking, shouting and cursing. They barked into phones and yelled at one another across the desks. Security quotes hung from hooks on a metal board on one side of the room, manually changed from moment to moment. Teletype operators sat in the middle, transcribing messages and shooting them from desk to desk on a conveyor belt that encircled the room.

Bloomberg took it all in as he headed to his interview: the noise, the action, the energy, the symbols of wealth—a partners' barber shop, the George Bellows oil of the Dempsey-Firpo fight in the lounge. The painting was rented, he later learned, but nonetheless an original, which highly impressed Mike Bloomberg, who had yet to throw off his small-town roots: "I had never seen real art outside of a museum."

Waiting for his interview, Bloomberg struck up a conversation with a fellow who introduced himself as "Billy." He was friendly and informal, "easy to talk to." He turned out to be

William R. Salomon, son of one of the three founders and the firm's managing partner. When it came time to choose, Goldman Sachs offered to pay more than Salomon. But money was one thing, already being on a first-name basis with "Billy" was another.

In those years, Billy Salomon set the company's tone. He was "a suave, dignified leader," according to William Simon, who joined the firm shortly before Bloomberg did. The future Treasury secretary admired Salomon for his ethical standards, especially for fully disclosing the company's finances to clients and banks when there was no obligation to do so. "Nobody else did that, but nobody else was Billy Salomon, and nobody else functioned like Salomon Brothers," Simon wrote in his memoir.

Salomon had always been proudly distinctive. It was born of controversy, a family feud centered on Ferdinand Salomon, the scion of Alsatian money brokers who immigrated to the United States in the late nineteenth century. He continued the family business in New York but suffered the defection of his three sons in 1910 because he refused to work on the Sabbath, when the markets were busy.

Wall Street was cliquish and dominated by elites in the early twentieth century, and so the Salomon brothers were forced to focus on selling boring bonds instead of sexy stock, and to serving institutions instead of individual customers.

The company wound up prospering by trading heavily in U.S. bonds during World War II, then went through a slow period until grandson Billy took charge. By the mid-1960s the company was thriving again, and growing.

In *Liar's Poker,* Michael Lewis would memorialize the Salomon Brothers of the crazed 1980s as the headquarters of the "Big Swinging Dicks," the crass, big-time bond traders. But in its golden age, the 1960s and 1970s, the firm was known for its aggressive risky trading and for its honesty; it was a fast, heady, competitive place. It featured big names—Simon; Henry Kaufman, an influential economist later known as "Dr. Doom" for his bearish forecasts; later James Wolfensohn, who would go on to head the World Bank, joined the firm. Yet in Bloomberg's early days, thirteen of the twenty-eight trading partners had not even gone to college, Lewis calculated.

The attitude was—yeah, so? What of it? "We had an inferiority complex," as one of those senior partners told me. "It was, 'Hey, we're gonna show you!' And we did."

In one sense, Michael Bloomberg fit right in. A twenty-three-year-old version of the Eagle Scout who had to control everything and the college student who had to run everything, he was as brash as his new employers, as scrappy as the most audacious traders. "Salomon was a band of warriors in the seventies and Mike had that warrior quality to him," says a former Salomon partner, Morris Offit. "He epitomized it."

But Bloomberg had something else as well: he was the firm's first Harvard MBA, and as a result, in the vanguard of change at Salomon and on Wall Street. His credentials set him apart and his colleagues did not let him forget it. Nor did he want them to. He had elbows and he used them.

Billy Salomon and John Gutfreund, the gruff, cigar-champing second in command, were charmed by the aggressive new man from Harvard. Younger, competitive colleagues saw a threat. "Mike was snippy, a little bit of a wise-ass kid, smart, knew all the answers. In some ways he hasn't changed a bit," says a former member of Salomon's executive committee, its inner circle.

Bloomberg started out counting securities in the sweltering "cage" one flight down from the trading floor, named for the tellers cages inherited from the building's bank days. The young clerk stayed there less than a year. He developed an appetite for selling and was assigned to the newer stock side of the firm, working with Jay Perry, the company's star equities trader. A fiercely competitive former bond man in his early thirties, Perry, from Hot Springs, Arkansas, was always in motion, punching the firm's 120-key telephone console connected to all major funds, shouting prices to institutional investors, erupting in triumph at every sale. And fighting with everyone.

So temperamental that he once spilled Bloomberg's desk drawers all over the floor, Perry finally had one fight too many, with a partner. He was transferred to Dallas in 1973, which made Bloomberg the head of Salomon's equities desk. After seven years, Mike had become a general partner and, at least on paper, a millionaire.

But he was kept out of the circle of senior managers, the executive committee. John Gutfreund remembers Bloomberg as "bright, aggressive, fast-talking," but not at the head of the class. "He wasn't ready for the executive committee," Gutfreund barked in an interview, speaking nonstop in staccato sentences, except when he turned to check the markets on two screens—both Bloomberg terminals. "One needs to be a decision maker and have responsibility for leading business in an overt way. Michael led in a way we didn't realize—the coming into the age of technology. We didn't recognize its potential." Bloomberg didn't either, in Gutfreund's view, though other Salomon alumni disagree.

Ultimately, it was politics that sidetracked Bloomberg—a combination of his brash manner and the resentment of Richard Rosenthal, one of Salomon's most successful arbitrageurs. The intemperate Rosenthal, who had never finished eighth grade, had taken an immediate dislike to Bloomberg.

Though they were close in age, he had seniority and from the start had treated the Harvard guy dismissively. "Bloomie," he would snap, "get me coffee."

It did not help that Rosenthal had also been a rival of Jay Perry, Bloomberg's early trading partner. The Dick vs. Mike feud simmered for years and finally spilled over when Rosenthal was promoted to the executive committee. He now oversaw the equities desk—Bloomberg's desk. That could never work—and was not meant to. Bloomie was being pushed out of the way to placate the more entrenched Rosenthal.

Thirteen years after he began at Salomon, Bloomberg was effectively demoted, transferred off the trading floor to the "information services" department, Tech Support. The firm had moved to more spacious quarters at 1 New York Plaza and Bloomberg found himself literally isolated from the action. "I was appalled," recalls Janine Hill, who joined Salomon's corporate finance department in 1976. "He got put on a floor all by himself, the forty-fourth floor, I think. A bunch of us kids would hang out with him on his floor. It was like a no-man's-land."

It was worse, recalls Kenneth Lipper, a friend at Salomon. "It was like death. It would be like assigning a cop to patrol the Lincoln Tunnel. It was a terrible thing in everybody's eyes, a terrible thing to do to a guy whose whole life was built upon a macho self-image."

Some Salomon traders expected Bloomberg to walk. He says he never considered resignation, he was a loyal Salomon man no matter what. And there were practical considerations: he had married and was a new father.

So he stayed, and if the demotion was a blow it nonetheless turned into another of those Bloomberg strokes of good fortune.

The computer age was dawning. Few on Wall Street realized the transformations the machine would bring. But Bloomberg had an early insight. He understood that technology was going to make trading easier and faster, that with computers every trader's information would be more accurate, more timely.

He knew it because Salomon already used a computer, the Quotron, and Bloomberg had improved it even before his exile to Tech Support. A dinosaur by later standards, the Quotron could spit out basic information about companies—like the history of dividend payments and stock prices. But it was static and could make no calculations. While still a clerk on the equities desk, Bloomberg went to Salomon and Gutfreund and proposed enhancing the Quotron. "They said, 'Look, you have to do your day job but if you want to, do it at night; you can take a computer programmer from upstairs.'"

So working after hours, Bloomberg upgraded the Quotron, developing what was called the "B-page," adding more data about stocks, bonds and company profiles. Then, during his two years in the Siberia of Tech Support, he made the B-page still more sophisticated and interactive. Salomon's traders could now ask it questions and the machine would respond.

As explained by Matthew Winkler, who wrote about securities for the *Wall Street Journal* at the time and later became Bloomberg's editor in chief, the machine's new talent was in handling the "what if's," the hypotheticals. "That's what made it valuable. What if the Fed raises interest rates two percentage points, what would that do for bonds Salomon owns today?; what if the Fed raised it half a percentage point? People could put in any number of assumptions and get a mathematical answer."

Though no one could know it then, Bloomberg had devised a prototype of the computer that would make him a mogul. It would also, incidentally, give Salomon a significant competitive advantage when the bond market exploded, after Bloomberg left the company. But it was only a primitive beginning. "The B-page was a predecessor to the Bloomberg terminal the way a monkey is to a man. It was very different, but you could see the DNA," said Thomas Secunda, now the head of technology at Bloomberg L.P.

Secunda, a slight, unprepossessing mathematician, was a minor player at Salomon in the seventies when Bloomberg invited him to dinner and asked him what he could do to make him more effective. Give him a computer at his desk, said Secunda, so he could save the time it took to get into the oversubscribed computer room. A terminal appeared at his desk the next morning. And soon enough, "Everyone who wanted them got them; productivity went way up."

Yet Bloomberg's reputation headed in the opposite direction. He was a threat to the old guard, especially by lobbying for more versatile desktop computers and debunking the large IBM mainframes favored by the technology brass. He was arguing that Salomon was spending a fortune on the wrong technology.

"Michael was showing what should have been done—that the little box was the future, not the mainframe," said Gedale Horwitz, a former Salomon partner. "It's a matter of instant access, the ability to instantly access information. He saw what none of us saw."

In fact, Bloomberg was beginning to shake up the culture of all Wall Street. Working at a computer used to be seen as demeaning to a professional, the job of ill-paid researchers. They were called "peckers" and they pecked at keyboards for the brass, virtually as secretaries. No bond or stock trader would deign to tap a keyboard. They took pride in trading with their gut. When they needed more information than their guts could provide, they would wait until a researcher had time to seek it in the oversubscribed computer room. That could take hours, delaying a transaction. Bond dealers used calculating machines to reckon interest rates, but they were clunky and had limited value.

Bloomberg recalls that at least a week's copies of the *Wall Street Journal* were always leaning against someone's desk leg on the floor because traders had to search them to track the recent record of some security. What sense did that make, he kept asking, making himself more and more unpopular with a cockiness still resonant years later when he talked to *Forbes Magazine:* "I kept telling Gutfreund I could run the goddamn company better."

In 1981 the Phibro Corporation, a publicly held commodities trading firm, acquired Salomon Brothers. All Salomon partners were summoned to the Tarrytown Conference Center in a leafy corner of New York's Westchester County to hear the news and learn what it meant to them.

The weekend began joyously because all sixty-two general partners would gain from the sale and get an immediate payment of their share in the company's net worth. Before the Phibro deal, they had to plough earnings back into Salomon's trading account while living on salaries and bonuses given out by the bosses. If they resigned, they would get a payout of their equity, stretched out over ten years.

Now they would be rich in fact, not just on paper. In a celebratory gesture, the partners were tossed T-shirts proclaiming them members in the new company's CRITICAL MASS. They grabbed at the flying shirts; some pulled them on, beaming at their good fortune. Bloomberg and five other general partners were left shirtless. They were fired.

Bloomberg got the news directly from Henry Kaufman and John Gutfreund. After fifteen years, he was out. "It's time for you to leave," Bloomberg was told. Dick Rosenthal had pressured the executive committee to drop his rival, and Bloomberg's Mike-knows-best manner had not earned him enough allies to save him. Rosenthal's triumph was not long-lived. He was killed six years later in the crash of a private plane he was piloting. Bloomberg recorded his reaction in his memoir: "Was I happy or sad? After all the years of bitter fighting, I am ashamed to say that the right word was ambivalent."

He left the rough-and-tumble world of Salomon Brothers schooled in the company's principals of openness and take-no-prisoners competition. He'd bought low and sold high, but as he was taught by example, he did not cheat and would not tolerate dishonesty in business or in government. He also left with about $10 million in cash and convertible bonds, Salomon's goodbye package.

After learning the news of his dismissal, Bloomberg ordered a sable jacket from an East Side salon to reassure his wife. Even in 1981 this was a dated gesture—costly baubles to please the little woman?—and it was foolish heresy to buy retail in the center of the nation's fur market. Flaunting his new wealth must however have felt satisfying. Bloomberg's was a sad drive home, but he admitted he was much too "macho" to let it show.

Though Bloomberg has always said that he would never have left voluntarily, he had in fact considered quitting earlier that year. He told Gutfreund, who advised him to stick around. Gutfreund does not recall if he already knew about the coming Phibro merger but allows that he could have been warning Bloomberg to cool off, to help him collect a bundle.

Gutfreund's advice was worth millions. If Bloomberg had left before the merger, he would have received about $5 million paid out over ten years. Getting double that amount in a lump sum allowed him to finance his own business venture—based on the machine he'd been begging to build at Salomon.

"When I got pushed out, I thought, why not do the same things? I could sell it outside. Nobody was rushing to offer me a job."

Former Salomon partners still shake their heads at what they missed—a revolution under their noses. "One of the dumbest things ever," said one. "This was all developed at Salomon and Salomon never laid claim to anything."

"We didn't know what we had," says Gedale Horwitz. "No question. We absolutely did not know."

CHAPTER 4

TERMINAL MAN

MIKE BLOOMBERG does not like movies. He'll go once a year if he must, but movies usually put him to sleep, and for a most Bloombergian reason. "I don't like watching other people do things. I don't want to watch Tiger Woods, I want to play golf! I want to hit the ball, not watch him do it."

Which is why it is a very good thing for him that he was fired from Salomon Brothers, the only place he had ever worked after graduate school. Propelled by failure, Bloomberg built himself a life that even a novelist would have trouble imagining, one that would eventually allow him to do almost anything he wanted. He used his $10 million in going-away money to start his own business, developing a unique computer terminal that assembles and digests financial information. The splashily handsome desktop became the machine that ate Wall Street, and the headstrong businessman would never have to work for anyone else again.

Innovative Market Systems, as the company was called at first, began with 4 people and grew to 10,500 people working in sixty-three countries by 2008. Its first product, a set of twenty-two small gray terminals that coughed up data for pricing bonds, was leased to a single company for less than $1,000-a-month each. That machine's successor spews out prices on nearly every public security, every variety of current and historical data on all listed companies in the world, and countless tools to analyze it all, colorfully augmented with interactive charts and graphs.

"The Bloomberg," as it quickly became known, runs news stories produced by 2,300 journalists and editors working in 140 bureaus around the world. It can also be mined for other information, including relevant legal decisions, mounds of financial records and even celebrity gossip.

By the spring of 2009, the company had about 280,000 subscribers on six continents who typically pay $1,590 a month for the Bloomberg's software. All get a Bloomberg e-mail system and did from the start, well before e-mail was ubiquitous, and handsome flat-screen monitors and user-friendly keyboards if they want them. They can also choose to identify themselves with a fingerprint and tap into the Bloomberg network—and even conduct trades—from anywhere in the world.

All customers have round-the-clock access to technicians and researchers who answer questions and solve problems, a pet initiative of the service-obsessed Mike Bloomberg that later inspired his call-311 system for New Yorkers.

The Bloomberg machine and services proved to be not just a notable improvement in data retrieval but a game-changer. It did for traders, investors and bankers what Microsoft did for the PC and what Google did for Web searching. It revolutionized the way business and financial information is delivered at breathtaking speed.

Only a few financial information systems existed before the Bloomberg, each providing limited data. Customers had to dial in and extract information piecemeal, the way a writer working on a biography might get one kind of article from the *Financial Times* and another from the *New York Post*'s Page Six. It was at best an ungainly routine that delayed and hampered business decisions.

Bloomberg saw a way to steal the data market right out from under the more established systems maintained by Reuters and Dow Jones. He set out to provide information with greater scope and depth, assembled in one place—on his at-your-elbow desktop machine.

As described by David Worlock, who studies the information and publishing industries for Outsell Inc., "He created a sort of walled garden, with his I-am-all-you need philosophy. He came to the market with an idea that one terminal could provide all the data you could need, allow you to analyze it on one screen, so one trader could look in a variety of different markets." Now routine in our information age, it was hardly routine then, notes Worlock, a former executive at Thomson, a Bloomberg competitor: "It was revolutionary."

Not even Mike Bloomberg knew in 1981 that the computer he envisioned with a few colleagues he hired from Salomon would become a global sensation. But he understood what traders needed because he had been one of them. And he knew what computers could do, because he had worked with them. Perhaps uniquely, he personified two cultures. Traders and computer engineers didn't talk in those days; they spoke different languages. "Unless you are a user, it is hard to appreciate the importance of certain kinds of features," says Andrew Lo, professor of Finance at MIT's Sloan School of Management. "Bloomberg was part of the process that designed from the bottom up. That is a hallmark of his success story."

One more experience was crucial in Bloomberg's success. Though a stock trader at Salomon, he also understood the bond market. The white-shoe firms that traded in glitzy stocks had left the less venturesome world of bonds to Salomon. Bloomberg, in mastering the Quotron, learned bonds inside out. The knowledge proved crucial when a new chairman of the Federal Reserve resolved to tame inflation. And lo! In the early 1980s, as Bloomberg opened his own company, the bond market exploded.

Innovative Market Systems was no overnight success. Bloomberg began by investing about $300,000 and went to work with three recruits he had met at Salomon—Thomas Secunda, who specialized in analytics; Chuck Zegar, who created the software; and Duncan MacMillan, the expert in customer needs. All three are still at Bloomberg L.P., wealthy but unsung heroes of the Bloomberg saga.

Their offices were three unadorned, cramped rooms on Madison Avenue. Only Bloomberg's boasted a window. Wall Street associates who ran into him in those early days saw a tense and anxious man, unsure that he could pull things off. Once, on a trip to California, he acknowledged his fears to a friend: he had assumed a daunting responsibility; what if it didn't work out?

It did, in part because of financial doings in Washington. Paul Volcker, the chairman of the Federal Reserve, had adopted a policy of letting interest rates float more freely than ever before. That change was enlivening the market in interest-bearing bonds. Investors the world over were focusing on bond trades as never before.

Once relatively safe investments for the risk-averse, bonds now became highly volatile. They were behaving like stocks, their values constantly changing, which meant that fortunes depended on their being valued correctly and quickly. And to value them correctly, traders and investors had to make informed assumptions about the underlying value of a company and its prospects.

That need created an opening for the computers and software being developed by the Bloomberg team. Better than any available tool, their machine would estimate both the actual and potential value of a bond, a vital check on the judgment of secretive brokers. Soon, the machine would also track other securities, but the test bed was bonds.

One of Wall Street's endless guessing games asks whether the Bloomberg terminal—and Bloomberg—could have triumphed if Volcker's change of strategy had not ignited the bond market at just that moment. There's no good answer. What is clear is that Bloomberg seized the moment and left his competitors far behind.

"Bloomberg just reinvented the field," says Floyd Norris, a *New York Times* financial columnist.

The largest financial information system then available, a Reuters product, was basically an electronic bulletin board that posted current rates and prices, then discarded them. Bloomberg set out to save the information, creating an expanding database to support sophisticated investment calculations. "This was the fault line on which Reuters' repeated attempts to compete foundered," wrote Brian Mooney and Barry Simpson in their 2003 book, *Breaking News: How the Wheels Came Off Reuters.*

Reuters—founded as a news-gathering operation—had not focused on what its customers did with its news after they got it. Bloomberg, by contrast, was obsessed with how to store up and manipulate information to improve traders' calculations. Confronted by fierce competition from the Bloomberg, Reuters's first reaction was to build a more comprehensive news service. Having missed the conceptual logic of the Bloomberg, Reuters found itself playing catch-up for years. By 1991, Reuters was claiming somewhat hysterically that a new machine it had developed would turn out to be the "Bloomberg Killer." Late and lame, it failed.

Bloomberg's advantage was not only a matter of timing—he had gotten out ahead of everyone—but of culture and temperament. In its early days his company was small, quick on its feet, able to pursue the vision of one financial daredevil, not of a bureaucratic executive board. Bloomberg was hungry; the larger established companies were not.

"The company was built off of Mike Bloomberg's ego, which is very big," says Douglas Taylor, who had been an executive with both Thomson Financial and Reuters before forming his own business management consulting firm. "It takes a lot of ego to start a company, prove it is as good as you say it is, and make it a success. I think he built a strong company in his own image."

Any number of information companies and news organizations had access to a lot of the same data and might have done what Bloomberg did. But journalists are better at telling stories than marshaling statistics. And data analysts were creatures of a market that offered no financial incentive to share information. The Goldman Sachses and Morgan Stanleys wanted to keep their customers dependent on them for bond valuations; they didn't want clients making their own calculations on a computer that sat right on their own desks. Bloomberg's machine was bringing transparency to a closed culture, giving buyers and sellers access to the same information.

"There are a bunch of reasons why Wall Street hated Mike Bloomberg," says Kevin Foley, who worked for him in the early nineties and now runs an equities trading business. "The biggest one was probably cultural. He broke ranks, you know? It was Robin Hood."

Bloomberg was no social reformer. He was in business to make money. His machine created an enormous franchise for itself. It benefited from the buzz that comes with being the first. It also benefited from Bloomberg's stubborn insistence on doing things his way.

He would only lease terminals, not sell them, becoming in effect a permanent landlord with lucrative real estate. He would give no discounts; he would not carve up his data as other companies did when they sold different basic and premium packages, like cable TV companies.

Bloomberg sold only his premium product. That created an allure; the Bloomberg became a status symbol as well as a necessity.

When Bloomberg's company was still suffering startup stumbles and setbacks, it took on some consulting work for Wall Street firms, among them Merrill Lynch. With a salesman's bravado, Bloomberg persuaded Merrill's executives that he could create a computerized system faster than they could build one in-house. He invested almost $4 million of his Salomon farewell money in that bet and in nine months—three more than promised—he delivered.

The Bloomberg got its eponymous nickname at Merrill, and it is there that it took off in time—it was not an overnight success—growing in capacity and moving well beyond its special bond skills. After just a few years of steady growth, Bloomberg got out of his exclusive deal with Merrill to market his machine around the globe. Merrill agreed because it owned a 30 percent share of his company and welcomed the added income. Bloomberg's company kept expanding, in size and depth, hitting its stride in the late 1980s when it began growing at a phenomenal rate.

In time Bloomberg could afford to buy back a third of Merrill's stake and when Merrill fell on hard times in the crash of 2008, he bought back the remaining 20 percent. That gave him 92 percent of the company's stock and set its value—at that moment—at about $20 billion.

The one advantage Reuters held over Bloomberg was its news wire. Traders needed real-time news to inform their decisions. Bloomberg had to pay dearly to get news feeds, always running the risk that Reuters or Dow Jones would damage his business by cutting him off. In 1990 Bloomberg hired the demanding Matthew Winkler, who had written admiringly about him and his company in the *Wall Street Journal,* and started his own news division.

In time, Bloomberg News would be joined by Bloomberg Radio and Bloomberg Television, would include a Sunday newspaper supplement, Bloomberg Personal, which failed, and a monthly magazine *Bloomberg Markets,* which has won awards. The Washington Bureau began expanding in 2005, under a new bureau chief, former *Wall Street Journal* reporter Al Hunt.

Bloomberg never intended to become a media mogul. His news operations—on his computer, on radio and on television—were all marketing tools, aimed at expanding his brand recognition and, as always, to give his customers what they wanted.

Bloomberg News was little more than a dry financial wire service at first, derided for its stilted style and no match for the more comprehensive and authoritative Reuters. It is still stilted and dry. The words that Winkler once banned outright—among them "but"—still make only rare appearances, and adjectives and adverbs are discouraged. In his heyday, Winkler enforced his rules rigidly, and developed a reputation for publicly delivered tirades, triggered by errors and the sin of being scooped.

The stressful Bloomberg newsroom, where reporters sit in crowded rows staring at multiple computer screens, is not a happy place for everyone. Many staffers complain that they are expected to put the company's promotion and sales of subscriptions ahead of reporting the news. They are also under great pressure to be first with the news but never to make a mistake that could result in costly trading errors.

In 2008, the company's new president, Daniel Doctoroff, recruited Norman Pearlstine, former editor of the *Wall Street Journal,* to be "chief content officer," and Andrew Lack, a former president of NBC News, to head Bloomberg's multimedia divisions. Winkler kept his title, but a new direction, and a new tone, were in the offing.

Despite his reputation as a bully, Winkler is credited even by detractors with creating a significant news enterprise from scratch, staffing it with inexperienced young reporters and shaping them to his needs. Bloomberg News found a niche—fielding a large staff, paying more than most other news organizations and expanding as others contracted—but it took a while.

In its infancy, Bloomberg News was so inconspicuous it was unable to get accreditation in Washington to cover economic developments vital to its subscribers. Where did its stories appear, the accreditation committee of journalists wanted to know.

Michael Bloomberg offered an inspired remedy: barter. He knew that financial writers at the *Times* wanted a Bloomberg but the paper had balked at his fee. So he offered a free terminal if the paper would credit Bloomberg when printing its news, just as it credited Reuters or the Associated Press.

Bloomberg got credit lines in the *Times,* its reporters got a terminal and his reporters got credentials in Washington. Soon 450 news organizations around the country got the same deal. And after five years of such barter, Bloomberg was able to charge them for what was once free. Most kept their machines even though they now had to pay for them, a former colleague recalled. "He told me, 'We'll give them free crack and they are gonna get hooked.'"

Floyd Norris became so addicted that when *Fortune Magazine* offered him a higher-paying position but no Bloomberg terminal, he chose to stay with the job at the *Times*—it had a Bloomberg. "It had information I could never get before. Say I was interested in American Widget: I could easily get up to date on what was going on with that company on the Bloomberg and nobody else was providing that data. It was a magical machine."

Bloomberg and his staff thrived playing the role of outlier. His original band labored long hours, six and a half days a week, reveling in the challenge of transforming their industry. They paid a price for their success. Personal lives were secondary and under stress. Secunda's weight plummeted, another colleague suffered intestinal ailments, Bloomberg's marriage felt the strain.

But they all got to be rich, moved to larger offices on Park Avenue and, later, when Bloomberg was mayor, to Bloomberg

Tower at Fifty-ninth Street and Lexington Avenue, a cool, glittery tribute to glass on glass.

In 1992, barely a decade after he started his company, Bloomberg appeared on *Forbes*'s list of the four hundred wealthiest Americans, worth an estimated $350 million. He was credited with at least $500 million two years later and hit *Forbes*'s $1 billion mark in 1995.

By the mid-1990s, Mike Bloomberg was a media wunderkind, the audacious bad-boy darling of the financial press. Newspapers and magazines wrote about his temper, his energy, his generosity. They called him "sharky," "an arrogant egomaniac" and "hot-headed," they romanticized his revolutionary innovations and admired his boldness, chortled at his vulgarity. THE BOOK OF BLOOMBERG: HAS CHUTZPAH SERVED HIM WELL? IS THE POPE BULLISH? asked a *USA Today* headline after Bloomberg tried to get a papal blurb for his memoir because, after all, the Vatican leased Bloombergs. He failed, but no matter. Everything Mike Bloomberg said and did was deemed intriguing.

A sampling: Bloomberg did not believe in titles at his company. He did not advertise in other media. He did not give volume discounts to customers, no matter how big they were. He did not have a secretary or an assistant. He made his own dinner, train and plane reservations. He was a control freak; he was a loyalty nut. He considered anyone who resigned a "traitor," never to be rehired. He boasted that he could do every job in his company. He was funny, he was down-to-earth, he was fast-talking, he was profane.

Even Bloomberg's psychosocial psychedelic decorating scheme became a fascination. Whether on Park Avenue, on Fifty-ninth Street or in stately City Hall, Bloomberg championed a combination of transparency and sensory overload that astonishes outsiders and energizes insiders even as it gives them headaches.

Bloomberg Tower, the company's futuristic headquarters on Lexington Avenue between Fifty-eighth and Fifty-ninth streets, was opened after Bloomberg became mayor, but it triumphantly projects his extravagant sensibility. Cesar Pelli's exterior design looms over midtown as another sleek and clean tower that reveals itself as a horseshoe edifice embracing a courtyard entrance.

Inside, Bloomberg's large stretch of offices is even more overwhelming, isolating employees in a media-mad world of their own, unlike any other. Ostentatiously futuristic, simultaneously cool and pulsating, Bloomberg's headquarters grandly echoes the walled garden that he had created with his unique machine. Just as the computer terminal, with its technological bells and whistles, is intended to give its clients all they need to conduct their business, the lofts of Bloomberg L.P. provide his employees with everything he presumes they need for creative—and incessant—labor. The computer-packed aisles, busy lobbies and food courts offer free chips, popcorn and apples for the stomach, flower vases for the soul, tanks of tropical fish for the mind and unending zippers of flashing news and equity prices to stoke the instincts.

A visit to Bloomberg L.P. is a provocative but unsettling experience, dominated by a sense of being under constant surveillance, which begins at the security desk in the lobby, where Orwellian men and women wearing big smiles consult a computer, take a picture and produce mug-shot passes that must be draped around the neck at all times. Guards at electronic machines protect the elevators: no pass, no entry. Employees "badge-in" and "badge-out," their comings and goings constantly registering in the system's computer.

A tour of the building, designed by Studios Architecture and Pentagram in collaboration with Bloomberg, reveals that there are indeed no private offices, not even for top executives, although a column here, a wall indentation there, gives them more protection than the average worker. The vast expanses that house 4,100 salesmen and women, reporters, marketers, techies and consumer counselors feature endless rows of desks, arrayed cheek-by-jowl in trading-room style, each workstation supplied with flat-screened terminals, as many as four-a-desk in the news room.

Overhead hang electronic scoreboards that update the number of customer calls answered, and log how quickly. Bloomberg's radio news echoes in the elevators, Bloomberg's television beams into the restrooms, flickering on a wall near the sinks. Bold modern art appears at every turn—a titanium-alloy sculpture suspended inside the curve of a winding escalator, a whimsical candelabra, a branchlike electronic mobile of delicate white lights.

Nothing is missing but calm and privacy. Some employees thrive in the relentless environment. Others run screaming (silently) to a nearby coffee shop to work in quiet when the overstimulation proves to be too much, risking demerits for being off the premises, as the computers will record.

The ideal Bloomberg atmosphere is supercharged and competitive. "Mike always made us believe we were fighting the establishment," says Jon Friedman, a media columnist with MarketWatch who worked at Bloomberg News in the 1990s. "We were Mike's people, we were on a crusade. He wanted to beat the other guy, he wanted to crush the competition. He didn't want to break even, he wanted to *crush* them."

Bloomberg developed a cultlike following among those employees who prospered in the demanding environment. They speak of the generous pay, the perks and the benefits—car services, museum memberships, annual bonuses tied to ever-growing sales of terminal subscriptions. But there was another dimension that explains the loyalty of men and women who loved working for Bloomberg. To them, he wasn't a conventional executive but a man with a cause, a flexible operator who loved risk and innovation.

To keep his customers and recruit more, Bloomberg kept growing the content of his machine, adding more lists, more charts, more graphs, more data.

Steven Ludsin, who had worked for Bloomberg at Salomon, had an idea for his old boss in 1989, when the Resolution Trust Corporation was beginning to liquidate the assets of savings and loan banks that had gone bankrupt in scandal. Ludsin, in business for himself by then, proposed advertising the foreclosed properties—homes, land and commercial real estate—on the Bloomberg. Why not, said Bloomberg. "It was Internet marketing before there was Internet marketing," says Ludsin, whose business grew, and enhanced the Bloomberg's reputation for providing reams of ever-expanding information.

Even years later, those who worked with Bloomberg in the heady days of his company speak of him in the awed tones that political workers use to describe their candidate during a feverish campaign, a combination of admiration, loyalty and fear.

"I used to say, I don't work for his company, I work for Mike Bloomberg," says one former sales manager. "I would say, if he told me to go to mow the lawn in Armonk [the Westchester town where Bloomberg and his family then lived], I would go up to Armonk and mow the lawn. You work for this guy personally."

Other employees, current and former, speak ambivalently of "velvet handcuffs" of unrelenting stress and ten- to twelve-hour days in exchange for generous pay, perks, benefits and bonuses. They found the company tense, the working conditions difficult, especially for women.

Before and after Bloomberg was running the company, many women accused Bloomberg and Bloomberg L.P. of sexism and sued, three of them when the future mayor was still in charge. When Bloomberg was in his second mayoral term, more than eighty women joined in a class action suit against Bloomberg L.P. The suit, filed by the Federal Equal Employment Opportunity Commission, charges the company with discriminating against women who took pregnancy leaves after Bloomberg left the company in 2001 to run for mayor, but asserts that "Michael Bloomberg is responsible for the creation of the systemic, top-down culture of discrimination."

The case is a sore point with the mayor, who refused to discuss it publicly, once snapping at a reporter who asked about it at a City Hall news conference that had shifted from the city budget to other matters, "What does this have to do with the budget? Next time, don't bother to ask us a question. Stick to the topic. Everybody else plays by the rules; you'll just have to as well."

His identification with his company is so strong that the subject of Bloomberg L.P. animates him like no other. In conversations with me, never was he more energized or engaged than when he was talking about it, citing current facts and figures and making informed observations about his creation.

Bloomberg left its day-to-day operations years earlier to run for mayor, putting trusted friends in charge—Peter Grauer and later Dan Doctoroff. But though he stayed in close touch, employees and media analysts said that the company's post-Bloomberg character changed in the way most maturing enterprises change, becoming less personal and reactive than in its brash youth when its founder exulted in pushing the envelope, perhaps to its detriment.

Analysts have periodically predicted that Bloomberg's expensive technology would be overtaken by less costly services, and that it would lose clients to free websites that grew more sophisticated as the Web expanded. Thomson Reuters, the giant created when the Thomson Corporation and Reuters merged in 2008, loomed as a serious competitor, but though Bloomberg slowed a bit in the recession, it remained the gold standard.

If Bloomberg L.P. ever does stumble, it will be long after its founder was celebrated everywhere for its success and hailed as Wall Street's "Terminal Man."

Bloomberg reveled in his corporate star turn. As he told *USA Today,* "You walk into a restaurant and see people mumbling and pointing—that's great stuff. Anybody who says they don't like it, c'mon!"

By the 1990s, the principal challenge to Michael Bloomberg was the success of his company. It could run practically without him. There was little new or challenging at Bloomberg L.P for him to do. He wanted to "make a difference," he told those around him, and that meant influencing more than bond trades and stock sales. He wanted to be someone in a larger realm. He wanted his opinions heard by a wider audience. Michael Bloomberg, billionaire business tycoon, was itching to reinvent himself.

CHAPTER 5

CRASHING THE A-LIST

ONE DAY IN THE MID-1990S, Barbara Walters got a call from Mike Bloomberg. She had heard of him—he was this madly successful businessman, she knew that. But that was all she knew, yet here he was on the phone.

"I had never met Michael Bloomberg, but he said he wanted to have lunch with me," Walters recalls. "I thought, 'That's interesting.'" They ate in a restaurant on Central Park South, near the Park Avenue offices that he wanted to show off, and went over to Bloomberg L.P. after they had their coffee. "I never saw anything like it, everyone working out in the open, everyone on phones—those fish tanks! I asked why he called and he said he wanted to meet interesting, different people. I can't think of anyone else doing that in such a direct way. I thought it was quite wonderful."

She could not have realized it at the time, but Walters was part of Mike Bloomberg's latest mission, a self-assigned task he was pursuing with the same discipline and drive he devoted to closing business deals.

He had resolved that his social role as a scrappy outsider had to evolve. But he had not yet paid enough attention to the social niceties required of New York's elite. So he set out to learn. By the time he dazzled Walters over their lunch, he was a billionaire in his early fifties, a celebrated mogul and once again a free-roaming bachelor. But wealth alone does not guarantee entry into New York's social aristocracy, and he wanted in.

"It was always on his mind," a friend recalls. "He had Wasp envy. He always wanted to become established, he wanted to be accepted by the Union Clubs. He couldn't wait to join the boards of Lincoln Center, the Met."

Bloomberg had gained his first glimpse of the good life fresh out of graduate school, in his apprentice years at Salomon Brothers, and he liked what he saw. When still an earnest clerk, a colleague once took him to dinner at La Côte Basque, then the grand dame of New York's see-and-be-seen French restaurants. He "couldn't stop gawking," Bloomberg wrote in his memoir. "A dozen people were seated around a table featuring the largest flower centerpiece I'd ever seen. And in front of me was more silverware per place setting than my family owned in total."

Soon after, he encountered expense account luxuries, which impressed him even more. "Sometimes, I thought I'd gone through the looking glass into another world. Once we cruised uptown in a big black limousine. The only other time I'd been in such a car was at my father's funeral. At our destination, someone tossed the driver fifty dollars—for what would have been a two-dollar ride in a cab! Funny world. Funny money."

In those days, Bloomberg was riding more subways than cabs. Home was a standard-issue bachelor apartment on Manhattan's East Side, small and functional. Social life was distinctly secondary. "We were kids—single, smart, hard working, driven," recalls Harvey Eisen, a Bloomberg client and summer-house buddy. "We all came from modest backgrounds and we all wanted money. We'd start work at six in the morning and leave at eleven at night and we'd date girls and mess around in the Hamptons. We were all *Portnoy's Complaint*—we all wanted shiksas. Mike always had one."

But money-making came first. It was not until he was thirty-four that Bloomberg was ready for marriage to Susan Elizabeth Barbara Brown of York, the twenty-eight-year-old daughter of Annette E. Morris and Donald W. J. Brown, a retired Royal Air Force wing commander. She had worked as a secretary in Salomon's London office, came to New York after her divorce from Charles Henry Meyer, and was living at the Barbizon Plaza Hotel for Women on Manhattan's East Side when a mutual friend introduced her to Michael Bloomberg.

They were married at midday on Wednesday, December 15, 1976, in the study of Rabbi David Posner, now the head rabbi at New York's elite, reform Temple Emanu-El. Bloomberg remained a member of the synagogue but his wife, whose mother was Jewish, "kind of raised us to be Church of England," says their younger daughter, Georgina. She also recalls the family celebrating the major Jewish holidays.

The newlyweds lived first at 2 Sutton Place South on the East Side, then moved to Armonk in suburban Westchester in the mid-1980s. About five years later, they made their primary residence the East Seventy-ninth Street town house that Bloomberg still calls home.

Their first child, Emma, was born in 1979, and Georgina in 1983. After graduation from Princeton, Emma worked for a time in her father's City Hall, then married and joined a nonprofit welfare agency. Georgina, who attended the Gallatin School of Individualized Education at New York University for several years, became an equestrian, with plans to compete in the 2012 London Olympics.

In 1993, after seventeen years of marriage, Susan Bloomberg precipitated a split from Mike. As she told the *London Daily Mail* years later, "I was the one who pushed for a divorce because he was working all hours of the day and night, and I was in a country that wasn't my own and very lonely."

Emma once commented that her parents "were not getting along because their lives are not compatible. My mother doesn't want to be social all of the time. She was perfectly happy to curl up with a book and not go out all week."

Georgina agrees. Her mother still is "very private," while her father "likes to go out and socialize." In her childhood, she said, her father "wasn't around a lot, but he was always good about calling, and he was always there for important things—if I had an important horse show or game, a practice. Just because someone is not around all the time doesn't make them a bad parent. I have no hard feelings about that, I am not one of those people who says 'poor me.'" Like father, like daughter.

The Bloomberg divorce was unusually amicable. Susan, Emma and Georgina continued to share in the Seventy-ninth Street town house with Mike for a few months after the couple split up, and they moved back in with him briefly again a few years later after a relationship of Susan's broke up. She worked in Bloomberg's campaign, celebrates holidays with him and their daughters and his companion, Diana Taylor, and has sat on the dais at his inaugurations.

"My father says he won't get remarried until my mother does," says Georgina, who thinks it unlikely that her mother will marry again. "They have a great relationship, they talk a couple of times a week on the phone, they are really great parents. They are just not married."

The divorce partly triggered the social reinvention of Mike Bloomberg. He was discreetly ending one phase of his life but conspicuously beginning another, crashing the top echelons of New York society with the same determination that took him up the corporate ladder and later into politics. He redirected more of his philanthropy toward New York civic organizations and cultural institutions. And he expanded his social life, focusing on people who could open doors for him.

A convenient source of contacts was the guest list of the *Charlie Rose Show,* which has long been recorded in a Bloomberg studio and proudly lists his company as a major contributor. "He would look at Charlie Rose's list every day and he would hang out. He wanted to meet people," recalls Paul Wilmot, a publicist for the fashion industry who brought designers and manufacturers to the program. Rose's guests also included political figures, sports stars and film celebrities. Bloomberg's employees still talk about the boss's adolescent excitement at the prospect of meeting Sharon Stone on her way to the studio.

He reached out to influential New Yorkers in his typically forward manner; friends now were more than friends, a party was more than a party, lunch was more than lunch.

After he charmed Walters, the two became friends; if she were younger, he's been heard to say, she would be the ideal second wife. Once, during a "fantasy wedding" segment of her television program, *The View,* Walters picked Bloomberg as her fantasy bridegroom and was pictured standing beside a cardboard cutout of him when Mayor Bloomberg rushed in from Staten Island and replaced the cardboard, saying, "Did you really think I was going to miss my own wedding?" His political advisers, worried about Bloomberg's low poll numbers at the time, were thrilled.

Walters and Bloomberg never dated. She was just one of many prominent women whom Bloomberg sought out with his candor, smarts and wallet. Another was Beverly Sills, the opera star then head of the board of Lincoln Center for the Performing Arts. Bloomberg appeared at her home on Martha's Vineyard one day in 1994 in the company of his then girlfriend, Christy Ferer, a television reporter and owner of her own media company. "She had never heard of him, but she had a nose for philanthropists, for people who wanted to help," says Ferer. "When I introduced them, she saw him immediately as someone who could be on her board. *She* pursued *him.*"

In quick order, Bloomberg won seats on the boards of Lincoln Center, the Metropolitan Museum of Art and the New York Public Library. He made the board of the Central Parks Conservancy after another phone call out of the blue to Betsy Gotbaum, New York City's parks commissioner. "Just like that, he asked me to dinner."

Though impatient with small talk, Bloomberg sat through society dinners night after night. Nancy Hass, a writer who befriended him after writing his profile for the *Forward,* in 1993, often accompanied Bloomberg on that early round of black-tie dinners. Married, she served as his escort.

"He was between girlfriends, he needed a walker. He'd call and he'd say, 'I'll pick you up at six-thirty.' The car would get there, he'd say, 'Okay, this is where we are going, this is what his father does, this is what his wife does, he's a member of the lucky sperm club.'" *The lucky sperm club?* "Meaning he is not that smart but his father was really rich." Hass felt herself more on a business mission than out for an evening of fun.

"That's what you do in New York when you reach a certain

level of economic success," says Bloomberg's old friend Harvey Eisen. "If you want to be on the circuit, which is defined as going to all these stupid dinners every night in black tie, if you want to be seen, you show up. He wanted to be a player, wanted to be a fancy guy in the city. He's not a phony. He's not a jerk, like [Donald] Trump. But he crossed over, you know? Do you have any idea of the dirty mouth this guy has? He used to be impossible. But you can't do what we used to do. He adapted."

Nothing has changed so much in the Bloomberg story as the shape of his personal life. Or so it seems; it's very hard to be definitive about someone who aggressively protects his privacy, and has the means to do it. For a public figure, Michael Bloomberg is unusually and insistently opaque.

The path of his personal life superficially followed a familiar pattern for ambitious, successful New Yorkers: bachelor dating, marriage, suburbia, children, divorce, social climb, celebrity dating. Then came serial monogamous relationships with bright, accomplished women, often taller and slim, usually not Jewish, and "age-appropriate." The "anti-bimbo billionaire," the *New York Post* declared.

As planned, by 1996 Bloomberg had become a boldface name in the social columns, and Barbara Walters could soon proclaim him a player: "The social set in New York has discovered him." He was attracting attention as the host of ostentatious parties at Elaine's, at Spago (with a live mermaid over the raw bar), of the after-party following Washington's elite Gridiron dinner, the annual press roast of the president and other political celebrities, and at the American Museum of Natural History.

In a city accustomed to extravagance, most over-the-top displays attract little notice. Not so the annual Bloomberg L.P. Christmas nights at the museum. They are remembered in exquisite detail by many of the staffers and guests—about six thousand of them—who partied in nearly every corner of the museum, among the lifelike displays of African lions and American bison in the Diorama Gallery, under the electronic stars in the Rose Center for Earth and Science.

"Actors on stilts greeted us in the lobby," recalls one guest. "They were dressed in costumes, on these huge stilts, Cirque du Soleil–like. And they were just the greeters. They are going around and they've got these silk scarves long enough to hit the floor. Extravagant. And every room has a different theme, different food, music, entertainment: Spanish food, flamenco dancing, or Chinese or Asian food. It was not at all generic, it was culture-specific. In the Whale Room there was contemporary music, dancing, strobe lights, a raw bar, waiters going around with food, lots of champagne flowing. And an element of sexiness. Two or three of the performers were dancers wearing some sort of leotard—skin colored. You do that double take—is this person naked?

"Mike went from room to room. He was a schmoozer. One or two lines and he is gone, wry and sarcastic, you know—'I am sorry you had to marry your husband,' and at the same time he is turning to someone else—but you felt like you connected for a moment."

The company's family picnics at the Bloomberg Westchester home in Armonk or at a city park on Randall's Island were equally extravagant, but kid-friendly. Clowns and costumed characters roamed the lawn, children rode on the Ferris wheel and roller coaster, visited the cooling tents with their clouds of mist, tried out the trampoline and flying trapeze, got paper party hats constructed by "Wacky Wendy," gorged on sliders, lobster rolls, dumplings, hot dogs, French fries and mountains of candy.

But the ne plus ultra of Bloomberg parties was no family outing. It was a "Seven Deadly Sins" frolic in 2000 for several thousand guests of the London office. The *Sunday Times* couldn't get over it: "The lavish themed bash was held in a disused office block that took 10 days to refurbish, renovate and prepare for the occasion. Among the attractions spread over four floors were massage and shiatsu rooms, manicure booths, a sushi bar, cabaret, casino, drag queens, a disco and live bands."

The Lust Room featured a twenty-five-foot-wide bed covered in purple satin, while the Avarice Room was bedecked with gold drapes, and entertainers circulated among the guests, waving bundles of cash and shouting, "Money—ain't it gorgeous?"

In a basement room, representing sloth, guests could get a massage, and gluttony took the form of a pseudo pig trough filled with truffles and other sweets. Guests ate and drank and watched entertainers who were lying on the floor having food shoved into their mouths.

The event, so large it required forty security guards, three first-aid stations, and an ambulance standing by outside, also featured the central attraction, "the American billionaire Michael Bloomberg," as the *Times* put it. "An inveterate networker, he regularly dines with such luminaries as Sir David Frost, Stephen Fry, Lord Archer and Julia Peyton-Jones, director of the Serpentine Gallery in Kensington Gardens."

In these carefree celebrity years, Bloomberg was seen with Liv Ullmann, Mary McFadden, Marisa Berenson, Diana Ross. Preparing to run for mayor, he boasted to *New York Magazine* that two of the city's most prominent social doyennes, Annette de la Renta and Jayne Wrightsman, "see me as their boy toy."

Fantasy, or just embroidery, also appears in Bloomberg's memoir, in which he boasts that before marriage, "I had a girlfriend in every city." His ex, Susan Bloomberg, begs to differ.

"That's maybe what Michael would like people to believe," she told the *Mail,* "but that's not the Michael who fell in love with me." She did observe that after their marriage ended, "I didn't like the person he was becoming. I didn't like seeing pictures of him at parties with all these social people, who latched on to him because he was wealthy."

But who was latching on to whom? Michael Bloomberg's visible social mixing was a conscious campaign to advance his rebranding. Just as his self-portrait as party animal in college does not match his friends' memories, the boy-toy image seems to have been camouflage for a more determined pursuit.

The wife of a Hopkins friend ran into him after his divorce. "I teased him, said, 'Well now you can go out with beautiful young models,' and he said, 'Look, how long does it take to make love? ten minutes?'—only he didn't say make love, if you know what I mean. 'Then what? I have to be able to talk to them. I don't want to be bored.'"

Post-marriage, Bloomberg has had just a few monogamous relationships. He seriously dated Ann Reinking, the dancer-choreographer, and Mary Jane Salk, a writer and widow of the child psychologist Lee Salk. Bloomberg's tax returns show that he provided generously for Ms. Salk with a $1-million trust fund and a Park Avenue condominium apartment he bought in 2000 for approximately $3.75 million.

In 2000, he met Diana Taylor, an investment banker, at a lunch. The tall, striking Ms. Taylor soon became Bloomberg's constant companion and hostess. Though a managing director of a financial services firm, she clearly maintains a flexible schedule, often traveling with Bloomberg out of town and appearing by his side, smiling and towering over him in stunning designer outfits.

"The best thing that's happened to the mayor is Diana

Taylor—she's funny, smart, and adores him," says Anna Wintour, the *Vogue* editor in chief and friend of the couple, who sometimes helps select Ms. Taylor's wardrobe. "She doesn't need help, it's more a convenience thing because she is so busy. She'll call, say 'I have such and such an event,' and we will point her in the right direction."

Taylor appeared on *Vanity Fair*'s 2008 International Best Dressed List, in the lofty company of Michelle Obama, Carla Bruni-Sarkozy and Ivanka Trump. When friends mentioned the honor to Bloomberg, he claimed some credit as well—for having paid for the Ralph Laurens and Giorgio Armanis that Taylor wore in her unofficial role as the city's First Lady.

Being available on a moment's notice and conforming to his lifestyle has been a long-standing requirement for Bloomberg's woman friends. Elizabeth Hayt, a writer who went out on only one unhappy date, recalls being warned by him that any woman in his life has to be able to throw a spontaneous dinner for ten or twelve, has to be available at the last minute to fly to Bermuda or anywhere else.

"If you want to live like that, you cannot have your own life," says Hayt. "It's pretty typical of powerful men. They want to get on these planes and go where they want to go. And they don't want to be with dumb women. Smart and pretty is much preferred over big, busty and blond. It reflects well on them."

Bloomberg's other customs are not unconventional. He has a passion for golf, for that childhood-inspired mélange of burned bacon and peanut butter, for steak and the roast chicken served at *Quatorze Bis,* an east-side Manhattan bistro, for lip-stingingly salty popcorn—at least he did until he expanded his public health campaign to wage war on salt. He admits to occasionally overindulging in red wine and he observes a permanent, competitive diet with uneven results, regularly comparing weight with his company's chairman, Peter Grauer. Whoever loses the least makes a donation to charity.

Bloomberg is a catnapper and says he does not sleep long. He reads a lot—the *Economist* and the *Financial Times* head his list—and is incapable of taking a night off, just relaxing alone. "He has ants in the pants," says his friend Nancy Hass. He frequently entertains in his town house, or meets friends for dinner on the Upper East Side or in a neighborhood restaurant in Queens or Brooklyn. Often, after a work-related dinner, instead of heading home he'll move on to a hotel or restaurant bar for hours of conversation about everything from golf to foreign affairs. "It's up to him," said one of his oldest friends, Michael "Mungo" Meehan.

Throughout his life, he had a way of almost acquiring people, subjecting them to a kind of special Bloomberg test of loyalty and competence. Those who pass are "in" and barring a breach of faith they stay in. Those who do not are "out" and they stay out. For his friends, they say, Bloomberg will do anything, from loaning money to helping a sick relative. "He is unbelievably loyal," says Meehan.

In Bloomberg's government, those who work for him admire the freedom he gives them, but all know that Bloomberg, while he might respect them, trusts only a very few people close to him—Patti Harris, Kevin Sheekey, Edward Skyler, who were all with him first at his company—and Daniel Doctoroff, who went to Bloomberg L.P. after he left his role as deputy mayor.

Friends and former dates pop up in ceremonial jobs, the children of friends get prized, unpaid internships.

When Bloomberg left the daily operations of Bloomberg L.P. to run for mayor, he tapped Peter Grauer, an active member of his board and a close friend for years, to run it. He and

Grauer had first met in the late 1980s when they took their daughters to horseback riding lessons. Bloomberg has had the same lawyer, Richard DeScherer, and accountant, Martin Geller, since his company was in its infancy. When the husband of his children's godmother was making a film, Bloomberg bankrolled it.

Bloomberg's closest friends tend to be like him, wealthy men rooted in high finance: Michael Steinberg, an asset manager; Meehan, a Salomon colleague he met in 1971; DeScherer; Michael Steinhardt, former hedge fund manager; Grauer; and Steven Rattner, who, at his company the Quadrangle Group, managed Bloomberg's personal fortune.

In sharp contrast to his public behavior, Bloomberg is reputed to be talkative with his trusted friends in private, openly sharing his views, candidly and often cuttingly critiquing the same public figures he treats mildly and neutrally in public settings. His own staff members assume that he is in fact the very source of the few confidential tidbits that have leaked out of his administration because he shares them with his dinner and post-dinner companions and people talk. That may be how objections of his closest advisers to his third-term plans got out, along with his criticisms of Barack Obama during the 2008 presidential race. Once Obama was in office and Bloomberg was in pursuit of support for New York—and support for his reelection from black New Yorkers—the mayor could not praise him or meet with him enough.

That is pure Bloomberg. He can adapt, adapt, adapt. It has been the motif of Bloomberg's life—personal and professional. He learned to fly his own planes and helicopters, but relinquished the controls when he became mayor. He joined exclusive clubs plainly closed to blacks and Hispanics, then quit when politics demanded it. After working so diligently to break into the social whirl of New York to make himself noticed, he quickly shed the flamboyant image to run for office.

Once elected, he insisted on combining his public life with a rigorous privacy.

Most of his constituents don't even know exactly where their $1-a-year mayor lives. In his best imperial manner, Bloomberg refused to move into Gracie Mansion, the creaky wooden riverfront residence of mayors since 1942. He deigns to visit only for occasional meetings and civic events. He has continued to live and privately entertain at East Seventy-ninth Street near Central Park, lavishly decorated by the mayor's celebrity designer, Jamie Drake, who also lent his ornate touch to Bloomberg's 6,000-square-foot waterfront home in Bermuda close to a golf course and his three-story London apartment on Cadogan Square (and to Madonna's baroque L.A. home).

The mayoral home is as ostentatious as his company offices but in European baronial rather than futuristic style. According to visitors, it features formal British furniture, flocked wallpaper, chintz upholstery, a foyer paved with Egyptian marble, Savonnerie rugs and trompe l'oeil ceiling paintings in the powder room.

The house, which Bloomberg has gradually expanded to 12,500 square feet by buying 5,000 additional square feet of space from an adjoining building, is reputed to boast a nineteenth-century pool table, Chinese vases, a twelfth-century buddha, a Fragonard and numerous twentieth-century paintings. One guest is sure he spotted a Rothko; another spoke of a wood-paneled library with leopard-print accents. After his first visit to the house, a former member of Bloomberg's staff was stunned to realize that "everything is real."

Most New Yorkers have seen only external pictures, if that, of the mayoral house—a reflection of security concerns and the

Bloomberg private mindset. It wasn't until halfway through his second term that New Yorkers learned their mayor had two stents implanted in a coronary artery the year before his first campaign. The heart blockage was revealed only because *Newsweek*'s reporters dug into health records during Bloomberg's presidential flirtation. The stock market did not shudder at the news. But in a city that heard Rudy Giuliani reciting clinical descriptions of his prostate treatments and Ed Koch loudly proclaiming his fitness seventy-two hours after suffering a minor stroke, the "none of your business" Bloomberg manner came across as defiant and disdaining.

Two weeks after the new mayor took office, he disappeared one Monday. It turned out he was touring new buildings at Johns Hopkins, his alma mater in Baltimore. When Bloomberg spotted a *New York Post* reporter trailing him, he threatened to call the police because the writer lacked a campus pass. "I have no interest in talking to you." That was 2002 and things never changed much.

Bloomberg's obsessive search for privacy produces frequent disappearances when he is not campaigning for office, none of them ever announced—a privilege the president of the United States does not enjoy. "We'd say Michael Bloomberg can defy time," explained a former City Hall aide. "Look at how it works: He does his radio show Friday morning. At 11:05, the latest, he is in his car. At 11:30 he is at the airport. His plane is in the air at 11:40, he's in Bermuda at 2:10. He's on the golf course by 2:30. He's back in New York Sunday evening before dinner. Almost every weekend, spring and fall."

If a crisis erupts in New York, as it inevitably does, he stays in touch by cell phone, delegates decisions to a deputy mayor or police or fire commissioner, issues a statement to the press from afar and flies back in time for the press conference. In 2007, when a fire in the Deutsche Bank building at the World Trade Center site took the lives of two firefighters, Bloomberg failed to appear for several hours—something that would have produced outraged headlines when Ed Koch, David Dinkins and Rudy Giuliani were in charge. The city did not notice. His absences are never even mentioned in news accounts. Polls show the public accepts his right to privacy, even if it contributes to what one adviser called his "out-of-touch branding."

Bloomberg has simply changed expectations, molding the job to fit his insistence on secrecy. In much larger ways, he has done the adjusting.

Bloomberg's Zelig-like ability to fit in, to make himself part of a new universe, is evident throughout his adult life. He has been bawdy on bawdy Wall Street, charming on charming Park Avenue, politically correct in politically correct City Hall.

He hasn't avoided tin-eared remarks and insensitive observations but he has learned to hide his crass side. He still delights in regaling other men and sometimes women with lusty reminiscences about celebrity conquests and equally colorful fantasies about how he would like to entertain Salma Hayek in Gracie Mansion. But the mayor of New York has not been caught making crude remarks in public. He has been respectful to the many women he named to top positions and never faced charges of sexism or sexual harassment, as he did at his company. Despite predictions that he would be the most social mayor since the jazz age's Jimmy "Beau James" Walker, the protean Bloomberg's routine with Diana Taylor is settled, safe, convenient.

Mike Bloomberg's pragmatism seems always to prevail over Mike Bloomberg's emotions, and a cold-eyed discipline over his frailties. Get a hold and get over it, as his parents instructed, and he does.

When Bill Clinton's dalliance with Monica Lewinsky was entertaining America, Bloomberg was indignant. Casual acquaintances were amazed to hear him vent angrily about the president. Clinton's behavior was not only outrageous, he would say, it was unacceptable; he should resign. Mike Bloomberg suddenly a prig? No way. He saw Clinton's offense not as immoral; it was self-indulgent, lacking self-control. Not the Bloomberg way.

CHAPTER 6

ENTER THE HIGH ROLLER

MIKE'S LIST: President of the United States. Secretary general of the United Nations. Head of the World Bank.

Those were three jobs Mike Bloomberg coveted as far back as college. He talked about them so often that friends were convinced that he wasn't fantasizing the way young people do, but actually planning ahead.

Plans change, though, and his life took a different course. Despite his early fascination with prominent public office, he made his way in private business and pretty much stayed away from politics. A Democrat, he made political contributions—modest ones given his wealth—to mostly Democratic candidates. But participatory politics was never his thing. In fact, he wrote in his self-admiring memoir, fittingly titled *Bloomberg by Bloomberg,* that when he was pondering a career change in his late thirties, "My impatience with government kept me away from politics. All elected officials could stop worrying."

In what could have been a broad hint, however, he also wrote that though being a legislator would bore him, "If I ever ran it would be for a job in the executive branch of government—mayor, governor or president. I think I would be great in any of these three executive jobs that mirror my experience."

His book was published in 1997, the same year Rudolph Giuliani was elected to his second and, under New York City's term-limits law, last term as mayor. The lineup of would-be successors was turning into a crowd, the list of likely candidates familiar, with one exception: Bloomberg. His name was on nobody's list but his own, and with good reason.

A Wall Street ace and computer entrepreneur, a political neophyte with an accent stuck somewhere between Boston and New York, did not fit the preferred profile. Slight of build and only five feet seven inches tall (though his New York State license reads five feet ten inches), Bloomberg could enter most rooms unnoticed. He could not deliver a speech anyone would want to hear, had never tangled with New York's ethnic and racial power centers or negotiated with any of its stubborn municipal unions. He had a crude mouth, a temper and no obvious public charm.

Still, his independence and smarts might appeal to many pragmatic voters. He could argue that by paying his own way and soliciting not a penny from contributors, he would govern on the merits, immune to pressure and free of the special interests and their selfish agendas.

Running even a stunningly successful business is not running New York, the toughest city in the country. It is not for nothing that many New Yorkers favor the theory that anyone who wants to be their mayor has to be a bit nuts. New York is infamously impossible to tame, politically treacherous and hard to impress.

The last privileged rich guy who tried to buy his way into City Hall—Ronald Lauder, the cosmetics heir—was crushed by Giuliani in the 1989 Republican primary after outspending him 5 to 1. Bloomberg was exponentially more savvy and potentially more salable than the grim-faced Lauder. Yet he was still a colorless manager, little known beyond the privileged precincts of Wall Street and Park Avenue.

New York's mayors rate celebrity status. They are, by law and practice, all powerful. The legislature, the city council, used to be ridiculed as weaker than a rubber stamp because it didn't even leave an impression. Since it was expanded and strengthened under a court-ordered reorganization in 1989, it has been derided merely for giving in to every mayor at just about every opportunity.

New Yorkers treat mayors as part of their dysfunctional family. They boo them at ball games, cheer them at tickertape parades, blame them for everything that goes wrong. Giuliani's predecessor Ed Koch used to say that if a sparrow died of a heart attack in Central Park, he would be held responsible. The city has a way of embracing its mayors when they first take office, then tiring of them and coldly rejecting them. And mayors have a way of trying to escape to higher office by running for governor or president. None has succeeded because what it takes to win in the city—a liberal agenda on social issues, street-smart candor and a nasty edge—is precisely what it takes to fail everywhere else.

That is because New York is unlike everywhere else. When I wrote a New York City column I used to say that if the town did not exist, it would never be invented. It is wondrous and purely ridiculous.

In the best of times the place is an unruly leviathan of eight million people chasing dreams and pursuing drudgeries in a multiethnic, multilingual cacophony of the very rich, very poor and very in between. The city houses clashing tribes of blue-collar workers and civil servants and striving immigrants, of artists and actors and students and drug dealers, of tourists who spend money and natives who wish they would do so invisibly, of street entrepreneurs selling seventy-five-cent coffee from a cart outside glittery Starbucks emporiums peddling exotic brews at triple the price.

New York's intricacies produce a mean brand of politics. Every constituency offers a rival agenda and none is shy about demanding it. Agreement is as elusive as a quiet city street.

The remnants of New York's Irish and Italian middle class want everything in their neat clapboard Queens neighborhoods to stay forever the same. Staten Islanders, anomalous Republicans at the other end of a ferry and faraway bridge, want to feel included and demand the resources that come with acceptance. The liberal Upper West Siders of Manhattan want everything to change unless change means replacing an old building with a new one.

In fact, most New Yorkers never want anything built in their neighborhood except a school, and never want anything taken away, especially a firehouse. The city's powers are as dissimilar as the people—ranging from real estate barons and municipal labor leaders, to the Reverend Al Sharpton, semireformed firebrand.

The job of bringing a semblance of order to the chaotic metropolis goes to the city's mayors, who have followed one after the other in a seesaw pattern of the weak and strong, the dull and vivid. New Yorkers have given the job to bland clubhouse accountants, like Abraham Beame, overwhelmed by the collapse of the city's finances, and to compelling showmen like Fiorello LaGuardia, who besides reading the comics to kids during a newspaper strike tapped into the New Deal's resources to nurse New Yorkers through the Depression. The city has romanced its chief executives and spurned them, loved them, hated them, built them up and torn them down.

No New York mayor has left City Hall unblemished. Even LaGuardia, still a beloved folk hero, retired an embittered man. He had streamlined the bureaucracy, chased after mobsters, lifted spirits in the trying decade of the thirties. But after he won a third term in 1941 and President Franklin Delano Roosevelt named him director of the Office of Civilian Defense, LaGuardia struggled to juggle the two jobs for a year, shuttling between New York and Washington. He really wanted a larger role in World War II but failed in his quest to be a general. Ill and frustrated, he left happier memories—and a mountain of debt—behind him.

A succession of clubhouse hacks and dutiful Democrats finally yielded City Hall to John V. Lindsay in 1965. The athletic liberal congressman with movie star looks wanted to preside over a benevolent government that would right every wrong in an atmosphere of racial harmony. But the social upheavals of that agitated decade left him dispirited and disliked. His "Fun City" turned sullen and depressed by racial unrest, strikes, violent crime and an imminent fiscal meltdown. The welfare rolls doubled, city prisoners rioted, taxes had to be raised, an experiment in community control of the schools began to fail, the middle class fled and took its taxes to the suburbs.

When Lindsay, who had left the GOP for the Democratic Party, pursued the presidency in 1972, he barely got off the ground.

After Beame, Edward I. Koch barreled into City Hall. A neocon Democrat who entertained New York with his bold showmanship and comedic touch, he also infuriated critics with his stubborn rectitude and big boastful mouth. He righted the city's finances, faced up to unpopular decisions and restored the city's brash posture.

But Koch, too, gradually fell from grace, victim of his abrasiveness and bad relations with black New Yorkers. He hurt himself with an ill-timed, ill-prepared run for governor, overcame that but then was further injured by a third-term corruption scandal that never involved him directly but tainted his reputation.

Then came the first black mayor, David Dinkins, to celebrate the city as a "gorgeous mosaic," only to have it shattered by ethnic strife, a bad economy and a roaring crime wave. He was defeated by the city and then by Rudy Giuliani, the first Republican mayor in a quarter century.

Giuliani gave New York a needed slap in the face, actually governing the supposedly ungovernable city. He went after crime, improved the quality of life, ruthlessly reduced the welfare rolls. But he had no patience for civil liberties or the First Amendment, damaged race relations with his unrelenting ferocity, was constantly attacking someone or something and governed with strict top-down discipline that discouraged creativity. He played politics with patronage appointments and repelled the public with his messy personal life.

By September 10, 2001, just 42 percent of the people said they would give him a third term if the two-term limit law did not prevent it. Only his grit in the weeks after the attack on the World Trade Center salvaged his reputation. Revived and riding high, he tried to become president of the United States. Yet like every other mayor who had chased higher office, Giuliani collapsed, failing to win a single Republican primary in 2008.

Even a casual reader of New York history could see that being mayor was a headache and a career ender. Why would a political neophyte like Mike Bloomberg want the job?

"It was time for a new challenge," he told me. "I'd been running my company for twenty years, it was time to go on." Friends said he told them he was bored. And he liked taking risks. As Bloomberg, the avid practitioner of Wall Street's salty patois, explained at a meeting to prepare for his campaign, the *New Yorker* reported, "I get slapped a lot, but I get laid a lot, too."

At the end of 1997, with the next mayoral race still four years away, he was quietly exploring a run for City Hall, confident enough to think he could succeed, wealthy enough to give campaigning a try and realistic enough to know that he was not about to get those dream jobs of his youth—leading the United States, the United Nations or the World Bank.

"Those three jobs, you can have an impact on the world," he told me when he was in his second term. "Now if I had to pick a fourth, and arguably more than one or two of the others, it is the mayor of New York City, because the city is so big. When I go overseas, you're not like a head of state but the press will be there and the government will receive you."

When he decided to switch careers, Bloomberg was not only a multibillionaire and noted philanthropist, he had assembled all the toys and perks of privilege. He flew his own planes, he owned, in addition to the lavish homes in London, Bermuda, New York, and Armonk, a farm in Westchester, a mansion in Vail, Colorado, and memberships in fourteen exclusive clubs in New York City, Maryland, and Bermuda, including the Harmonie, Bond, Harvard and Brook clubs and the Century Association in Manhattan; the Coral Beach and Tennis Club in Bermuda, the Golf Club of Purchase, New York, and the Caves Valley Golf Club in Maryland.

Bloomberg also spent his money generously, giving more than $100 million to about six hundred charities in 2000, the year before he ran for mayor. He was a benefactor of civic groups, hospitals, synagogues, social programs and especially of his ever-grateful alma mater, Johns Hopkins. He contributed his way onto the boards of Lincoln Center for the Performing Arts and the Metropolitan Museum of Art. And he lived the life of a desirable, divorced bachelor, an overactive member of the New York cultural and social elite.

When he first thought about City Hall in 1997, *Forbes Magazine* estimated his net worth at $1.3 billion. And the source of his fortune, Bloomberg L.P., was growing rapidly. He did not have to work another day in his life. That, of course, was the problem.

As far back as the 1980s, Ken Lipper, a colleague at Salomon Brothers and later an aide to Mayor Koch, remembers Bloomberg speaking longingly of a public career. "When I was in City Hall, I remember Mike saying, 'I'm gonna copy your life.' I had the impression that he would run for office. He had the means to run, he had the desire, he thought he could do a better job than other people, he really believed that. And he liked the idea of the glamour, the attention, all of that."

Other billionaires put their names on buildings and concert halls, endow hospital wings, join boards. Bloomberg did his share of that and openly enjoyed the recognition that his money bought him.

But the Hopkins- and Harvard-trained engineer who had revolutionized Wall Street wanted to do something still more important, and something new.

"You gotta do something with your life," he said, recalling his decision to go into politics. "And public service was something I hadn't done."

Bloomberg experimented with Hollywood, financing a film based on an Arthur Miller novel about anti-Semitism, *Focus,* which opened in 2001. Backing the film was about friendship, not about shifting to show business: the director, Neal Slavin, married an old friend of Bloomberg, the godmother of his children. "He told me he had seen ten films in his whole life," recalls Slavin with a laugh. "*Blazing Saddles* was his favorite. I think he can't sit still for that long."

So he was not going to make films. Besides, there are many film producers at one time, only one mayor. Friends who had served in government had always told him they found public service electric, whether Lipper and Nathan Leventhal, another Koch alumnus, or the most influential, the late Steven Fenster, a Harvard classmate who had worked as one of Defense Secretary Robert McNamara's "whiz kids" before becoming an investment banker.

The first media mention of Bloomberg's political aspirations appeared in the *Financial Times,* during his 1997 book tour, slipped into an interview, it would seem, by one Michael R. Bloomberg. "He would quite like to be president of the US, but accepts it could be a tall order to arrange," wrote the reporter, Raymond Snoddy. "Instead, he is thinking about running for mayor of New York." That article, all of 497 words, generated a buzz. Bloomberg says friends called, that his sister, Marjorie, teased him about the insulting presumption that he could run for mayor but not for president. Well, what's wrong with being mayor?

Once planted, dutifully reported and repeated, the notion of a mayoral run developed a life of its own, with substantial encouragement from the antsy Bloomberg and from fellow business tycoons who feared that after Giuliani the city would revert to clubhouse rule and labor union dominance, that crime would rise again and trigger a destructive cycle. The barons loved the idea of their energetic friend running City Hall and watching out for their interests. Given his resources, he could rise above the sordid politics of New York, buy the best consultants, pollsters and advertising mavens and ride a media blitz into office.

Others thought he was delusional. What would happen when reporters searched through the news files and learned about Bloomberg's sarcasm and short temper, his testosterone-fueled crudeness, wit, or the sexual harassment charges brought against him and his company? He'd find unflattering revivals of quotes like one from a 1996 *Guardian* interview: "I like the theater, dining and chasing women. Let me put it this way: I am a single, straight billionaire in Manhattan. It's like a wet dream."

A journalist friend remembers telling him, "'Mike you are crazy, the reporters will kill you with your own words.' He wasn't worried. He said, 'If it didn't stop Clinton, it won't stop me.'"

He would face other problems. The mayor would inherit a dysfunctional public school system; no more places to dump the city's garbage; racial tensions rubbed raw by Giuliani's truculence; gridlocked traffic and mounting municipal debt. Bloomberg would have to preserve Giuliani's success in reducing crime and welfare payments, find a way to build more affordable housing, unfreeze archaic zoning laws.

And winning did not look easy. Bloomberg's chances of getting the Democratic nomination were nil; too many better known Democrats were itching to retake the city from Giuliani. The Republicans, always hungry for attention and money and a plausible candidate, would welcome a wealthy turncoat, but their label represented a serious handicap with voters who registered 5 to 1 Democratic. Only three non-Democrats—LaGuardia as a "Fusion" candidate and Republicans Lindsay and Giuliani—had succeeded in the last seventy-five years. Betting against the odds, Bloomberg quietly switched his affiliation to Republican.

He was a stranger to New York's Republican establishment, though, the professional politicians who could talk up a candidate, give him credibility at least on the inside, with the party's power brokers.

Bloomberg had to connect the dots from his crowd to theirs. He had to network, and that tapped into one of his talents. He was a good networker who had developed a habit of holding on to old friends and lovers, keeping his connection to them even if just tangentially with an e-mail here, an invitation there and later, a mayoral appointment to some honorary position. He even kept ties to the old Salomon crowd that had spurned him.

His approach, helped by the magnet of money, the allure that wealth always confers on the wealthy, was effective. By instinct or design, Bloomberg generated loyalty by never burning bridges. That is a useful technique for someone interested in politics, the profession of connections and interconnections. To break into Republican circles, he turned to friends, including a former girlfriend, Christy Ferer. Ferer, who met her husband through Republican senator Alfonse D'Amato, had befriended the senator's trusted aide, Zenia Mucha.

Ferer called her friend Zenia about Mike as he prepared to run for mayor. By then, Zenia had become the closest adviser to New York Republican governor George Pataki, and was happy to invite Bloomberg to lunch. It went well, she told Pataki, and that's how he met the governor. That went well, too. And why not? The Republicans lacked a strong candidate for mayor. Bloomberg was smart, and wealthy, a potential contributor and a candidate able to pay his own way.

"The fact that he was willing to finance his own campaign

made it much easier to actually see a possible win," Mucha remembers. "In New York City, it is very difficult to raise the kind of money a Republican would need to challenge Democrats. The demographic is not there."

The governor gave his blessings and alerted the Republican troops and business allies. Bloomberg also connected some dots to Guy Molinari, the borough president of Republican-friendly Staten Island. In the 2000 presidential campaign, Molinari had managed New York for Senator John McCain of Arizona, a social friend of Bloomberg, and Molinari, too, welcomed the wealthy new benefactor, who contributed handsomely to his Staten Island clubhouse.

As he networked, Bloomberg prepped. To learn about the city, he hired an army of consultants and tutors. His philanthropy had exposed him to some civic and political leaders and their programs. But the vital requirement was a team of experienced political operatives, and the pivotal partner was right at hand: his most trusted employee at Bloomberg L.P., Patricia "Patti" Harris, a former director of the city Art Commission in Mayor Koch's City Hall.

A study in competence whose permanent smile belies a steely resolve, Harris had joined Bloomberg's company in 1994 to manage his philanthropy. Recommended by yet another Koch alumna, Harris soon became her boss's confidante, fiercely loyal and unequalled in power, his "velvet hammer." She influenced top staff selections and just about every aspect of his life—and death. She even picked his burial plot, Bloomberg revealed airily one day—somewhere in New York City, though he does not know where. He does not have to know. Patti Harris does.

All powerful people need an anchor, someone secure and confident enough to utter uncomfortable truths. Spouses often do the honors. For the divorced Bloomberg, the role was Harris's. When the political bug bit her boss, Harris was a married mother of two children in elementary school and a stepson in his twenties. She might have preferred her gracious corporate life on Park Avenue. Suddenly, she had to assemble a campaign staff fast.

As it happened, help came knocking at the door in the person of Kevin Sheekey, a young Democrat who worked for Senator Daniel Patrick Moynihan in Washington but wanted a change. A wiry Irish pol with darting eyes and a talent for spinning both journalists and fancy tales, Sheekey can sit for an hour-long interview without answering one question directly, deny he did any such thing and convince his questioner—momentarily, at least—that he is right. He flits from subject to subject without notice, drops ideas from the frivolous to the creative like a manic gardener scattering seeds, deflecting anger with humor.

The job-hunting Sheekey had decided that Bloomberg L.P. needed a lobbyist on Capitol Hill, connected with Harris through a mutual friend and so met Bloomberg in June 1997. "I sat down with him and he asked me if he should run for mayor. He clearly had been thinking about it before I got through the door." Sheekey told Bloomberg he didn't know, but under no circumstances should he tell anyone he was *not* running for mayor "because it is a great [business] promotion."

With help from Sheekey, Harris and other connections, the candidate-in-training met not only with the pooh-bahs of the GOP but with a parade of elected officials, political scientists and journalists: people like Congressman Charles Rangel of Harlem; former police commissioners Raymond Kelly and Robert McGuire, former schools chancellor Frank Macchiarola. He connected with consultants, academicians, union leaders and preachers, tapping talents and picking brains. Some were dazzled. Barnard professor Ester Fuchs, a former adviser to Mayor David Dinkins, asked him why he wanted to be mayor. "He said, 'I want to fix public education, everybody deserves a good education.' He said that then!"

Others were not immediately impressed. Calvin Butts, the influential pastor of the Abyssinian Baptist Church in Harlem, remembers his reservations before he became a fan and beneficiary of generous Bloomberg donations. "I met with him in his offices at Bloomberg, open, all glass, the way he likes it. He was asking me what it means to be mayor, and I was trying to tell him, but he was in the mode of push-back. He was kind of like, 'I really don't care what you think, let me tell you where I'm going with this.' I said to myself, gee that is kind of arrogant. I remember saying someone should tell this guy to listen, but I was told that is a characteristic of people with this kind of money. I found out later he does reach out, but there are certain things he believes he must do and will go bull-headed and try to do them."

At least Bloomberg did not need to solicit campaign contributions. But he had to decode New York's dizzying array of neighborhoods and special interests and the sensitivities surrounding issues he never before considered.

His learning, though facilitated by his quick mind, was complicated by his stubbornness. He could not understand at first the law that barred expulsion of a disruptive student, why New Yorkers have a legal right to shelter, why the parents of underage girls seeking abortions should not be notified. In his business, codes of conduct had been for him to prescribe. Now he had to learn the city's ways and means.

In 2000 as he geared up to run, Bloomberg directed more of his contributions to city endeavors, participated in more civic events and more assertively than before, identified his company with volunteer efforts. His charitable giving doubled to $100.5 million and of two hundred new recipients, seventy-nine were in New York City. At about the same time Bloomberg News created a new division to cover city news, and the company employees—long encouraged to volunteer in schools, museums, parks and programs for the disabled—felt a renewed emphasis on doing good works around town.

Some at Bloomberg L.P. are convinced they were made part of the boss's "rebranding." As one employee put it, "There are those who believe that Mike and Patti plotted his political career by winning the loyalty of all the cultural and social organizations, causes and charities that he supported, developing a reservoir of social ties, good will, creating a buzz that became a potent, silent base of support spanning a broad range of the city's ethnic and political terrain." It certainly sounds like politics.

Bloomberg's advisers bristle at that interpretation. As Patti Harris sees it, the company's expanding good works, and new focus on city news, were extensions of Bloomberg L.P.'s growth and prosperity in its hometown: "He felt the company was growing at such a fast rate, and it should give back to the city that was contributing to its success. And I think he wanted employees to also know they could help make the city a better place."

Maybe so. But the policy still had political value, spreading his name and goodwill.

Bloomberg exposed himself to his spreading network of advisers and local factotums. A secular Jew who had dutifully contributed to New York's many Jewish causes, he even visited Israel for the first time two months before declaring his candidacy. (He had, just five years earlier, quipped to a reporter for the *Jerusalem Report* that he saw no reason to go to Israel because "there's no good skiing there," boasting that he had said precisely the same directly to Benjamin Netanyahu, Israel's future prime minister, then the Likud leader, when he saw him in New York. But he made no issue of his faith, telling the *Forward,* "Am I glad to be born a Jew? I never even thought about it in that context. You are what you are. Would I like to be six foot tall and able to throw a football like John Elway? Sure, I would like that."

As the election year approached, Bloomberg's circle developed concentric rings of workers, advisers, consultants. Mitchell Moss of New York University schooled him in the city's economy and ethnic diversity. Fuchs and others advised him on education and city-state relations, and Amanda Burden, member of the City Planning Commission and a friend of Patti Harris, took him touring to dilapidated corners of Brooklyn.

Jonathan Capehart, hired away from the *Daily News*'s editorial board to write a column for Bloomberg News, became a policy adviser and tutor. "I made up these flash cards," recalls Capehart. "Facts and figures about the city school system, the Metropolitan Transit Authority, Albany, who everybody is. I would give them to him. I would breeze by his desk and ask, 'What is the size of the school budget?'" Capehart also introduced him to fellow journalists, African Americans and gay New Yorkers.

Harris and Sheekey recruited Edward Skyler, a former Giuliani press aide, William Cunningham, a former Moynihan operative, Douglas Schoen, an experienced political pollster, Maureen Connelly, a public relations consultant and Koch press secretary, and Bill Knapp of Washington to design TV commercials.

Bloomberg personally wooed the curmudgeonly David Garth, the city's political guru. Brusque and street-smart, Garth had been a fixture in New York campaigns for decades, guiding

Lindsay, Giuliani and Koch to victory. No longer the feared, all-powerful campaign autocrat, Garth was still sought after for bragging rights. His support lent Bloomberg's campaign much-needed credibility and kept Garth away from the competition.

Garth remembers meeting Bloomberg and thinking, "This was a guy in love with himself. He's a prick, all right? But he also has empathy for people—blacks and Jews, you know? And I never liked the people around him. Except for Kevin, who knows politics, and Patti, who has excellent instincts, these are faceless guys that have made money." Nonetheless, underwhelmed by the Democrats lining up to run for mayor, Garth went with Bloomberg. "I figured it would be interesting." Also, remunerative. Though Garth says he signed without discussing his fee, he knew the affiliation would be worth his while. Not that he thought Bloomberg could win; he didn't. Who did?

Logically, he shouldn't have won. But it was not the first time that fate unpredictably shaped Bloomberg's future—and New York's.

CHAPTER 7

TRAGEDY TRUMPS POLITICS

If Mike Bloomberg had known what he was getting into when he considered a run for mayor in 2001, he might well have run the other way, right back to his fine company in its shimmering glass redoubt, wondering what had ever possessed him to consider participatory politics, in New York of all places.

Even the smoothest campaigns in New York City test endurance and upend logic. "There is an October surprise every month," says Edward Koch, the former mayor. "You gotta be nimble, on your feet, able to dance with a new partner every day."

And that is in normal times. The campaign of 2001 set a new standard, for reasons everyone would like to forget. It was, as ever, a mix of the familiar and the unprecedented, of vivid characters and tribal conflicts, of warring egos and petty rivalries. And it was, as never, overwhelmed by terrorism—the September 11 attack and its aftermath.

Mike Bloomberg's successful journey to City Hall came to depend on the campaign's improbable twists and turns. And on two distinctly New York characters who were not even running: Rudy Giuliani and the Reverend Al Sharpton. They helped the new candidate in ways he never could have envisioned—in ways no one could have envisioned.

Before 9/11, by no known political logic did Mike Bloomberg have a chance to become mayor. He could be the Republican candidate all right; his only primary opponent was former congressman Herman Badillo, who had no money, no base and no chance. But early polls showed that Bloomberg would lose to any of the Democratic candidates—by 40 points! Few voters knew anything about him, only about half had even heard his name. People he recruited to work for him routinely asked if he was prepared to lose. "He said, 'I've thought about that and I think I can handle it.' He didn't sound all that sure," said Kathleen Cudahy, then a city council aide who joined as a consultant.

Bloomberg himself was buoyed by insights from a focus group in December 2000 that left him more hopeful than his many advisers. The group interviews revealed that the leading Democratic aspirants weren't much better known. Only about half the group had heard of Mark Green, the city's public advocate, though he was a frequent candidate who had been elected citywide to an ambiguous ombudsman-like role. Fernando Ferrer, the Bronx borough president, had even less recognition.

Bloomberg? He was wealthy. That was all the voters knew, if they knew that. Did he even know the cost of a quart of milk, some wondered? If not, he sure found out fast. He also learned what voters wanted in their next mayor: a good manager, a fiscal conservative, a conciliator but someone strong enough to say no. They wanted crime to keep declining, better schools, more housing and more jobs. They wanted another tough Giuliani, without his bullying.

As Giuliani's two tempestuous terms drew to a close, it felt like an election for the Democrats to lose. The campaign was to a large degree a referendum on Rudy. He still had a cadre of support, but it had been thinned by his combativeness. After several racial incidents and repeated complaints of police brutality, Giuliani was anathema to blacks and Hispanics and even former supporters had grown weary of him.

But the mayor remained a factor. He had tamed crime and welfare payments. Even Times Square shed its filth after decades of futile reclamation projects. Its comeback spanning three mayoral administrations and two decades was hardly Giuliani's doing, but he was in charge when it arrived and got considerable credit. The "ungovernable" city was turning downright genteel—a stunning transformation from the decaying late 1970s and 1980s.

Back then people made elaborate calculations about how late they dared to ride the subway. Gunshots echoed all night in deteriorated neighborhoods. The phrase "drive-by shooting" entered the city lexicon. Prosecutors had a difficult time seating juries because nearly every hand went up when judges asked who'd been a crime victim. Purses were swiped from restaurant chairs. Parents gave their children mug money to appease assailants on their way to and from school. Women bought skinny "wallets on a purse" to secrete beneath sweaters and jackets.

In 1990, a record 2,245 people were murdered in the city, and more and more middle-class residents—the spine of any city—were escaping to the suburbs. "I felt there was nothing on the horizon to redeem the city from an ever-downward spiral," recalls Joseph Berger, a reporter with the *Times* and book author who grew up in Manhattan and the Bronx. He had never thought for a moment about moving out of the city. But he and his wife, a psychoanalyst, reluctantly left for Westchester County in 1991. Their experience was typical. They had a lovely apartment in an art deco building on Manhattan's West Side near the Hudson River, and were savvy enough to find the best public schools for their daughter, then four. But the daily tension defeated them.

New York's reclamation was no overnight phenomenon; it took more than thirty painful years. Incrementally, the city restored the steep cuts in service and in the municipal workforce, a legacy of the fiscal meltdown of the mid-1970s. Mayors grew more disciplined; everyone learned to do more with less. The city also benefited from social and economic trends beyond any mayor's control, from the merciful collapse of the crime-radiating crack epidemic to sweeping demographic shifts. Vibrant, striving immigrants replaced some poorer, less educated African Americans from the rural South and Puerto Rican New Yorkers. Most important, flourishing Wall Street pumped big bucks into the city treasury.

The climb out of the depths came in fits and starts, crystallizing under Giuliani, who was elected after one of the city's worst periods, a time of rising crime fueled by drug wars and sharp black-Jewish tensions. DAVE, DO SOMETHING a *New York Post* headline screamed at Giuliani's beleaguered predecessor as mayor, David Dinkins.

Taking advantage of the racial polarization, Giuliani defeated Dinkins in 1993 and disciplined the city with his tough policies. But after two terms—a new law limited mayors—Giuliani's truculence had soured even his most ardent supporters. The Democrats felt cockily ready to reclaim City Hall.

"Republicans are elected every thirty years in the midst of a crisis," said Fred Siegel, a historian and admiring Giuliani biographer, on the eve of the 2001 party primaries. "We just had Giuliani for eight years, and there's no crisis."

Reasonable, but wrong. There would be a helluva crisis, and Giuliani did not go quietly.

The Democratic primary shaped up as a conventional contest among familiar faces and factions: Bronx president Ferrer, hoping to be the first Puerto Rican mayor; Public Advocate Green, a liberal veteran candidate now painting himself as a moderate; City Comptroller Alan Hevesi, an experienced official hampered by accusations of mismanaged fund-raising; and Peter Vallone, a visibly tired Queens leader driven out of his job as city council Speaker by the two-term limit. It was a good bet that none could get 40 percent of the vote to avert a runoff between the two top contenders.

Green and Ferrer were in the lead as primary day arrived.

Bloomberg, meanwhile, had just about made it through the summer. Herman Badillo, a former congressman, gamely brought some interest to the Republican contest, but mainly it was Bloomberg vs. Bloomberg. The businessman was a terrible candidate. He was stiff in public, impatient with retail handshaking, awkward with voters and accustomed to saying whatever he wanted and whenever he wanted to say it. Even his own advisers saw the problem. "He started off as a terrible candidate, then got to be a so-so candidate," said one of them.

Could the rigidly private Bloomberg turn himself into a public figure? Retail campaigning was no longer central to a campaign. Television ads, radio ads and direct mailings counted for more than kissing babies or eating hot dogs. With his money, Bloomberg could build a heavily manipulated offstage identity and his minders worked hard to limit and control his public appearances.

On June 6, 2001, Mike Bloomberg made it official, after months of teasing the public with hints that he would run, and once scooping himself by spilling his plans to gossip doyenne Liz Smith at a charity dinner.

But he had to make a public announcement, and did—first saturating the airwaves with a "Hi, I'm Mike" TV ad when he was out of town at his older daughter's graduation. Then Bloomberg announced his candidacy directly, at the Ridgewood Senior Center, in a blue-collar corner of Queens.

It was not an auspicious debut. Facing a phalanx of photographers armed with clicking shutters and flashing strobes, Bloomberg begged for order. "Would it be easier if I just wait for some pictures and get that out of the way?" Pause. "That's not going to stop, no matter what I do? Well, thank you very much for coming. Ahhh—I'm Michael Bloomberg, and I'm running to be the 108th mayor of the City of New York."

Bloomberg could not hide his awkwardness or break out of his self-referential business mode. "Our customers think we walk on water, and I can do that for the city," he pledged. "I can find ways for the average Joe to get to the person in government that can make a difference."

"Wizard of Oz–like," sneered Ferrer. Green, supremely self-confident, airily dismissed Bloomberg with an impatience that bordered on derision, convinced that voters were not about to elect a dull Republican businessman who barely knew the city.

Bloomberg gave his opponents ample ammunition. Well into the campaign he marveled at his discovery of Fordham Road: "It is amazing how much business activity there is in that part of the Bronx," he gushed. "The streets are mobbed, the stores, people are coming and going. There were no empty stores."

With similar innocence, he told the Women's National Republican Club: "That's the other thing that has just amazed me as I've gone around the city. Forty percent of New York City is foreign-born. That's not someone that comes from outside New York City; those are people that come from outside the United States!"

More startling were his politically incorrect sentiments. Relying on statistics but ignoring sensibilities, he praised garbagemen for doing more dangerous work than policemen. Invoking small-town nostalgia, he saw nothing wrong with public school students daily reciting the Lord's Prayer as he had as a boy in Medford, Massachusetts; so what if Jewish students had to recite the beloved Christian words? It hadn't hurt him.

"When he walked back into the office that day, Mike looked like somebody had shot his dog," recalls one campaign adviser. "He was pretty upset. He would say something stupid like that every day."

When he was endorsed by Governor George Pataki, Bloomberg chided Mark Green, by then his opponent, for being too liberal—before conceding to a surprised governor that "I am a liberal, yes, I think in many senses I am a liberal."

Bloomberg was hard to budge from his willful ways, even refusing, with expletives, to give up his tasseled loafers for more Everyman shoes. "It was, 'I am either going to win this or lose this, but my way,'" a staffer recalls.

The newspapers focused mainly on Bloomberg's wealth. When the *Times* began asking about his private clubs, he was forced to resign from four mostly white ones—the Harmonie and Racquet and Tennis clubs in Manhattan, the all-male Brook Club, also in Manhattan, and the Century Country Club in Purchase, New York.

Editorial boards chided him for eluding limits on campaign spending by relying on his own funds; by early August, he had spent $16 million, more than all the other candidates combined.

He grabbed up more than a dozen Web domains to keep NoBloomberg.org and IhateBloomberg.com out of hostile hands; he had his own, handsome website and spoke mostly through his expensive commercials.

Pundits could not contain their glee. "Voters' first impression of the campaign," wrote Gail Collins of the *Times,* "is going to be that the city has a hologram running for chief executive."

Primary day was scheduled for Tuesday, September 11, which dawned sunny and warm, a late summer gift. Then, disaster.

Elections were the last thing on anyone's mind after a plane hijacked by Islamic terrorists crashed into the north tower of the World Trade Center at 8:48 a.m. Eighteen minutes later a second plane plowed into the south tower; a third struck the Pentagon and a fourth crashed in Pennsylvania. Not long after, the burning New York buildings both collapsed, killing more than two thousand workers and hundreds of firemen. The voting was cancelled, the primary reset for September 25.

The candidates gradually resumed dispirited campaigning. Two weeks later, as predicted, Bloomberg trounced Badillo while Ferrer edged out Green without reaching 40 percent. There would be another sixteen days of Democratic combat.

But the mayoral candidates had become political footnotes. The city, indeed the entire country, focused now on only one issue—9/11—and on only one New Yorker—Rudy Giuliani. As if he had prepared his whole life for an enemy equal to his aggression, Rudolph Giuliani rose from his lame-duck torpor to preside over the city with confidence and sensitivity.

Critics would later raise doubts about some of his decisions before and after the planes struck. But in the days after 9/11, he consoled and steadied the city and the nation, becoming "America's Mayor." Chants of "Rudy! Rudy" echoed wherever he went. Even the irreverent David Letterman, his eyes wet with tears, bowed to Giuliani.

Despite his sudden stardom, Rudy was on his way out of City Hall, the first mayoral victim of the term-limits law. Or was he? One day after the inconclusive primary, Giuliani threw the three remaining candidates a curve. He thought he should remain mayor longer than the law allowed, to manage the tragedy and guide the city toward recovery.

Giuliani pondered a number of scenarios, finally coming up with a plan to stay in office an extra three months. The governor and state legislature would have to agree, and so would the candidates. The election could be held as scheduled, but a successor would not take the oath until April 1, 2002.

Giuliani personally delivered his proposal to the three candidates, summoning each to a separate meeting at his makeshift emergency command center on a West Side pier. He met first with Bloomberg, then Green, just before they began observance of Yom Kippur, the most holy day on the Jewish calendar. Bloomberg, in avid pursuit of Giuliani's support, quickly agreed. Green was initially noncommittal but resistant, reminding Giuliani that Lincoln held a regularly scheduled election in 1864, during the Civil War. An outraged Ferrer said no way.

Later that evening, as Green's family gathered for the holiday, they discussed the mayor's proposal. His older brother, Stephen Green, a wealthy real estate investor, felt strongly that it made sense to agree. Mark Green thought about it a little longer, then called Giuliani and gave his consent.

It was a decision that would haunt him throughout the rest of the campaign. He had been running strong among blacks and white liberals who admired his criticism of Giuliani's tactics and tolerance of police misconduct, then suddenly sided with their nemesis.

Maybe he hoped to appeal to centrist voters, but most likely, Green wanted to appease and neutralize Giuliani's sudden popularity. If he had resisted, the mayor might have been angry enough to try changing the law so he could run for a third term, and if he did that, Green wouldn't have a chance.

Whatever the impulse, Green's "ninety-day decision" became a self-inflicted wound, perhaps fatal. In the campaign's "overnights"—its private tracking polls—Green's standing with black New Yorkers plummeted by 15 points, from 80 to 65 percent, and among white liberals by almost 20 points to 50 percent. He regained some ground with both groups, enough to defeat Ferrer. But he did not regain all that he had lost. Siding with Giuliani became the first of several gaffes that undermined Green's quest for badly needed minority votes.

"He never gained back his moral suasion," said Hank Sheinkopf, an experienced Democratic consultant and in a minority among Green advisers. "I knew we were done. I really felt it would be the end of the campaign. Part of what he had was the moral argument—he stood up to Giuliani. By doing what he did, Mark Green became a political hack."

In retrospect Green's former campaign manager, Richard Schrader, who initially supported the move, came to agree that it had been a mistake. "A shadow hung over us all through the campaign."

Giuliani's gambit to extend his reign eventually died. State legislators balked, responding to the powerful Democratic Speaker of the assembly, Sheldon Silver. Thoroughly alienated by Giuliani over the years, as were many of his fellow Democratic lawmakers, he never let the idea come to a vote. And that was the end of the odd but powerfully resonant episode.

Fueling the anger at Green were racial passions. Race always figures in New York campaigns, and it was central in 2001. Ferrer, looking to build a black-Hispanic coalition, courted the Reverend Al Sharpton, a formidable agitator for black rights then at the height of his political influence.

The large, loud Reverend Al, "The Sultan of Spin" as the *Times* of London called him, has never been elected to office but shapes New York politics as surely as any old-time political boss, and just as effectively, if not more so. A huckster to some, a statesman to others, Sharpton first made his name in 1987 when he defended a young black woman named Tawana Brawley, whose claims of abduction and rape by a group of white men were ultimately exposed as a cruel hoax.

Sharpton never admitted error, parading instead as an in-your-face voice of the disaffected. He could inflame passions one moment and soothe them the next. By 2001, his velour outfits had been replaced by business suits and his shoulder-length hair by a trim cut. But his spleen continued to vent on cue, especially in campaign season.

Giuliani refused even to talk to Sharpton. Many Jews suspected him of anti-Semitism; the business community worried that if his candidate Ferrer won, Sharpton would have too much influence in City Hall. Others saw him as a fact of New York life while still others venerated him as a genuine representative of the poor, the abused and the disaffected. Ferrer, by aligning with Sharpton, risked losing as much with one group as he could gain with another.

The Sharpton-Ferrer coalition had managed to get Ferrer into the runoff but now, against Green, Ferrer needed more white support. With Green's encouragement, the Sharpton connection alienated many white voters.

Ferrer added to his problem by proposing diffuse and costly remedies for the city's struggle back from 9/11. Could he really revive and rebuild New York, especially given his ties to Sharpton?

In the runoff, liberal Mark Green found himself the anomalous choice of Rupert Murdoch's right-wing *New York Post,* usually among his harshest critics. But now he was the lesser of evils and a possible mayor.

Murdoch himself met with Green before endorsing him to urge that he denounce Ferrer's Sharpton connection more explicitly. Green briefly held back, but when polls showed the runoff tightening, he delivered harsh blows—"Can New York afford to take a chance?"—which Ferrer decried as ugly and unfair, as playing "the fear card."

And then, inevitably in New York campaigns, came dirty tricks. Leaflets were circulated in mostly Jewish areas of Brooklyn that featured a *New York Post* cartoon depicting Ferrer kissing the rear of a grossly overweight Sharpton. Green denounced the flyer and denied responsibility. But he declined to immediately investigate the source. In yet another miscalculation that deepened hostility against him, he said he preferred to spend his time planning the city budget.

On September 25, Mark Green became Bloomberg's November opponent by defeating Fernando Ferrer 52 to 48 percent, with the electorate largely divided along racial, ethnic and class lines. An exit poll showed Green winning 84 percent of the white voters while Ferrer won among Hispanics by the same margin and among blacks by 71 percent.

With the general election campaign truncated to a mere twenty-five days, the betting and polling still, however, favored Green over Bloomberg the Republican. Despite his blunders, the split among Democrats and a vague public discomfort with

Green, whose self-confidence could veer into hubris, he was a strong speaker, quick on his feet, comfortable with reporters and in front of cameras. Bloomberg was not. He never became a smooth candidate that year. He held his own in debates and other forums only because of his intelligence.

In a normal election year, Green would have won despite his mistakes and Bloomberg's money. The Republican candidate showed no ability to charm voters. But he did not have to. The luring was done for him. The Wall Street mogul found his candidacy buoyed by circumstances well beyond his control.

CHAPTER 8

MONEY, MONEY ON THE WALL

MONDAY, NOVEMBER 5, 2001—one day before New Yorkers were to elect their 108th mayor after a chaotic and sad campaign that could not end soon enough. It would not be over, though, until one more bizarre episode played out.

In the campaign's closing days, candidate Mike Bloomberg had improbably closed the gap with Mark Green, even though the city is overwhelmingly Democratic and Bloomberg had entered the race as a long shot. The prospect of yet another Republican mayor after Rudy Giuliani's two terms alarmed Green's loyal backers, among them Queens-born Harvey Weinstein, the Hollywood mogul. The excitable Weinstein, whose ego matched his girth, decided that despite the late hour, the feuding Democrats could still be united. He appointed himself peacemaker, and over the next several hours starred in a melodrama worthy of one of his movie plots.

Weinstein summoned disaffected Democrats to a lunch at the Four Seasons—Fernando Ferrer, his mentor, Bronx leader Roberto Ramirez, and the Reverend Al Sharpton. Also present was Kenneth Sunshine, a public relations whiz whose clients range from Bronx pols to Barbra Streisand; he was there because he knew everybody—and their cell phone numbers.

Weinstein proposed a big unity photo to end the campaign and had Sunshine invite Green and former president Bill Clinton, by then working out of an office in an admiring Harlem. Green was unprepared for Weinstein's eleventh-hour stunt and balked. He had already held his final campaign event with Clinton and Senator Edward Kennedy; besides, he had no desire to appear in an election day photo with Ferrer and Sharpton, an irritant in many precincts, especially Jewish ones.

"Stupid I am not!" Green exploded.

Weinstein would not give up. He kept ordering insanely expensive pizzas from room service as he stubbornly worked the phones. "It was like a combination of a Marx Brothers film and Fellini," Sunshine remembers. Finally Clinton drove up to the hotel for what he thought was a private meeting. When he saw a crowd of reporters and photographers, no doubt tipped off by Sharpton, he feared a hostile publicity stunt and turned away. That was the end of peacemaking.

Furious at the turn of events and even more furious at Green, Weinstein called Edward Skyler, who was escorting Bloomberg to a final rally atop the Empire State Building. "Tell Mike I want to talk to him, I'm endorsing him," Weinstein said. The droll Skyler thought to himself—*now,* on the eve of the election? He shrugged and handed his phone to Bloomberg, who listened and said, "Thanks."

Years later, the would-be peacemakers still marvel at that

Four Seasons debacle. It was a fitting denouement to the mayoral campaign of 2001.

Senator Ted Kennedy's presidential aspirations took a fatal tumble in 1979 when Roger Mudd of CBS News asked him, "Why do you want to be president?" Kennedy couldn't give a persuasive answer. Mike Bloomberg in 2001 had a similar problem.

Why did he want to be mayor of New York, anyway? What was his rationale? He cared about education, yes, but who didn't? He promised to bring the management skills that made him a billionaire to City Hall, but selling computers for a private company did not seem to the average New Yorker like good preparation for fighting crime and jousting with a balky state legislature.

Why did Bloomberg choose to run? The first-person pronoun got an inevitable workout when he discussed the decision with friends. He routinely referred more to himself than to civic policy. As William R. Brody, the president of his alma mater, Johns Hopkins, remembers, "He said to me, 'Bill, if I take my billion dollars and put it on Park Avenue and light it on fire tomorrow, nobody will call me.' He felt that the way the world valued and recognized him was as a billionaire. He didn't want to be known as a billionaire, he wanted to be known as someone who makes a difference."

Still, escaping a stereotype and pledging to make a difference do not a political platform make.

When the general election began, Green was well ahead in the polls. A Cornell- and Harvard-educated lawyer, the tall, athletic Green was bright, quick and knowledgeable. But he suffered from the arrogance of being the smartest kid in the class, conveying a cockiness and sense of entitlement that had hurt him in previous campaigns.

This time, though damaged by the bitter primary fight, he seemed to have a stronger claim to the mayoralty than Bloomberg: the recovering city needed an experienced political hand. "Michael Bloomberg has as much experience in government, to bring us together, as you or I have in running Bloomberg Financial News," Green told Gabe Pressman of WNBC. The next mayor would have to wring funds from Washington and Albany, wrestling with elected officials and power brokers. Green knew his way around. Bloomberg? He came from an alien world.

But Green and many others, looking through the conventional political prism, were missing something. The terror attack, and the resulting collapse of an already weakening city economy, had given Bloomberg the rationale he was lacking. He was a manager, he understood money, he was a part of the business world—strong credentials for guiding the city back to health. And he had the resources to deliver that message to the voters. His polling numbers had moved up slightly even before 9/11. The catastrophe brought the opportunity to talk up his strengths.

"We sort of wheeled the résumés," says William Cunningham, an adviser. "We suspected it and our polling picked it up. People began to say, 'Who is going to keep the city functioning? Do we need a pol or do we need a manager?'"

Bloomberg hadn't changed. He could still offer little more than his record as a successful, self-made entrepreneur. But after 9/11, he could argue that his experience dovetailed with the city's needs. The moneyed class—his world of big business and the social-cultural elite—aggressively plugged his candidacy. And he spent massively on television ads and direct mailings.

Bloomberg's vulnerabilities as a candidate could well have doomed his campaign in normal times.

The largest of those vulnerabilities turned on the complaints of women about sexual harassment and discrimination at Bloomberg L.P. While preparing to run, Bloomberg had told his advisers about the cases and they tried preemptively to bury the subject—by airing it in public.

Three months before Bloomberg announced his candidacy, he disclosed that a polygraph test, administered by an expert he had hired, proved he had been truthful when denying the sexual harassment allegations of a former employee. The contents of the test were never made available, just the expert's conclusions. In her 1997 suit the plaintiff, Sekiko Sekai Garrison, had charged that when she told Bloomberg she was pregnant, he had said, "Kill it!" and then muttered, "Great, Number 16"—an apparent reference to fifteen other recent office pregnancies.

Garrison also charged that Bloomberg and other company executives subjected women to "repeated and unwelcome" sexual comments and overtures, that Bloomberg regularly made offensive comments about women employees, such as "I'd fuck that in a second," "I'd like to do that" and "That's a great piece of ass." At one point in 1996, Garrison alleged, Bloomberg told a group of workers at a sales conference, "I would like nothing more in life than to have Sharon Stone sit on my face."

As the candidate's handlers expected, news stories about the polygraph would belabor all three harassment lawsuits filed against Bloomberg and his company. Garrison's suit was settled a year before he became a candidate; he did not admit guilt, and she was paid an undisclosed sum and legally bound to remain forever silent.

A second suit, by a woman who charged that "male employees from Mr. Bloomberg on down" harassed and degraded women, was dismissed after her lawyer failed to meet court-imposed deadlines. A third was withdrawn by the plaintiff after her husband, another Bloomberg employee, pleaded guilty to stealing more than $1 million from the company. (A large class-action suit charging discrimination against pregnant employees who took maternity leaves was filed against the company when Bloomberg was in his second mayoral term and no longer running Bloomberg L.P.)

For the 2001 election cycle, Bloomberg's aides had effectively defused the issue and the public was fixed on more immediate troubles anyway. But a few other ghosts appeared.

Michael Wolff, then a caustic columnist at *New York Magazine,* obtained a compendium of racist, sexist and homophobic jokes that employees had heard from Bloomberg over the years and assembled in a booklet to celebrate his forty-eighth birthday in 1990. It was meant as a lighthearted gesture, but no candidate for mayor in 2001 wanted to be mocked for saying, "If Jesus was a Jew, why does he have a Puerto Rican first name?" or "Make the customer think he's getting laid when he's getting fucked" or "If women wanted to be appreciated for their brains, they'd go to the library instead of to Bloomingdale's."

Bloomberg belittled the comments as feeble Borscht Belt humor and said he did not recall making any of the quips. When company colleagues said he had made them all right but probably didn't mean any insult, his lawyers delivered a stern warning to at least one talkative former employee. But Bloomberg need not have worried; the embarrassing magazine column ran in the September 10 issue of *New York Magazine* and though news of its content circulated a few days earlier, the whole matter quickly faded after 9/11.

One more ghost appeared in October, when a *Village Voice* article quoted Bloomberg's sworn deposition in the case of a woman charging rape by a company employee. She described Bloomberg's office as a "hostile environment of persistent sexual harassment and the general degradation of women." Bloomberg testified that he would credit an allegation of rape only if the rape were witnessed by a third party—a condition as sexist as it is unlikely.

Green tried to exploit the Garrison case with a TV spot that aired the day before election and featured an announcer grimly saying, "Kill it! Kill it!" It just made Green look desperate. Luckily for Bloomberg, the public remained intensely focused on the city's survival and had little patience for backward glances.

Bloomberg also benefited from his unimposing demeanor. The short candidate with the serious mien just did not look the part of a crude predator. He looked more like your Jewish uncle.

Avuncular he is not. He is sarcastic and profane in the best (or worst) manner of Wall Street. He does not suffer foolishness and he does not hide his angers. His employees calculated precisely how far his phone cord extended so they could stand out of reach when the boss took to phone-throwing. There is no question that he told off-color jokes and made sexual comments, which intimidated some younger women around the office and offended even more secure women as insulting to their professionalism.

Especially in his business days, Bloomberg did enjoy shocking people. Former subordinates still remember a crude joke he once used at a large gathering to mock First Lady Hillary Clinton's attempt to reform health care in 1993. "Mike always liked to be outrageous," says one former bureau chief. "It's only for show. But I think it does matter, it does give insight into his character. You're running a large company, you would think at some point he would realize he can't get away with that stuff."

A journalist, who went to an all-male off-the-record dinner with Bloomberg and others after his election, was so taken aback by the mayor's language that he would not repeat it, even if guaranteed anonymity. "I've been around guys all my life, I know what people say, how they talk, but this was—holy Jesus—and it wasn't just that it was the mayor talking. It's almost like time stopped for him in that area when he was twenty-three."

The signals are manifestly contradictory. Bloomberg never dated an employee or, it appears, tried to. Sexual banter, however awkward and even threatening, seems to have remained just that. After he became mayor, women's rights groups regularly supported him, rating him strong on defending abortion rights and in fighting domestic violence. Bloomberg has also set a pattern of giving some women significant responsibility in his company and in government. Patti Harris is the most obvious, his top adviser at his company and at City Hall; Katherine Oliver, who managed his foreign television operations, became his commissioner of film, theater and broadcasting. A few women swear with straight faces that they have never heard an off-color remark from him.

Bloomberg obviously watched his words during the mayoral campaign, but he could slip. One television makeup artist vowed never to powder him again after he asked about her favorite sport and quickly said that his was sex.

The public has not seen the crudest side of Bloomberg and not only because of his self-discipline. In his first venture into politics, voters saw as little of him as possible. He kept his distance from the public and the media, shielded by an army of consultants, and let his television ads and mailings define him. His aides worked hard to keep prying eyes, voice recorders and microphones away. He was the only candidate who refused to be interviewed for a campaign documentary for PBS. "Too much of a risk," one aide explained. "He was used to dealing with the press on his terms. He would decide whom he wanted to meet with, how long he wanted to talk to them, what would be public, what he wanted to tell them."

Bloomberg's resentment of certain press inquiries would linger for years. During the 2001 campaign, for example, the *Daily News* looked into Bloomberg's claim that he had tried to volunteer for military service in Vietnam. When he was completing Harvard Business School, as his student draft deferment expired, he had indeed applied to the army's officer training program—assuming that a second lieutenant would be a safer rank than infantry private—but he was rejected for having flat feet.

He was still subject to call-up by his hometown draft board, whose recruiting quota had tripled. Yet the board also invoked the flat feet and classified him "1Y"—draftable only in a national emergency. How the board learned about the flat feet without ordering its own medical exam remains a mystery. Bloomberg insists he was not the source, and the officer training program would not normally be.

In his memoir Bloomberg wrote that he was "trying to do the right thing—serve my country—while also trying to maintain a measure of control over my life." His campaign literature rang with the same patriotic theme. Years later, he sounded more practical than patriotic, like millions of others who tried to get through the Vietnam era in one piece, their reputations also intact.

"I don't know that anybody wanted to serve, that I wanted to serve," the mayor told me. "I thought I had to and I was gonna go do it. Did I have a burning passion to go to war like some of these young kids do? No. But it was just what you were gonna do." Asked a few more questions about his draft board's decision, he suddenly tore off his loafers and stood in stocking feet. "Look, those are my feet," he said, his voice rising. "Do you see an arch?" Indeed he has no arches.

Neither sexual harassment nor flat feet figured significantly in the 2001 campaign. Nor did much else said by or about Bloomberg. New York was in mourning, on edge and focused starkly on recovery.

A month after the terrorist attack came the scare of anthrax attacks, New York's economy went into a further decline and the city remained on edge. Did it really matter that Bloomberg would let reporters look at his "reconstructed" tax returns for only five hours while other candidates released theirs? Or that after learning that an aide said Mark Green had written "a defense of Joseph Stalin" in one of his books, he not only failed to repudiate the red-baiting but called Green a "liberal, leftist kind of guy," adding, "I don't know whether he is a Stalinist."

It did not even matter with voters that, to get a second ballot line so that dedicated Democrats who wanted to vote for him would not have to pull the Republican lever, he formed an alliance with the controversial Independence Party to win its endorsement. One of its leaders, Lenora Fulani, had made anti-Semitic remarks but Bloomberg heatedly defended the association and his financial support of the fringe party and a Fulani youth program. "So what! I'm not anti-Semitic!" he snapped.

Bloomberg's over-the-top spending also seemed a non-issue. Just about every reference to his campaign spending called it "a record," which it was. By the end of summer, Bloomberg had surpassed Ronald Lauder's $13.7 million war chest of 1989 and by election day he acknowledged expenses of $74 million—not counting his ancillary but supportive philanthropy. Not even Nelson Rockefeller lavished that kind of money on his campaigns.

New York had never seen anything like Bloomberg's saturation mailings of glossy, color brochures tailored to people's computer-determined interests, religion or ethnicity.

Black New Yorkers received brochures depicting a casual Mike in baseball cap (though baseball thoroughly bores him), flanked by smiling black children. Jews were treated to an old photo of young Mike and his little sister posing with their parents plus a list of Bloomberg's many generous contributions to Jewish causes. Italians got a picture of Bloomberg marching in a parade beside Rudy Giuliani. Other mailings catered to Latinos and women, some promised education reforms, some assailed Mark Green.

Bloomberg's pollster, Doug Schoen, had tracked the city's electorate for years and learned that voting preferences were less predictable along racial and ethnic lines than they once had been. Bloomberg's fortune allowed him to exploit that trend. Schoen compiled a computerized profile of just about every voter and divided the electorate into economic groups. For example, given the growth in the number of Latino homeowners in the Bronx, the standard ethnic appeals to them were augmented by the middle-class economic appeals also aimed at Jewish homeowners in Brooklyn. The Bloomberg money let Schoen mix and match messages.

Bloomberg still trailed Green in late October, but he was gaining, and not just because of his money. Divisions were growing among Democrats, where nothing was going as planned. Green hurt himself—and handed Bloomberg fodder for a TV ad—when he boasted that he would perform "as well or better" than Giuliani in the aftermath of 9/11. And when Green met with Freddy Ferrer's top supporters to make peace after their bitter primary runoff, he said, "I don't need you to win; I need you to govern," whereupon the group—including

Sharpton, Congressman Charles Rangel, of Harlem, Roberto Ramirez, the Bronx Democrat, and Dennis Rivera, the president of the hospital workers union, stalked out in a rage.

"We couldn't have won without Mark's help," one Bloomberg aide said. "We sat back and watched the Democrats destroy each other."

Well, they didn't quite sit around. Bloomberg's operatives reached out to disaffected Democrats. They and their candidate, who had already met privately with Rangel, now sat down with other Ferrer supporters to assure them they could live with a billionaire businessman in City Hall. The unhappy Democrats listened, not only to punish Green, but to protect themselves. Some were seeing the handwriting on the wall: Bloomberg could be mayor.

In his private contacts with them, he was reasonable even if he was a nominal Republican. Most of his policies fit theirs. A Democrat in all but label, he favored abortion rights, gay rights and gun control, was pro-immigrant and opposed the death penalty. Many Democratic activists knew that he had, in the previous year, given to many more civic and cultural organizations in New York. If this were a sign of things to come that could benefit them and the people they cared about, they would meet Green's opponent halfway.

Despite some optimistic signs for Bloomberg, his tracking polls showed Green leading throughout the general election. His own advisers prepared for defeat. Even Rupert Murdoch's conservative *New York Post* accepted the conventional wisdom that it would be a Democratic year and rather than endorse Bloomberg, hedged its bets and took a neutral editorial stance. The *New York Times* endorsed Green. Of the major dailies, only Mort Zuckerman's *Daily News* took a chance on supporting Bloomberg.

Ten days before the election, Bloomberg got some help from Giuliani. America's mayor gave his fellow Republican a low-key endorsement. Focused on the city's recovery, he seemed subdued. No matter. David Garth was there with his cameras to record the event for a television commercial, and Giuliani's support was welcome and helpful.

News accounts persisted in describing the Bloomberg campaign as "troubled" and in need of more of a lift than the current mayor's cool endorsement. But the story was roiling and changing.

Something was happening. In the campaign's last chaotic week Green's numbers dropped by an unusual 6 points. The week had been Green's worst: Ferrer refused to go to a Democratic unity dinner; Green's "Kill it, Kill it" ad had boomeranged and his prominent supporter, movie mogul Harvey Weinstein, had messily failed to get Ferrer, Green, Sharpton and Bill Clinton together for an eleventh-hour supportive photo op. By the last weekend, Bloomberg's polls showed the two men in a virtual tie; Green's late tracking polls gave Bloomberg a slight lead.

The race almost looked like a toss-up. But even the Bloomberg camp expected a Green win. He was the Democrat, he had the demographic edge, New York was New York.

On election day, November 6, 2001, Bloomberg told his ninety-two-year-old mother, Charlotte, that the election would be close. If he lost, he assured her, "Don't worry, you are not going to be embarrassed."

The first round of exit polls in midafternoon, based on a sampling of 867 voters, showed Green leading by 2 percentage points. That was within the margin of error, but 2 points is 2 points. Schoen and Sheekey recommended a final effort—robotic phone calls—("robo-calls") featuring Bloomberg's voice promising middle-class Democrats an economic revival and Giuliani's voice urging conservatives to think about the city's security and crime rate.

Bloomberg immediately okayed the $150,000 tactic, and in the next six hours, the hastily recorded calls went to 1.5 million homes. The campaign estimated that 70 percent were answered.

Their effect can never be measured but even on election day, Bloomberg's open-ended budget had struck again.

Bloomberg awaited the results in a suite at the Hilton Times Square, across Forty-second Street from a jazz club where fans and campaign workers had assembled. With him were his family and prominent supporters, including Patti Harris, Kevin Sheekey, Jonathan Capehart, Doug Schoen and Maureen Connelly, Governor Pataki, Giuliani, former mayor Koch and former Republican senator Alfonse D'Amato. In a small bedroom on the second floor of the suite, Doug Schoen and other operatives including Stanley Schlein, a seasoned Bronx Democrat, worked the phones, getting returns from the Board of Elections and sources with advance information.

At one point, with the Florida 2000 debacle in mind, they thought a close result might require impounding the election machines for a recount. "You have to get the cops so the machines are not tampered with," recalls Sheekey. "We had the mayor, Giuliani, talking about calling the police commissioner and everyone starts having conversations about calling lawyers. We're saying, 'Where is Bob Bennett? Who did Gore use? We need to get them.' We started to get phone numbers around midnight on Tuesday." And then, in what seemed like minutes, they relaxed. "The numbers kept coming in and we knew we didn't need to impound machines."

They knew, about an hour ahead of the media, that their

man had beaten Green when they saw his big lead in the city's reliably Republican borough, Staten Island. Sheekey walked out into the hallway with Bloomberg, reached into his pocket and pulled out two speeches—one a concession speech, one a victory speech—and carefully handed the mayor-elect the right one.

Sheekey can't recall how Bloomberg reacted at the moment of victory. Significantly, nobody else who was in that suite can. Nor can Bloomberg. Years later, he remarked, "I didn't jump up and down cheering, I can tell you that—that's not me."

What he did do was to reach out to New Yorkers who could help him govern and keep ethnic peace.

Al Sharpton, whose antagonism toward Green had significantly helped Bloomberg, says he heard from the mayor-elect that night: "My cell phone rings and it's Jonathan—Jonathan Capehart—and he said, 'Hold on a minute.' A voice comes on and says, 'Hello, this is Michael Bloomberg. I want you to know it will be different with me as mayor. We will not agree on everything, but you will have access to City Hall.' I was stunned. It was clearly a reversal in how City Hall was going to deal with us." (Capehart thinks he placed that call on election eve, but confirms the substance.)

Green got 46.6 percent of the vote to Bloomberg's 48.9 percent—a gap of 35,539 of the total 1,520,443 votes cast. Green's support in minority districts was unusually low for a Democrat. Blacks were his strongest supporters, but with only 71 percent instead of the customary 90 percent for a Democrat. And Bloomberg had almost half the votes of Hispanics because many shifted from their usual support for Democrats while others stayed home. Roberto Ramirez, the Bronx Democratic leader, failed to bring out his troops for Green, recalling with a laugh, "That is historical fact. I chose not to."

Green and his advisers blamed Bloomberg's stunning financial advantage; his spending was almost five times Green's—$74 million to $16.5 million. His resources let him take advantage of every error and every angle—from 9/11 and Giuliani's vital backing to Green's "ninety-day decision" and the Sharpton wildcard. Without any one of those factors, Green might have squeaked in.

But he didn't. A city in trouble took a chance on a man it hardly knew. Almost by accident, Mike Bloomberg became its 108th mayor.

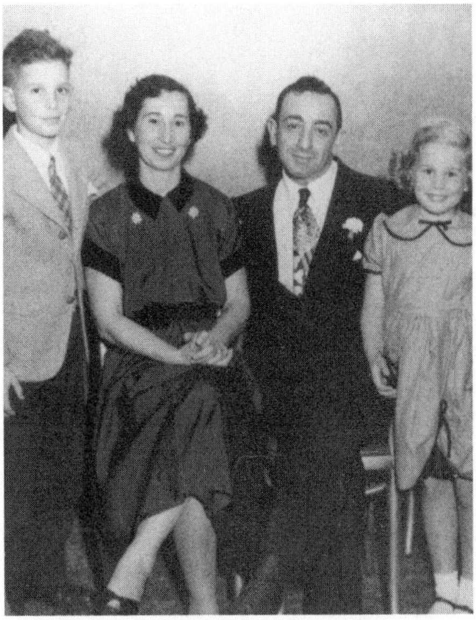

Mike on his trike; Charlotte and William Bloomberg, flanked by Mike and Marjorie; the Eagle soars, age 12; "argumentative" Mike, Medford High class of 1960

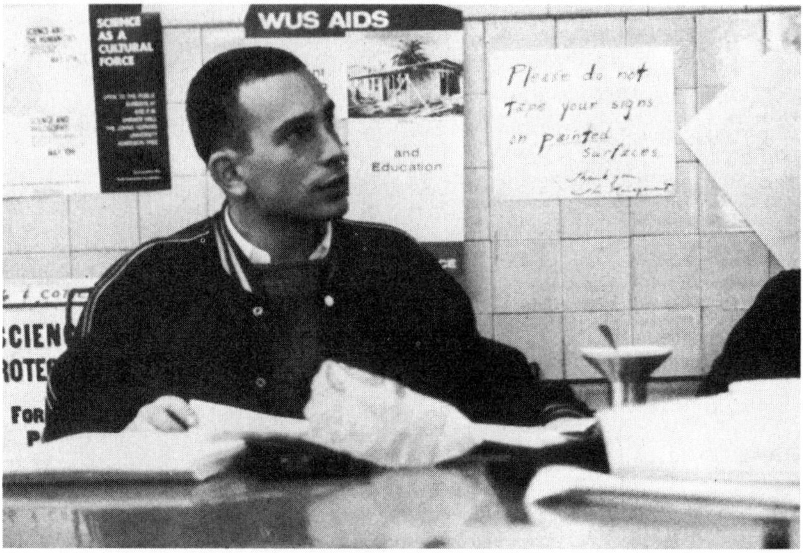

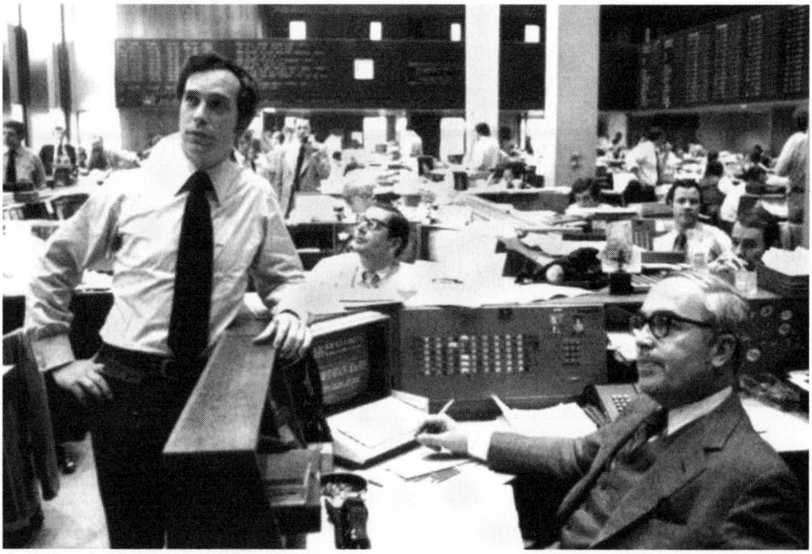

Frat chat at Johns Hopkins; with Salomon's John Gutfreund

Bloomberg in front of Bloombergs, 1994; a fateful hug from Rudy Giuliani, 2001; I, Mayor Mike, with Mom Charlotte, Chief Judge Judith Kaye and daughter Georgina holding the Bible

Not-too-ex Susan Brown Bloomberg and daughters Emma and Georgina, at 2002 inauguration; with Diana Taylor at a fashion celebration, 2008; with Social Sherpa Barbara Walters, 2006

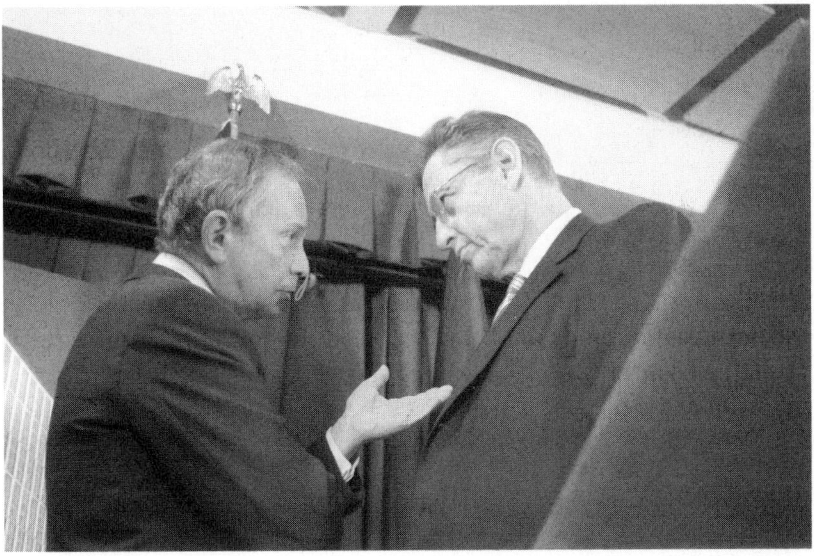

Mom and Sis help dedicate a rescue center named for dad in Jerusalem, 2007; Speaker Sheldon Silver likes to speak last, 2005

Let them eat cheesecake, 2008; best of friends? 2008

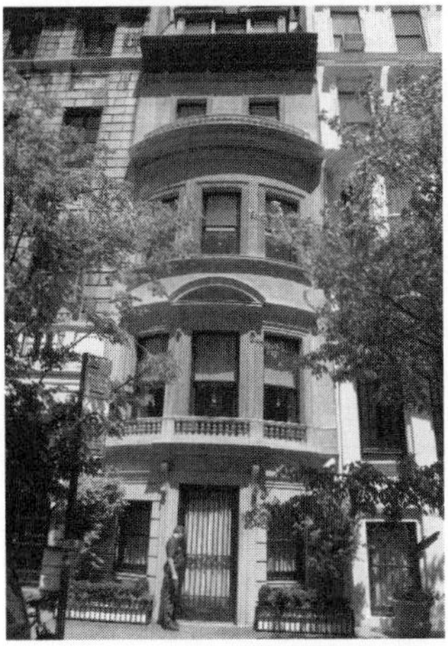

Home Sweet Homes. Medford, Massachusetts (top); East 79th Street, Manhattan (middle left); Cadogan Square, London (middle right); Bermuda waterfront (bottom)

Bloomberg, the company, towering over New York. Bloomberg, the mayor, absorbing debate over his third-term strategy.

CHAPTER 9

MANAGING CITY HALL

MIKE BLOOMBERG SWORE to be a good mayor on New Year's Day, 2002, the coldest, bleakest January 1 New Yorkers could remember. His friends, family, fawners and favor-seekers sat shrouded in wool blankets, sipping hot cider from insulated mugs, shivering and wondering. Their troubled, wounded city was burdened by a huge budget deficit. Tax collections were down, unemployment was up, storefronts were shuttered and the fear of new terror attacks was keeping tourists away and residents on edge.

New York ached in every way, and there stood this slight stranger who'd bought his way into office and promised, like the Eagle Scout he was, to revive his adopted city and govern impartially, apolitically. Really? In New York, the mother of Tammany?

How could a rich mogul without visible charm or political roots devise new policies to bring New York back to life? Was this serious businessman, who was to showmanship what

Madonna was to subtlety, going to lift the spirits of a citizenry that loves its leaders colorful, loud and entertaining?

His fourteen-minute inaugural speech offered no more clues than the boilerplate prayers that opened and closed the chilled assembly. Bloomberg's flat, twangy baritone promised belt-tightening, no tax increases and, well, he would bring people together. Even his loyal campaign aides didn't know what to anticipate from Mayor Bloomberg. "There was lots of crying when we won," one of his consultants remembered. "It wasn't joy, it was fear. We didn't expect to win. What would we do now?"

By instinct, or inspiration, Mike Bloomberg resolved to do a great deal, and to do it fast, while the public still relished the idea of a new start with a new leader and new hope, before resistance congealed and the entrenched power brokers re-grouped. Mike Bloomberg had never thought small and he was not about to think small now.

For starters, he was going to win control of the public schools, liberate 1.1 million students from a deadly bureaucracy and a greedy teachers' union—a goal that had defeated his three immediate predecessors. Getting kids through high school at last, with diplomas they deserved because they really learned something, was going to be his enduring contribution to a future America.

Besides education, what Mike Bloomberg cared most about was health. He had, as mayor, a chance to do more than underwrite a major school of health, hospital or research lab. He would revive New York's neglected public health system and maybe start off by forcing New Yorkers to stop killing themselves with cigarettes. Oh, and there were all those rotting neighborhoods of abandoned factories and collapsing warehouses; maybe he could rewrite the city's zoning codes to turn decayed manufacturing sites into residential blocks, and get the real estate barons to transform eyesores into luxury suites. Maybe, too, there were better ways to ship out the city's garbage and to unchoke its traffic.

He promised to make City Hall as transparent as his company, incongruously transforming an antiquated meeting hall into a cubicle-filled bullpen for him and fifty staff members, complete with Bloomberg terminals on every desk, a free snack bar, tropical fish and, after a second-term modernization, a 103-inch plasma TV with multiple screens that flash breaking network news feeds, traffic footage and 311 statistics.

Not all innovations were allowed to displace the past. Bloomberg wanted the city's reduction in crime under Rudy Giuliani to go further. And he wanted a more sensitive police force and a new civility in dealings with black and Hispanic New Yorkers. He would do away with patronage, turn a deaf ear to the lobbyists and special pleaders and, as the law demands, balance the budget. Bloomberg suddenly had a comprehensive agenda for New Yorkers of all kinds, one that sent a clear message: Trust me. Let me get on with the job. I am all you need.

Bloomberg's first job was to pick his team. Patti Harris would be central, as she was in the campaign and at his company. The graduate of Ed Koch's City Hall staff, Harris was called deputy mayor for administration but Bloomberg relied on her loyal judgment at every turn; she was really deputy mayor for Mike. She would look after everything that touched on him, his life and his philanthropy. Both feared and respected, Harris and often only Harris could get her headstrong boss to change his mind, and it is she who deserves credit, or blame, for the administration's unusual discipline; every disloyal act would invite her disapproval, every misstep her raised eyebrow.

In the days when Bloomberg was still more mogul than

mayor it took only one stare from Harris to reclaim him from "one of his moods," as insiders call them. "An attractive woman would walk into the bullpen and the mayor would say 'nice tits'—he just couldn't help himself," recalls one top aide. "And Patti would give him the eye, like, 'Behave!'" But she never cured him of his habit, a rare Harris failure.

When a Bloomberg appointee to the Landmarks Preservation Commission broke the rules and shared an opinion in print, when a deputy mayor derided the concept of working in the open in the mayor's beloved bullpen, it was Harris who expressed disapproval.

Edward Skyler became Bloomberg's spokesman, sharing the press wrangling chores with communications director Bill Cunningham, another campaign alum. Kevin Sheekey brought his political skills into City Hall, becoming Bloomberg's Karl Rove, or David Axelrod; anything with a political angle was his, from running the 2004 Republican Convention for the mayor when it came to New York, or lobbying recalcitrant state legislators. Ester Fuchs became an adviser and policy wonk, but to run the government Bloomberg recruited seasoned pros to whom he could delegate authority, in his preferred leadership style.

To find them, he relied on Harris and her former colleague under Koch, Nathan Leventhal. They screened and Bloomberg selected, interviewing most candidates himself. Marc Shaw, an experienced technocrat, became first deputy mayor, a central voice on Albany politics and budget strategy alongside the experienced director of Management and Budget, Mark Page.

For the all-important role of police commissioner, Bloomberg selected the highly regarded Raymond Kelly, who had held the same job in David Dinkins's government. Nicholas Scoppetta, who'd worked for his first mayor in the 1970s, was named fire commissioner. John Doherty, a former sanitation commissioner under Giuliani, returned to that post. Dr. Thomas Frieden, a former assistant health commissioner, returned from working on a tuberculosis project in India to head the city's Health Department (he would later be tapped by President Obama to head the Centers for Disease Control and Prevention). And Dennis Walcott, former head of the New York Urban League, became deputy mayor for policy and one of few high-ranking African Americans in the Bloomberg government.

What would prove to be two of the most influential posts went to government outsiders. Daniel Doctoroff, a successful investment banker and founder of the campaign to bring the 2012 summer Olympics to New York, was asked to invest his disruptive and enthusiastic style in the task of stimulating the city's economic revival. And Michael Cardozo, a former head of the City Bar Association, was chosen to be corporation counsel, advising on virtually every issue.

Bloomberg's provocative recruiting style could be fully focused or rudely distracted. A judicial candidate up for a mayoral appointment hotly recalled Bloomberg fiddling with his BlackBerry throughout the interview. Cardozo, meeting with the mayor in his East Seventy-ninth Street home, got Bloomberg's undivided attention. "Bloomberg says to me, 'Michael, you know I fly a helicopter, and looking out of my window, I realize that if I cut down two or three trees in Central Park, I could build a heliport there. What do you think about that?'" When Cardozo gently insisted that the idea was illegal, Bloomberg asked if he would then defend him. "I told him if he was involved in a civil case, it would depend. Lawyers have a rule that you cannot defend a frivolous civil case. He play-acted a little; he said, 'You mean if you are my corporation counsel you wouldn't defend me?' I knew he was ribbing me but I thought he was getting at a point. Then he suddenly turned to Nat and said, 'Why didn't you have the guts to stand up to Giuliani on the Brooklyn Museum?'"

By twitting Nat Leventhal, who had declined to condemn the former mayor's meddling in museum affairs lest he lose subsidies as head of Lincoln Center, Bloomberg deftly signaled his expectations to Cardozo.

His team in place, Bloomberg plunged into his agenda. First: the schools. Mayoral control was an idea whose time had come. The city's decentralized system, introduced in 1969 after decades of mayoral leadership, had been fully discredited by corruption and incompetence. To appease public opinion, state legislators had already eliminated the hiring powers of local school boards in 1996—one of their own rich sources of patronage. They were finally willing to yield to the clamor for mayoral control, but the Democrats would not give the prize to the irritating Rudy Giuliani.

Bloomberg, though also a Republican, was another matter. Albany being Albany, he still needed several months of haggling and arm-twisting, Bloomberg's best salesmanship and the patience of his Albany-savvy deputy, Marc Shaw. The cunning leader of the Democratic assembly, Sheldon Silver, characteristically playing hard to get, insisted in a last-minute maneuver that the law be subject to renewal at the close of Bloomberg's expected second term.

But the new mayor mostly got what he wanted.

Gone was the balkanized Board of Education, seven people appointed by six city officials who used their votes to bargain for extraneous benefits. Gone, too, were the powers of the thirty-two community school boards to treat the city's children as afterthoughts. One person—the mayor—was now to be accountable for their education and he alone would select the schools chancellor. Bloomberg picked Joel Klein, a blunt, hard-charging Washington lawyer (and graduate of New York City public schools) who had even less patience and fewer political skills than his City Hall sponsor.

Flushed with his initial success at gaining control of schools, Bloomberg, the public health advocate, opened a citywide offensive against smoking at the passionate urging of his health commissioner, Dr. Thomas Frieden. When the administration was just a few months old, Frieden urged Bloomberg to broaden Koch's ban on smoking in restaurants and public buildings by extending it to bars and smoking sections of restaurants. He warned Bloomberg that the fight would be a tough one. Bloomberg, the reformed smoker, advised him not to undercut his case. "He told me, 'The first rule of business is once you make a sale—leave.'"

Bloomberg's anti-smoking campaign infuriated barkeeps, worried the tourism industry, and frustrated protective mayoral aides worried about championing a smoking ban with the city still in recession and recovering from 9/11. The policy was fine with them, but not the timing. "What are you thinking?" Edward Skyler, Bloomberg's press secretary, demanded of the health commissioner when they ran into each other on the second floor of City Hall.

"The Mommy Mayor," thundered a *New York Post* editorial. NANNY BLOOMBERG complained a headline in the *Wall Street Journal.*

Bloomberg persisted and, ultimately, the gamble paid off. Bars and restaurants survived, and public opposition dwindled. The number of adult smokers declined by 350,000 New Yorkers in seven years, attributed as much to sharp increases in city, state and federal cigarette taxes that ultimately brought the cost of a pack in New York to $10 as to the new law.

At the time, though, "We got killed," says Sklyer. Bloomberg's emerging style was two-edged—independent from the customary clubhouse pressures, but stubborn to a fault. Pleading the weak economy, the mayor tabled Giuliani's plans for new stadiums for the Yankees and Mets. Yet he insisted that the expensively renovated Tweed Courthouse become the headquarters of his new Education Department and not, as long planned, of the Museum of the City of New York.

Political independence was a valuable commodity. Owing nothing to social services advocates, Bloomberg could anger them by housing homeless families in a former jail when the city ran out of more acceptable spaces. Willing to alienate merchants and hotel owners, he could relieve congestion by stopping drivers from making turns on some midtown streets. Ready to rile neighborhoods all over the city, he planned to build garbage transfer stations on formerly sacred turf.

But while trading on his independence, Bloomberg fell victim to his brashness and inexperience. He almost lost his anti-smoking campaign by neglecting to clear it with the city council. He no sooner appointed a diverse new education panel than he barred its members from speaking in public: "I would not tolerate it for thirty seconds."

He had no patience for sentiment. Traumatized survivors of 9/11 complained that Bloomberg was insensitive because he advised them to "move on." When grieving families grew worried that the remains of loved ones might be buried in Trade Center debris and carted to the city's garbage dump, he told them coldly that he had only visited his own father's grave once, and intended to leave his own body to science.

Christy Ferer, Bloomberg's official representative to 9/11 families and herself a 9/11 widow, had to paper things over, explaining that the mayor was not callous, just realistic. "This is a man who believes in the greatest amount of good for the largest amount of people," she said. "You live for the living. That was always Mike's attitude." But she conceded, "Perhaps he could have handled it in a more sensitive way."

New Yorkers expect tough love from their mayors. Bloomberg was tough all right, but he failed in the love department. He made bold moves without connecting with the public. As he saw it, he had serious work to do. When a water main broke in the Bronx and left two thousand people without water, he did not see the value in showing his concern by rushing to the site. "I'll be in the way," he told an imploring aide.

Disdaining the showboating of his predecessors without accepting that it could also help him and reassure the public, Bloomberg could go days without making the local news. He was conducting what presidents call a hideaway Rose Garden strategy at City Hall, rarely visiting neighborhoods, taking few phone calls from listeners on his weekly radio show, flying off secretly to Bermuda on weekends.

Having drained any warm and fuzzy feelings that his election might have engendered, he went one step further. He felt compelled to commit the mother of all political offenses: raising taxes. Although he had warned as a candidate that raising taxes would "destroy this city" and pledged no higher taxes in his inaugural speech, Bloomberg broke his promise. To protect city services and budget shortfalls, he decreed the highest property tax rate in the city's history, settling with the city council on an increase of 18.5 percent. And he raised the taxes six months sooner than necessary, to collect more revenue faster. "We raised taxes on a balanced budget," says Marc Shaw.

Owners of single-family homes, co-ops and condominiums

had to pay about $200 more in property taxes even before Bloomberg finished his first year in office—and double that amount in the next full year.

Bloomberg's popularity polls, already slipping, began to spiral down. As 2002 ended, 46 percent of the public disapproved of the mayor, double the number that disliked his performance a year earlier. By June 2003, after he infuriated more of the public by closing six firehouses, his approval rating fell to 24 percent, the lowest since the *Times* began polling on mayoral performance in 1978. His dismal numbers cut across all races: only 31 percent of whites were approving, 15 percent of blacks, 19 percent of Hispanics.

Headline writers were having a jolly time. The *Daily News* screamed, MAYOR: WHAT, ME WORRY? and CITY LIKES ANYBODY BUT MIKE. The *New York Post* shouted, WORST POLL YET IS A "LOW" BLOW TO MIKE. The news was national, too. N.Y. MAYOR WATCHES FORTUNES FALL, said the *Chicago Tribune.*

The public, always dyspeptic about government during a bad economic patch, was giving the mayor no quarter, and his distant style was no help. In fact, it was confusing. He would do as he wished, but quietly. He would pursue irritating policies, but without confrontation. He did not lose his temper in public, did not rail at Albany when it blocked his path.

His voice was barely heard when Washington slighted the city, even when officials failed to relay a tip about a terrorist plan to smuggle a small nuclear bomb into his city. Though an obviously false rumor, Bloomberg mustered only a polite criticism. "I do believe that the New York City government should have been told, and it was not." Bloomberg was coming across as diffident, or worse. Did he care? Did he get it?

At the early stage of his mayoralty, the contrast between his demeanor and reputation inside and outside government could not have been sharper. Though frustrated by the boss's public style, officials respected his pattern of deciding issues on the merits, yielding little to the customary political lobbyists, interest groups and of course nothing to campaign contributors since there was only one—Bloomberg himself.

Gretchen Dykstra, his first consumer affairs commissioner, remembers a call from Bloomberg after one of his friends, Ken Langone, complained that her department was suing his company, Home Depot, for illegally selling box cutters and spray paint to minors. "The mayor called me and said, 'Hey wait a second, what's going on? I just got a call.'" She told him the company had been warned but persisted. "He said, 'Sue the hell out of 'em. Bye!'" (The company eventually agreed to pay a $125,000 fine.)

That was typical. Bloomberg aimed to select strong department heads and let them run their agencies even, sometimes, when he disagreed.

For example, he opposed a Law Department decision to allow part-time work to accommodate working mothers. The mayor believed in government, as he did in running his own company, that part-time programs were wasteful and inefficient. But he did not stop the Law Department's plan, which would have undercut Cardozo, and might also have hurt Bloomberg, vulnerable on women's issues because of the sexual harassment charges at Bloomberg L.P. Nor did he force his first traffic commissioner, Iris Weinshall, to install a stoplight where he had demanded one—on a street bisecting his favorite Staten Island golf course; to his frustration, her engineers said it would be dangerous to drivers. He whined for years about the resulting danger to *him,* but did not overrule the decision.

Though controlling in his business's earliest days, he grew to disdain micromanagement. "His attitude is, if you need me to make a decision, bring me facts, bring me options, tell me who I have to talk to, who I have to sell," said Peter Madonia, the mayor's first-term chief of staff. "He's a salesman, right?"

For his own appointees, this freedom from political interference more than made up for the trials of working for a moody, exacting boss. Coming to him ill-prepared or with wrong information could evoke a sharp tongue-lashing in the open bullpen. He encouraged innovation—paying students who score well on tests, expanding the number of charter schools—and stood by subordinates if their risky efforts failed, as long as they tried.

His tolerance of his team also had a downside. Reluctant to dismiss anyone or admit error, he let weak commissioners stick around long after any other mayor would have dumped them, especially if they were criticized in the press. "We joke that getting the *Post* to demand our resignation is the ultimate job protection program," said an adviser.

The starkest example of Bloomberg's style was his loyal support of Fire Commissioner Nicholas Scoppetta after his department failed to adequately inspect a bank tower severely damaged on 9/11. The demolition of the building was broadly bungled by several city and state agencies, leading to the death of two firefighters in 2007 and charges of negligence against contractors.

The Bloomberg administration admitted the city's complicity in the deaths of the firefighters and made reforms to prevent a similar disaster. There was plenty of blame to go around and to single out Scoppetta would have amounted to scape-goating, Bloomberg argued. Critics thought every aspect of the tragedy showed that Bloomberg had failed a test of his vaunted management skills.

The mayor's commitment to loyalty was only one holdover from his pre–City Hall years. So was his fondness for engineering. That side of him had not disappeared either, to the frustration of some of his aides, who had to endure his headstrong notions. He fiddled and fussed with the creation of his call-311 citizen complaint system. And he was intrigued by the problem of garbage disposal: how to rid the city of over twelve thousand daily tons of solid waste after Giuliani had closed the last landfill without providing an alternative. Bloomberg drew numerous sketches of garbage schemes and had his staff running in circles investigating not only upstate landfills but even the possibility of hauling garbage in submarine-like barges to Caribbean islands. (He finally settled on the less exotic if politically sensitive solution of containerizing the waste and exporting it to landfills by rail or in covered barges.)

In an unspoken rebuke to the pattern set by Giuliani, Bloomberg's patronage was trivial and strictly personal. He hired a few former employees he considered competent and two members of his family. His older daughter, Emma, then twenty-two, became a program coordinator in City Hall; his sister, Marjorie Bloomberg Tiven, a social worker, became the commissioner of the city's Commission for the United Nations, Consular Corps and Protocol. Like the mayor, his relatives were paid government salaries of $1 a year.

Bloomberg, of course, had another way to show his appreciation—his personal checkbook. He gave his own money to cultural and social service organizations, some directly, some indirectly and anonymously, though everyone in politics and philanthropy knew the "secret source." He contributed to the fringe Independence Party and one of its youth programs, a reward for its endorsements. He made many generous donations to the Republican Party even after he changed his registration to independent, most notably to Albany legislators when the city needed their votes.

New Yorkers knew little about the inner workings of Bloomberg's government, or much else about it. He got little credit for his considerable achievements. He was reorganizing the school system and, for a short time in that first term, did the nearly impossible and got concessions from the teachers' union. He had buoyed the confidence of business owners and kept them from fleeing a demoralized city. The crime rate continued to drop. Vital services were still well financed because Bloomberg, convinced that the city's quality of life came first, would not slash them.

He was, in those early years, pulling the city together, but almost as a stealth mayor. New Yorkers wanted a leader as well as a city manager. Where were his vaunted skills as a salesman?

He had deployed those skills impressively in one direction: On the morning after his election, he had met with Dennis Rivera, then the influential leader of the largely minority hospital workers' union, and with Fernando Ferrer, the mayoral candidate defeated by Mark Green in the Democratic primary. And days later he had also invited the Reverend Al Sharpton to take a photo with him, at a business dinner sure to get plenty of media coverage. "I said, 'Are you serious about this?'" recalls Sharpton. "He said, 'I want to send a message to the black community that I am open.' He and I shook hands and of course it was on the front page of the *New York Post,* something like, 'he sold us out already.'"

The handshake that implied political and maybe even financial support neutralized Sharpton and turned him into a sometime-ally. "I got the one-day nasty editorial from the *Post,* and it was over," recalls Bloomberg. "Rudy had the same albatross around his neck for years with Sharpton, and if he'd done that once it would have gone away. The fact of the matter is when you have a racial problem Sharpton's on your side, quieting things down. He'll yell and scream a little bit, he has to do that for his audience, but personally, you know . . ."

Bloomberg also continued to meet quietly with black preachers and community leaders, developing personal relationships with them, donating to their causes. That would serve him well when, inevitably, racial tensions erupted.

Yet as sensitive as he was about racial relations, Bloomberg proved himself clumsy in interactions with most New Yorkers. At times, even when trying hard, he got it wrong. Preparing for a threatened transit strike, he bought himself a bicycle to pedal to work—a good idea. But the bike he bought cost $600. "It should've been fifty dollars," muttered Ed Koch.

Halfway through his second mayoral year, the *New York Times*'s City Hall bureau chief, Jennifer Steinhauer, wrote that "the feeling is that Mr. Bloomberg is an enigma wrapped in a Paul Stuart suit, a wealthy businessman whose good fortunes have left him out of touch with ordinary New Yorkers."

Maybe the skeptics had been right all along, that in fact no businessman could possibly serve effectively as mayor of New York. What good was his lonely independence? Not owing anybody meant nobody owed him. Speculation grew that Bloomberg was good for one term only, that he was better suited to being a mogul.

CHAPTER 10

OLYMPIAN DREAMS

HALFWAY THROUGH his first term, Mike Bloomberg faced the unacceptable: failure. His reelection campaign was two years away and the city was not warming to him. What to do? What would circumstances let him do?

His advisers implored him to try to lead as well as manage, to get out into neighborhoods and listen to people and their problems. He would try—and a poignant opportunity soon presented itself that let him do more than try.

Next, could he find a way to take the sting out of the real estate taxes that Bloomberg had chosen to increase instead of cutting services? One alcohol-fueled meeting produced a shrewd and promising ploy.

But true to form, Bloomberg wanted more than public relations and payoffs. He wanted grand projects that left his mark on the metropolis, bold schemes like the ban on smoking and, most of all, a campaign to lure the 2012 Olympics to New York. The opportunity to show a newly human Bloomberg face presented itself just before 6:00 a.m. on a spring day in 2003. Alberta Spruill, an African American woman of fifty-seven, was in her Harlem home getting ready for work when police officers threw a concussion grenade into her apartment, crashed through her door and cuffed her.

After complaining of chest pains, she was being ferried by ambulance when her heart suddenly stopped. Two hours after the raid she was dead—literally frightened to death by police who had acted on an informant's erroneous tip about guns and drugs.

Reacting swiftly and with sadness, Mayor Bloomberg called what had happened tragic and "a terrible episode," visited the city office where Spruill had worked as a clerk for twenty-nine years, and spoke with apology and candor at her funeral.

In the past, such tragedies had become flashpoints, generating anger, racial turmoil and unrest. A public accustomed to Rudy Giuliani routinely giving the police the benefit of every doubt greeted Bloomberg's apologetic tone, and Police Commissioner Kelly's, with surprise and gratitude.

The city stayed calm after Alberta Spruill's death. And it stayed calm over the next few months despite two more police encounters with innocent African Americans, each of which provoked similarly soothing and rapid reactions from Bloomberg.

Anticipating such racially raw episodes was one reason the mayor had opened the door early to the Reverend Al Sharpton and others who could help him contain anger and resentment. Drawing on the counsel and connections of Deputy Mayor Dennis Walcott, he met with black religious and civic leaders in their neighborhoods and invited many to city events. "He wanted to have a relationship so when there were problems, people could feel comfortable reaching out to his office," recalls Leroy Comrie, a councilman from a black Queens community.

Word of Bloomberg's openness spread through the political, religious and civic networks of African Americans. His purposeful strategy paid dividends not only in his first year but most notably in his second term, when Sean Bell, an unarmed African American, was shot dead by the police outside a Queens bar after his own bachelor party. Through a bitter time of despairing protests, Bloomberg could count on being shielded by Sharpton, Comrie and many others.

His welcoming approach proved to be of invaluable help to Bloomberg years later, when his strongest opponent for a third term was a black candidate. He still got many endorsements from black church and community leaders.

By making it clear that his City Hall was open to black New Yorkers, the mayor hinted for the first time that he was not altogether imperious or unfeeling. He loosened up a bit and visited neighborhoods more frequently. Soon the media was speculating that on-the-job training was taking effect. Yet the real estate tax increase continued to sting, holding down Bloomberg's popularity ratings. He needed another scheme to buoy his reelection chances.

The mayor's clever response was born one night in a bar near Gracie Mansion, where Deputy Mayor Marc Shaw and Bill Cunningham, Bloomberg's communications director, sat unrecognized and bemoaned their shared problems. Cunningham's job was politics—getting Bloomberg reelected. Shaw's job was economics—keeping the budget in balance. By the time the two men were in their cups, they had fixed on a mutually satisfying remedy: money.

Why not appease New Yorkers, who'd been angered by Bloomberg's 18.5 percent real estate tax increase, by returning some of the money to the angriest city voters? The city could afford it. In the fourteen months since the higher tax was approved, the economy had turned around, tax revenues had grown and the budget was in surplus.

So Bloomberg opened 2004 by offering a voter-friendly tax cut on residential property, worth about $400 a year for every owner of a private home, co-op or condo. That would cost the city only $250 million of the $1.8 billion produced by the Bloomberg tax increase because the break went only to residential property owners. They happened to be his sharpest critics. The mayor gave no relief to the owners of utilities, large apartment buildings, office buildings, stores and factories.

Bloomberg took all the credit for the timely gift. "We recognized that tough times call for making tough—and sometimes controversial—choices. And we made them," he said. In fact, the city's finances usually rise and fall in sync with the national economy and Bloomberg's role in the comeback was limited.

New York's economy was rebounding because the national recession had ended, priming Wall Street's pump.

Bloomberg deserved credit for helping to restore business confidence, for having chosen higher taxes instead of a decline in services and for raising taxes sooner than strictly necessary to build a cushion.

The billionaire mayor could appreciate the political value of the rebate but only with a degree of insensitive contempt. To him, $400 does not even qualify as chump change and he sneered at the sum's importance to his constituents. "It's a dollar a day—come on!" he said years later, at the public outcry when he threatened to withhold the rebate payments during another downturn.

Minding his public words in 2004, Bloomberg got the rebate through the city council and, as if someone had hit a START!

button, his popularity ratings in several polls began a gradual rise. By February they were at 44 percent and in June they hit 50 percent, a long way up from that all-time low of 24 percent two years earlier.

Bloomberg was also settling into the job. He won praise for his firm handling of a devastating Staten Island ferry crash and of a debilitating summertime power failure. Even managing the city's inevitable crises with skill was not, however, enough for him. He had a larger agenda. He wanted to advance grand schemes for the city, as he had at Salomon Brothers and in his own business. He wanted his mayoralty to be defined by those big moves—the ban on smoking, the revitalizing of the schools and most spectacular of all, luring the 2012 summer Olympics to New York.

The appeal for the Olympics bid would be to a tough international panel, but the ultimate test of Bloomberg's diplomatic skill required the wooing of a homegrown power, a figure more formidable than a dozen Olympic gods.

New York has never hosted the Olympic Games. Starting in the 1970s, mayors and business leaders tried several times to rally public interest in a bid, but to no avail. The very idea of staging the Olympics in New York drew yawns from people who feel no need for more excitement; they live permanently with noise and chaos, the casinos of Wall Street, the kaleidoscope of Broadway, the angry polyglotism of the United Nations. While New Yorkers backed the idea of the Olympics bid, there was no excitement, no wellspring of support for it in a city where the average citizen would not mind if the klieg lights dimmed now and again.

Deputy Mayor Daniel Doctoroff was having none of New York's trademark diffidence. He'd had a lightbulb moment in

1994, while watching a World Cup soccer match at Giants Stadium, and became an instant Olympics enthusiast. "The stands were packed with screaming, flag-waving Italian and Bulgarian New Yorkers. I wondered, why hasn't New York ever hosted the Olympic Games?"

Doctoroff founded NYC 2012 to promote an Olympics bid. Mike Bloomberg became a donor, a board member and his mentor. Tall and handsome with curly hair and a broad smile, Doctoroff left a managing partnership of an investment firm to join the administration as the mayor's $1-a-year deputy for economic development.

Doctoroff and the mayor quickly became a team within a team. Associates said the mayor saw a lot of himself in his forty-four-year-old deputy, that Doctoroff was the son the mayor never had and was profoundly influenced by him—unduly so, as far as critics were concerned.

The two entrepreneurs certainly spoke the same language, the language of successful, wealthy risk-takers. Unafraid, even eager to break the rules and ignore the conventions of government and politics to get things done, they only gradually learned that the entrenched powers of government, politics and politicians were not easily rolled over. But first, they dreamed, and they dreamed big.

Doctoroff's Olympics pursuit was a mix of the quixotic and the practical. He knew that mishandled, the Olympics could be a drain on a city's finances. But handled right the games could remake a city, as happened in Barcelona in 1992. As Doctoroff saw it, sections of New York, particularly old manufacturing areas, the waterfront in Brooklyn's Williamsburg and a section of Queens for which he envisioned the Olympics village, would stir to life merely in preparation for the games through upgraded zoning and infrastructure improvements.

His centerpiece would be the Olympics stadium, an ambitious plan to transform a neglected section of Manhattan into a sparkling new neighborhood, the linchpin of what was called the Hudson Yards Master Plan.

The area of promise extended from Thirtieth to Forty-second Street west of Eighth Avenue, a low, dark stretch of parking lots, warehouses, small shops, some apartments and huge rail yards long begging for development. The Olympics plan was to be a catalyst for new roads, a Park Avenue–like boulevard, office towers, hotels, high-rise luxury apartment buildings, parks, a subway extension and expansion of the long inadequate Jacob Javits Convention Center.

At the heart of the plan would be a "multi-use facility" with a retractable roof to lure the Olympics, to return the Jets football team from New Jersey and to accommodate trade shows and conventions. The Jets were to contribute to the stadium's cost, but it would take at least $600 million more in public funds and one more element: the approval of the state power brokers in Albany—the infamous "three men in a room."

Just about any major undertaking in New York State involves the governor and the leaders of the two legislative chambers. They control the obscure Public Authorities Control Board that must coordinate all public spending, and any one of the three has veto power.

Governor George Pataki, a Bloomberg ally, posed no problem. The leader of the Republican-dominated senate, Joseph Bruno, could probably be won over if the leader of the assembly came along. Unfortunately for Doctoroff and Bloomberg, the third member of the Albany troika was the Speaker of the overwhelmingly Democratic assembly, the powerful, elusive and cagey Sheldon Silver.

When it comes to almost anything of political importance in

New York State, the frustrating guessing game is always the same: what will Shelly do? Silver, in his late fifties when Bloomberg became mayor, and in his eighth year as Speaker, plays his hand with such skill and guile that nobody fully understands his approach to difficult issues and the influences upon him. And newcomers to New York politics usually underestimate him. Slowly but surely Bloomberg mastered many of the quirks of New York politics. But to his repeated chagrin, he has not mastered Shelly Silver.

Silver knows politics like Bloomberg knows finances. It took the mayor a while to realize it, but he had met his match.

Silver is the antithesis of Bloomberg, his polar opposite personally, culturally and politically. Bloomberg talks fast and reasonably; Silver speaks circuitously and laboriously, as if through a mouthful of molasses. Bloomberg disdains the routines of politics and party-shops to suit his convenience. Silver, a personal injury lawyer, is an old-fashioned, party-first Democrat. Bloomberg, Wall Street whiz, is an assimilated, divorced Jew with extravagant houses around the world. Silver is a married father of four, grandfather of grandchildren numbering in the "double digits," and lives in an apartment in lower Manhattan and a modest country house in the Catskills.

Sensitive to slights, real and perceived, Silver suspects Bloomberg of patronizing him and his lifestyle. Bloomberg thinks Silver does not bargain in good faith. Both deny the other's aspersions. The relationship has never been comfortable. Sometimes they agree: Silver was Bloomberg's ally on mayoral control of the schools at crucial points. Often they do not.

The starkest difference is in their view of political power. Bloomberg extolled principle and, with his my-way-or-the-highway style, would take risks to do what he thought was right. For Silver, principle is often a synonym for Democrat. He puts party first because he believes in Democratic tradition and power. Once he cost the city an annual bundle by supporting repeal of a tax on commuters, to help the election prospects of suburban Democratic candidates for the legislature. A product of the clubhouse, he does not make a move if it will endanger his party's majority in the assembly, his job as its leader or his hold on his district, which has been returning him to Albany since 1976. Complicating the woes of his rivals, Silver is very smart.

Doctoroff and Bloomberg, impatiently pursuing the Olympics, skirted multiple layers of public approval. They ignored the local community boards, bypassed the city council, and focused instead on gaining support from high-rolling business executives and construction unions who were predisposed to love the idea. Their strategy, however efficient and fast, failed to build consensus. Their project arrived in Albany with few allies, leaving Silver even more flexibility than usual. Developing the far west side of Manhattan was not to his liking.

Doctoroff had also thought, early on, that he could get financing for the project in a way that would bypass the Albany triumvirate and avoid Silver entirely. That proved impossible: political leaders as skilled as Shelly Silver do not lightly surrender power at key moments. Silver wanted state resources funneled to his region of lower Manhattan. Ground zero, the huge crater where the World Trade Center towers once stood, lies in the heart of his district, as does Chinatown, which suffered greatly after 9/11.

The rebuilding of downtown was dragging, and Silver resented a tacit agreement between the mayor and the governor: Bloomberg attended to development of the West Side while Pataki took charge of downtown. Though the Trade Center site sat as a blight on his city, for most of his mayoralty Bloomberg abdicated responsibility for reviving it, instead centering on the West Side where he would have less layered competition from the state, a bi-state New York–New Jersey agency and the emotions of 9/11 survivors. It is impossible to imagine Giuliani doing the same, but Bloomberg came to the party late and knew he would have a fight over ground zero, one he could well lose.

The West Side rail yards became his baby, to Silver's frustration. The Speaker thought that the West Side project would hurt his district by siphoning off resources, giving uptown an unfair advantage in competing for development with downtown. Months passed before Bloomberg and Doctoroff realized the Speaker had to be energetically wooed if he could be wooed at all—and by the time they tried, it was too late.

There was no shortage of Bloomberg administration officials who understood Silver and spoke the language of Albany, but Doctoroff was in charge and had the mayor's trust. "Dan is the Music Man," said William Cunningham, the mayor's first communications director, with an appreciative laugh. "He's selling you nonexistent uniforms for a nonexistent band sometimes. Dan didn't listen to advice from people like Marc Shaw and others on how to deal with Albany. They told him." Doctoroff later said he regretted his inattentiveness to the legislature. He was not sure anything would have helped, though, and was probably right on that.

The Olympics plan had plenty of opposition, as development always does in New York. In the late 1970s, even the seeming gift horse of federal financing for Westway, a proposed underground highway to be topped with waterfront parks, generated such strong opposition that the plan collapsed in litigation and the "highway" is now a busy six-lane surface road of whizzing traffic that people have to cross to reach the waterfront parks.

Community residents and some city planners were sure that an Olympics-sized stadium was far from the best use of such valuable land, while businesses and leaders of industrial unions embraced it as a generator of jobs and economic activity. The meetings and protests, for and against, were raucous and emotional, and the mayor grew increasingly stubborn. Public opposition to the stadium grew, and so did Bloomberg's impatience. "I'm sixty-three years old and I'm not going to spend my life pandering to anybody," he said to a group of business executives during the height of the fight. "I'm going to do what I think is right for this city and I'm going to lead from the front and not the back."

The battling factions might have neutralized each other if not for the most potent of the opposition. It came from members of the rich and powerful Dolan family, motivated not by the needs of the community itself or the niceties of city planning, but by the imperatives of commerce.

The Dolans, Silver contributors, control Cablevision and Madison Square Garden. They saw the stadium as competition to their arena and mounted a costly campaign against it. They formed an odd-couple alliance with grassroots opponents and, practiced players, enlisted an army of lobbyists, among them Patricia Lynch, an unusually close and trusted Silver confidant, and Kenneth Bruno, son of the senate leader.

As time went by, Silver raised concerns about the plan but portrayed himself as neutral, the better to wrench a series of concessions from Bloomberg, who worked overtime for the Speaker's vote.

As his associates winced at the spectacle of the proud mayor pandering to the manipulative Speaker, Bloomberg attended the bris of two Silver grandsons, paid a condolence call when the Speaker's brother died, participated in a Chanukah celebration, often held upbeat news conferences in Silver's district, renewed his support for a new public school downtown, endorsed a package of generous business subsidies and other incentives for lower Manhattan. The mayor's grab bag of goodies came so late in the maneuvering that Silver feigned insult, but he pocketed every gift while still keeping everyone guessing about his decision.

What would Shelly do?

The day before the crucial vote in Albany, Bloomberg and Silver both attended a charity breakfast in the Roosevelt Hotel. The two met in a side room and the mayor, ever the persistent salesman, pushed, cajoled, persuaded, and refused to give up. By then, Bloomberg's aides had figured out what Shelly would do. They knew Silver would do nothing. He was defiant, immovable.

Bloomberg himself could not believe it. He insisted that Silver would come around, that it was too good a deal to refuse. His aides didn't budge: Shelly was not interested, he wouldn't support it, he was never going to support it. Bloomberg insisted later that day that "everything always has progress in it. Things are, you know, always moving along," even as Silver somberly intoned, "We have no deal."

Next day, Silver and Bruno's representatives to the Albany control board abstained from voting to fund the stadium. And so it died. Silver got all the credit, or blame, since it was widely believed that Bruno would have assented if Silver had wanted his vote.

When asked if the stadium deal was really dead, Silver replied with a wicked grin, "It was never alive . . . Am I supposed to turn my back on lower Manhattan as it struggles to recover? For what? A stadium? For the hope of bringing the

Olympics to New York City?" The project, he said, was "a shield to shift the business and financial capital from lower Manhattan to the West Side."

Bloomberg was furious. "You think you have an agreement with him, and then Shelly puts out his hand and says, 'Wait a minute, one more thing.' The city suffered at Silver's hand," he charged.

Jay Cross, president of the Jets, shook his head in frustration. The vote was never about sports, he said. "It was about metro-politics."

By the time the International Olympic Committee met to select the 2012 host city, New York's submission no longer had its dream stadium. An Olympics bid without a stadium? The Doctoroff team scrambled to produce a new plan for a stadium in Queens, but the Olympics dream, always a long shot, collapsed. New York was ranked fourth among applicants and the designation finally went to London.

Bloomberg and Doctoroff insisted that the failed bid came with a saving grace: it had quick-tracked the zoning changes and would now spur development. They had a strong point. Cities are typically paralyzed by inertia; mayors are typically reactive and crisis-driven. The Olympics pursuit created a sense of urgency, broke through the paralysis, liberated "the last frontier" in Manhattan from outdated zoning and, as a result, an ill-used, wasted area of the city could eventually be built into a new neighborhood, filled with new development. But what kind of development?

Critics complain that instead of zoning for the neighborhood, the Bloomberg administration had zoned for the Olympics, in a classic case of the tail wagging the dog. The remaining plan, for instance, includes a grand, diagonal promenade—

originally called Olympics Boulevard—leading to the phantom Olympics Square, in front of the phantom Olympics stadium. Locals call it "the boulevard to nowhere."

To save on costs, the subway line extension will have one less stop than planned and as far as critics are concerned, it now follows the wrong route, since it was set originally to accommodate the lost Olympics. There is also debate about the proposed density of construction, an evergreen objection in New York, and about the soundness of the financing plan.

Bloomberg angrily rejects the criticisms and was never consoled about the Olympics loss. "You are never going to get big things, you are never going to get great things, if you just avoid the risk," he said. Years later, on the slightest provocation, he would still rail about his defeat, complaining that it had cost the city jobs, investment and opportunity.

The mayor and Doctoroff believe the city has been left light-years behind where it would have been with the stadium because the parochial, self-interested powers in Albany let the perfect be the enemy of the good. The unsightly rail yards, a huge gash in Manhattan's side, would have been decked over at public expense; the city would have had a year-round, world-class convention facility, connected underground to the mediocre Javits Convention Center. Quite a vision—unrealistic by New York standards, though the city will never know what might have been.

What eventually happens to the area will not be known for decades as the city passes through more cycles of boom and bust. Before the crash of 2008, construction had begun on the subway and a few sleek residential buildings had risen, sparkling incongruously above an otherwise bleak neighborhood. But the area is primed to eventually grow, slowly and incrementally like other parts of New York, instead of the dramatic, centrally cast way favored by the team of Bloomberg and Doctoroff.

The stadium failure stands as Bloomberg's greatest miscalculation and embarrassment. Maybe because they are both non–New Yorkers—Doctoroff from Detroit, Bloomberg from a Boston suburb—they misjudged not just the politicians but also ordinary people.

The public did not want that stadium. One poll found that 58 percent of New Yorkers opposed the stadium and an even larger percentage was less likely to vote for Bloomberg because of it. At a public hearing on the plan in 2004, when a Bloomberg official told local residents, "This will put us on the map," the roomful of three hundred New Yorkers erupted in laughter. New York already sat securely on every map. The city didn't need Bloomberg for that.

Paradoxically, Shelly Silver knew not what he wrought. By shattering Bloomberg's Olympics dream, he saved Mike Bloomberg from himself. His veto was cast five months before election day. It removed the greatest obstacle to the mayor's re-election, while shielding Bloomberg from being blamed by the labor unions and developers who wanted the stadium. Shelly did that, not Mike.

"We sent flowers to Shelly Silver," said his delighted communications director, Bill Cunningham. "Big, red roses."

CHAPTER 11

YES FOR MAYOR, NOT FOR DINNER

With the stadium elephant removed from his path, Bloomberg was rid of his greatest obstacle to reelection. He had it won before the campaign even began, though that's not how he played it.

The mayor cast himself as the underdog, prepared to sell hard as always and spend unlimited millions, even though he found himself running against a weak opponent and had history on his side. New Yorkers always reelect scandal-free incumbent mayors who avoid major failure. In recent memory, they denied only Abe Beame, in the center of the fiscal meltdown of the 1970s, and David Dinkins, undone by a bad economy and a bitter racial flare-up. There was no reason for Bloomberg not to have expected a second term.

If anything, he was in a stronger position than most. The city was not just recovering its confidence after 9/11; it was booming, the beneficiary of a strongly rebounding national economy and sound guidance from the mayor. Bloomberg could boast about his now popular anti-smoking legislation and of winning control of the schools—with still uncertain benefits for students but public appreciation for taking on a burden most other mayors had ducked.

The mayor's tax rebate was moving budget surpluses into consumers' pockets; so were his generous settlements with municipal labor unions, over conservative protests. And, dropping his objections to a Giuliani promise, he rebounded from his politically lucky Olympics loss with new plans for costly stadiums for both the Yankees and Mets.

There were lingering irritants. New Yorkers, most of them still Democrats, objected to Bloomberg's handling of the Republican National Convention in the summer of 2004, when eighteen hundred people were arrested and held in a large detention center, some guilty of no more than standing on a street during a police sweep. Never a conspicuous civil libertarian, the mayor, in a talk with me, brusquely dismisses the issue of the treatment of demonstrators, and privacy in general, justifying himself and his Police Department, pitting his pragmatism over the principles of others: "Number one, there's a camera watching you at all times when you're out in the street, the civil liberties issue has long been settled," he says.

As he sees it, those who were arrested put themselves at risk and in effect got what they deserved because the police were reacting to threats. "What are you gonna do, say one yes, one no? I'm sorry, if you get caught up in a crowd where everybody's throwing rocks and you get arrested, that's just the real world! You have to be stupid to be in that crowd!" There have been no allegations of rock-throwing, but his point is clear. He feels he owes no one any apologies.

The Bloombergian pragmatism came at a price. Five years after the convention, the city had spent $6.6 million to defend the lawsuits, an additional $1.7 million to settle ninety claims and still faced lawsuits filed by hundreds of plaintiffs. About 90 percent of the people arrested had their charges dismissed outright or dropped after six months.

Despite the litigation, the matter passed without dimming the mayor's reelection prospects. Neither, ultimately, was he hurt by the public's impression that Mike Bloomberg was not the kind of leader who understood or much cared about the concerns of the average New Yorker, that he was too focused on development and Manhattan's wealthy and, frankly, was something of a pill. Quinnipiac University, having some fun with its polling, asked New Yorkers a few times if they'd want to have Thanksgiving dinner with Bloomberg; nearly 60 percent said no thanks.

But those same New Yorkers gave him stronger and stronger approval ratings, responding to his spending onslaught and effort to demonstrate some empathy. They were also responding to his opponent.

All candidates benefit from luck and Bloomberg had plenty—most especially in the weak rival the Democrats threw against him. Fernando Ferrer, the former Bronx borough president who had lost the primary to Mark Green four years earlier, handily won the four-way Democratic primary, but not before crippling himself with a self-inflicted wound.

Courting favor with an organization of police sergeants, he asserted that death six years earlier of an unarmed African immigrant, Amadou Diallo, in a hail of police bullets had not been a crime. Even though Ferrer had made criticism of the police in the Diallo case an important issue in his 2001 mayoral campaign, in 2005 he suggested that prosecutors, by indicting the four police officers for second-degree murder, had overcharged them.

Diallo's death had rocked the city, crystallizing resentment of Rudy Giuliani's tough tactics among minorities. The killing remained a raw wound, particularly in the black community where Ferrer needed to run strong.

Ferrer's latest opinion on the Diallo case may have been legally sound—the four policemen were ultimately acquitted—but he was resented for changing his tone and using such a sensitive case to advance his ambition. Bloomberg shrewdly said little about the Diallo death, just, "This was a great tragedy and I'm not going to politicize it."

In March 2005, before his comments, polls gave Ferrer a slight lead, 46 to 40, over Bloomberg—a predictable showing in a Democratic city not yet bombarded with campaign messages. By April, however, after Ferrer's comments, Bloomberg pulled ahead 51 to 38. Many voters, including Democratic ones, saw Ferrer as a sacrificial lamb.

Running against the billionaire took fortitude, recalls Luis Miranda, Ferrer's senior political adviser. "Every morning you sort of had to put in your coffee enough doses of denial, euphoria and intellect—it was the only way to go through the day." There was not enough money, leading Democrats were defecting or, as with Bill Clinton, telegraphing halfhearted support for Ferrer. "And at three every afternoon there was the barrage of press inquiries. They did lots of research, negative research—obscure things. You always held on to your desk to see what happened at three when every reporter in City Hall would call."

Bloomberg's resources raised negative research, a standard campaign technique, to a new level; his people could debunk Ferrer's claim on his campaign website that he had attended public schools for most of his education—he attended mostly Catholic schools—or merely keep reporters busy chasing down an awkward remark he'd made in the 1980s.

As the campaign went on, the mayor just ran over Ferrer. The challenger could not deny that the city was much stronger than when Bloomberg took office, even if he disapproved of several mayoral policies and questioned claims of great strides in education. Ferrer lost all four major newspaper endorsements to Bloomberg. And he could not come anywhere near his spending.

By the end of the campaign, the mayor had spent $85 million of his own money—about $10 million more than in 2001—while Ferrer, operating under the limits of the city's public financing program, spent only a painfully raised $9 million. On an even larger scale than in 2001, the mayor's glossy mailings targeted individual New Yorkers by demographics and ethnicity. He ran ads in Spanish, Russian, even Mandarin and Urdu; he ran ads featuring celebrities like Kathleen Turner and Magic Johnson; he carpet bombed radio and television with ads.

Bloomberg's spending came to about $100 a vote, not counting staff bonuses or his personal contributions to charities, churches and cultural and civic organizations, at least some of which brought him more than gratitude.

With his messages dominating the airwaves, Bloomberg could duck one debate against Ferrer and consent to just two heated exchanges late in the campaign. An obviously frustrated Ferrer played to his Democratic base, rebuking Bloomberg for his Republican ties and for what he called serious policy failures on education and affordable housing. Bloomberg, boasting of achievements in education, reduced crime and greater prosperity, accused his opponent of doing "nothing" as borough president.

Still a Republican in a Democratic town, Bloomberg also gave himself cover by running as the candidate of the helpfully mistitled Independence Party and of the usefully named Liberal Party, an already moribund splinter group that was neither liberal nor much of a party.

Bloomberg's margin on election night was 20 percentage points—a landslide, especially for a Republican. He drew about half of the black vote and three of every ten Latino votes. It represented a resounding mandate.

The mayor's implicit mandate in New York City, plainly, was to use his power over the schools to advance education, to exploit prosperity to attack poverty, homelessness and to build affordable housing, to keep renewing decrepit neighborhoods, to go on containing crime, driving more guns off the streets, painting himself green with tree plantings and an assault on traffic.

But the election returns evoked a dream in Kevin Sheekey's mind, which gradually seized Bloomberg as well. It was the dream of an even louder summons: perhaps the rest of America was now ready to listen to a pragmatic Republican who had shown he could tame the wild natives of New York.

At the least, he could take his show on the road and interest the country in urban issues that national politicians routinely ignore, helping him run New York and helping other cities. At the most—well, who could tell? Nobody had given him a chance to be mayor in the first place and here he was, the magnate-turned-mayor, serving his second term after winning in a blowout.

Building on his first term, Bloomberg broadened his scope and once again thought big and bold. He sued out-of-state gun dealers, accusing them of illegally selling handguns that were later used to commit crimes in New York. He did battle against weak federal gun laws, created a national coalition of mayors to fight illegal weapons—useful to raise awareness, although really effective gun control demands national legislation. His suits were often settled and drew the fury of the National Rifle Association, whose magazine pictured the mayor as a menacing octopus and held a "Bloomberg Gun Giveaway" to help dealers pay the legal fees defending against Bloomberg's lawsuits. His demonization by the NRA was priceless in liberal New York, a risk on the national stage, though it certainly got Bloomberg attention beyond the city's five boroughs.

A year into his second term, he ginned up his administration to go green, putting Dan Doctoroff in charge of creating PlaNYC 2030, an ambitious twenty-five-year blueprint to reduce air pollution, build housing, improve mass transit and develop abandoned industrial land. The proposals ranged from the innocuous—planting one million trees—to the contentious—charging drivers a fee to bring their cars into midtown Manhattan, a toll system called congestion pricing.

"If we don't act now, when?" Bloomberg asked, making his announcement on Earth Day, at an event that via video heard California governor Arnold Schwarzenegger introduce the mayor and British prime minister Tony Blair praise him for "a brave act of leadership."

Most chief executives do not spend much time planning for the future, when they will no longer be in office to claim credit. That's why bridges fall down—from neglect by politicians worried about their today, not a successor's tomorrow.

But PlaNYC's 127 projects, regulations and innovations—an agenda so ambitious that Bloomberg likened it to the designs for Central Park and the construction of Rockefeller Center—rely heavily on political cooperation, public funds and a strong economy. That made it a nettlesome proposition, likely to be much harder to realize than it had been to announce with ceremony and celebrity videos.

The toughest proposal was congestion pricing. Bloomberg had long shied away from charging cars admission to mid-Manhattan, as London and other cities do; as he readily observed at his Earth Day event, it was "the elephant in the room," an affront to drivers from the other boroughs of the city and from the suburbs—and to their aroused legislators in Albany where, as always, the state's power brokers would get the last say.

Once again, Bloomberg found his ambitions pitched against the political guile of Assembly Speaker Sheldon Silver. This time Bloomberg was determined to get it right. He won a federal subsidy from the Department of Transportation. He lined up support from ecology-friendly organizations and enlisted the lobbying talents of Patricia Lynch, the Silver confidante who had worked against the Olympic stadium plan. He put the affable Kevin Sheekey in charge of negotiations, in place of Doctoroff, who had irritated legislators. He secured support from the Republican majority of the state senate by giving their leader, Joseph Bruno, $500,000 to help the GOP stay in power—to no avail, as it later turned out.

Then, when everyone said that congestion pricing was dead, he flew to Albany and personally brokered the outlines of a three-way deal by sketching it out on cocktail napkins left over from a take-in lunch of burgers and popcorn in Bruno's offices. Albany being Albany, each player wanted something: Bruno already had his $500,000; Governor Eliot Spitzer wanted support for campaign finance reform; Silver wanted a pay raise for his members and a say over spending on public transportation in members' districts.

Fleetingly, it seemed as though Bloomberg had mastered the arts of political brokerage, but in Albany, a deal is not necessarily a deal. Little of consequence is accomplished in less than a decade, or two—or three—in New York's retrograde state capital. Just beginning to revise the harsh Rockefeller drug laws took more than thirty years; returning the city schools to the mayor's control took over twenty. Bloomberg's congestion pricing plan was brand new. He had proposed it early in his second term and it was heading for a quick vote by Albany standards—a year later.

As the plan ran into trouble, critics complained that Bloomberg and Sheekey had been distracted, traveling around the country on their unacknowledged presidential sortie. Others complained that Bloomberg had uttered threats, or shown insufficient deference to individual lawmakers, under the mistaken belief that everything depended on a constituency of only one—the all-powerful Silver.

What he still did not realize was that Silver, careful and self-protective, led from the back; he took his cue from his members, because they keep him in power. Or not.

Actually, Silver supported congestion pricing—his lower Manhattan district is not heavy on commuters with cars. But assembly Democrats from Brooklyn, Queens and the suburbs fought the idea, resenting it as a scheme favoring the Manhattan elite. Some confided that the proposed $8 fee to drive into parts of Manhattan would hurt them in the wallet. "You're going to cost me forty dollars a week," one Brooklyn lawmaker grumbled to a supporter of the mayor.

The Speaker also had to keep an eye on an ambitious Westchester assemblyman, Richard Brodsky, who pined for Silver's job and opposed congestion pricing. Offending suburban and outer-borough lawmakers, and encouraging a rival in the process, is not how Silver had retained the Speakership since 1994. So he wielded his favorite passive-aggressive tool, a handy device to bury hot issues. Saying there were not enough votes to pass congestion pricing, he never brought the bill to the assembly floor.

Once again, Silver had outgamed Bloomberg.

The mayor did not hide his fury. "It takes a special type of cowardice for elected officials to refuse to stand up and vote their conscience on an issue that has been debated, and amended significantly to resolve many outstanding issues, for more than a year. Every New Yorker has a right to know if the person they send to Albany was for or against better transit and cleaner air."

Bloomberg could take comfort in a happy side effect of his battle, a reason, some thought, he'd made it the centerpiece of PlaNYC 2030 in the first place: his bold initiative had strengthened his national profile. With the big campaigns against gun dealers, for school reform, for the PlaNYC, and even the futile Olympics bid—a captivating idea outside of New York—Bloomberg was registering as a national figure at an opportune time.

The mayor who had predicted so many years earlier that he would be the first Jewish president was gaining stature just as the country was starting to search for a new commander in chief.

CHAPTER 12

SEE MIKE NOT RUN

THOSE WHO WITNESSED the curious moment would call it the Night of the Cheesecakes.

It was the night when Mike Bloomberg hand-delivered three trademark confections from Brooklyn to the college town of Norman, Oklahoma. It was also the night that marked the beginning of the end of Bloomberg's stealth presidential campaign.

The journey had been long and devious.

The day after Bloomberg won reelection by a landslide in 2005, his political maestro and stalking horse, Kevin Sheekey, dropped a bomblet on NY1 News, New York's 24/7 cable television station. Asked about the mayor's future, he did not hesitate. "Obviously, Bloomberg 2008—we'll roll right into the presidential as we move forward," Sheekey said to his stunned interviewer, Dominic Carter. "Dominic, don't you think the mayor should run for president next with his unique view on how to solve the problems in urban America?"

With that began the will-he-or-won't-he parlor game, promoted aggressively by Sheekey, coyly by Bloomberg, helpfully by Bloomberg's money. Would Bloomberg be an updated version of H. Ross Perot, the wealthy Texan who ran as an independent in 1992? No, the mayor kept saying crankily for more than a year, and into the presidential season that ended with the election of Barack Obama. No. No. No. Wink. Wink. Wink.

"Which letter in the word 'no' do you not understand?" he said at press conferences. "I am not going to run for president." Once, when pressed to cite the circumstances under which he might run, the mayor answered, "If everybody in the world was dead and I was the only one alive."

Yet at the same time, his aides let it be known that Bloomberg could spend whatever he wanted on running for president. It would be "a billion-dollar campaign," Sheekey told *Newsweek*. At every opportunity, he talked up the idea of his boss running as a third-party candidate, a message echoed by Bloomberg's pollster, Douglas Schoen, who, surely by coincidence, was writing a book about the impending death of the two-party system and parallel rise of political independence. It would not have been hard for the mayor to silence both men. He did not.

In June 2007, Bloomberg, the lifelong Democrat who had become a Republican to run for mayor, quit the GOP and declared himself an independent. He spoke about his decision the next day, at a ceremony marking the fifty-millionth call to 311, his proudly installed citizens' service system.

"I'm really thrilled that people care so much about 311 and its ability to deliver services, and I'm sure that will be on the front page tomorrow," Bloomberg said, a sardonic edge to his voice. Asked at least a dozen different ways about his presidential gambol, he insisted he was "not a candidate" and had left the Republican Party to become unaffiliated only because "if you are independent, it just gives you a flexibility, and the more I thought about that, the more I think it felt right."

The pros met denial with helpful (to Bloomberg) speculation. "Maybe he's telling the truth," wrote the *Washington Post*'s Dana Milbank. "But there is circumstantial evidence to the contrary, including his recent move to quit the Republican Party—a necessary precursor to mounting an independent presidential candidacy." Noting that Bloomberg could "buy his way into contention," he concluded that the mayor could be revving up a "niche" candidacy. Unidentified mayoral aides dribbled out tantalizing bits of unverified information to feed the rumor mill. They said they had worked for two years laying the groundwork for an independent candidacy; that they were collecting technical data on the requirements to put Bloomberg on the ballot in fifty states; that the mayor was closely studying Perot's independent candidacy in 1992, when he won 19 percent of the vote.

The true scope of Bloomberg's covert campaign has never been disclosed. A company called the Symposia Group, which had a client of one—Mike Bloomberg—had created a Bloomberg for President website on Sheekey's instruction. Mayoral sources were quoted in news accounts saying Symposia was preparing to analyze voter preferences nationwide if Bloomberg ran. They also said they were polling around the country. It remains a well-guarded secret how far that went, what Bloomberg paid for preliminary "micro-targeting," travel, salaries and polling, or what he learned. Since Bloomberg personally underwrote his non-campaign, he could spend what he wanted without creating the standard paper trail of public candidate reports.

Unknown, too, maybe to everyone but himself, is Bloomberg's state of mind at the time.

"He was conflicted," says Gerald Rafshoon, the former aide to President Jimmy Carter and a founder of Unity '08, a reform group that was looking for a bipartisan presidential candidate early in the campaign season. Bloomberg had attracted the group's interest.

Rafshoon remembers speaking with the mayor early in the summer of 2006 at Ben Bradlee's birthday party in the Hamptons: "He told me he had to decide what he was going to do after he was mayor. He said, 'I could do more good as president than I could at philanthropy.'" To Rafshoon, Bloomberg seemed intrigued and flattered by Unity 08's interest in him, but worried. He did not, he emphasized, want to be a spoiler: "He didn't want to be responsible for electing another right-wing president."

Rafshoon told him that he and his colleagues were convinced that in a polarized blue-state, red-state country, an independent candidate could parachute into the broad middle and win. It would all depend on who emerged from the Republican and Democratic primaries.

Sheekey agreed. As he saw it, a country frustrated with partisanship and the dysfunctions of Washington might embrace a third-party candidate, especially one who could spend $1 billion on his cause. He thought Bloomberg could appeal to the center if the Republicans nominated, say, the conservative Mike Huckabee, former governor of Arkansas, and the Democrats nominated John Edwards—or Barack Obama.

"I used to say if it was Huckabee and Obama, I'd write the filing checks myself," said Sheekey, reflecting the preliminary and, as it happened, erroneous view of Obama as a standard liberal who would not appeal to independents. Sheekey told others his man could run if Hillary Rodham Clinton became the Democratic nominee. Sometimes it seemed that at least on the Democratic side, any candidate argued in favor of a Bloomberg run.

Others were more dubious about Bloomberg's chances.

At about the same time the mayor spoke with Rafshoon, he was introduced to Al From, a founder of the Democratic Leadership Council, the centrist group that had promoted Bill Clinton's election. Summoned by his friend Michael Steinhardt, the former hedge fund tycoon-turned-philanthropist and a former DLC chairman, From came to Steinhardt's art-filled Fifth Avenue duplex just north of the Metropolitan Museum of Art. Present were Bloomberg, Sheekey, Patti Harris and Ed Skyler. From their two-hour discussion, From said he did not find Bloomberg "chomping at the bit" to run for president.

Nor was he sure that the mayor would make a good candidate. "A presidential candidate needs to galvanize. My friends in New York loved him because he can get the job done. But presidential campaigns tend to be about cause and ideology, and process never trumps cause. He had to think about whether he could adapt the qualities that made him a good mayor to exciting people in a presidential campaign."

The DLC founder recalls Bloomberg as noncommittal and playing devil's advocate at one point. What chance does "a short, Jewish, divorced billionaire" have on the national stage? he asked.

That was only part of his burdensome baggage. He was a traditional urban liberal—anti-gun, pro-immigrant, pro-choice, a secular New Yorker who supported gay rights. The suits against him and his company charging sexual harassment—though settled and old news in New York except for one still-pending class action lawsuit suit against his company—would be national media fodder. He had never articulated an Iraq policy, then the central issue in the campaign, and bristled when anyone questioned his foreign policy credentials: "I know more about foreign policy than any of the candidates. I've negotiated deals around the world, I've dealt with politicians in every one of these countries, we do business with their companies and with their governments."

Bloomberg had also steadfastly refused to bow to the country's demand that national candidates make a display of religious faith, and he showed no willingness to leaven his position. "I think everybody's religious beliefs are their own and they should keep them private," he said to me when speculation about his presidential aspirations was growing intense. "This business of bringing religion into everything is just bad because if you really believe in religion you should be the person out there championing separation of church and state. If you don't care about religion, then no harm, no foul."

One can only speculate how that message, delivered by an unapologetically secular Jew, would have played in a campaign that featured the melodrama of Barack Obama's flamboyant minister one moment, and lengthy interviews of both Obama and John McCain by an evangelical preacher the next.

Bloomberg, unlike the declared candidates, was never subjected to bruising scrutiny, either. A sympathetic and comprehensive *Newsweek* cover story about Bloomberg one year before the election thrilled City Hall. Even Patti Harris and Ed Skyler, dubious about their boss running for president, figured the mayor's growing visibility was good for New York.

Bloomberg's every comment about issues—infrastructure, the dangers of smoking, illegal guns, inner-city schools—drew exaggerated attention, giving him and issues important to New York a national airing and simultaneously hoarding his power in the city. Without his non-campaign he would have been a weakening lame duck, as the spotlight of attention shifted to prospective successors, because of the city's two-term limits law. Instead, network hosts interviewed him, newspapers everywhere quoted him—the presidential venture made him more of a celebrity than ever.

Bloomberg stayed purposefully loose. In August 2006, he had endorsed Joseph Lieberman, the Connecticut Democrat who lost his party's primary and was running as an independent; the mayor was no doubt hoping for a return favor, should it come to that. Bloomberg's out-of-town traveling escalated, growing from an average of eleven trips in each of his first four years, to twenty-five in 2006, thirty-nine in 2007. He always flew in one of his company's corporate jets, comfortable twelve-passenger planes with reclining seats, individual electronic screens and a well-stocked galley.

In 2007, as speculation about his presidential possibilities hit a high, some of his travels took him to Beijing for a China-U.S. "innovation conference" and to Shanghai to speak at a university; to Washington, DC, to talk about public health on one visit, capital markets on another; to Mexico for meetings on finances; to Amman, Jordan, to see the king; to Cincinnati to meet with a group he created, Mayors Against Illegal Guns; to Paris and to London, to Blackpool for a British Conservative Party conference. His visits to Washington alone tripled between his first term and the first three years of his second.

Back home, he seemed less engaged in the inner workings of his administration, delegating even more than in his first term. His government was running smoothly, but pundits were starting to wonder whether at some point, the Hamlet-like performance would backfire and make the mayor seemed frivolous.

Despite his disclaimers, Bloomberg was seen as poised to run for the White House if the opportunity arose, and the speculation about his intentions reached a crescendo in the last week of 2007, with news that he would join a bipartisan conference of elder statesmen and women at the University of Oklahoma, billed as an effort to pressure the major party candidates to renounce partisan gridlock. "Our political system is, at the least, badly bent and many are concluding that it is broken," read the invitation.

The participants included former Democratic senators Bob Graham and Gary Hart, and Republicans Christine Todd Whitman, a former governor of New Jersey, and senators Bill Brock and John Danforth. Also attending were two men frequently mentioned as possible Bloomberg running mates—former senators Sam Nunn, Democrat of Georgia, and Chuck Hagel, the maverick Nebraska Republican.

When first announced, the conference seemed destined to take place while the presidential race was still fluid, so it attracted wide attention. Anything could happen, it seemed, as the 2008 election year finally dawned.

On January 6, Mike Bloomberg flew to Oklahoma on his Falcon 9 jet, an entourage in tow—Sheekey, Harris, Jim Anderson, his communications director, and Stu Loeser, his press secretary. Arriving for dinner at the campus home of the university president, former Democratic senator David Boren, the mayor was soon surrounded by reporters. Was he running? Was this the moment? Bloomberg smiled in silence. The reporters tried again. Silence. Retreating to trivia, they asked about the three boxes he was carrying.

"I always bring a house gift and I could not think of anything more appropriate than three different cheesecakes," he said. "Are they bipartisan cheesecakes?" a reporter asked. Actually they were Junior's cheesecakes, once unequalled Brooklyn confections that had long since lost their quality, but still coasted on warm memory.

As Bloomberg disappeared into Boren's house, the media pack clarified the flavors of the high-cholesterol offerings (plain, raspberry swirl and chocolate swirl) and tried, but failed, to resolve the other burning question of the evening—whether the color of the mayoral sweater was rose or salmon. One journalist reported with certitude, however, that the mayor wore red, the University of Oklahoma's official color.

It had come to that. There was an unspoken sense that evening in Oklahoma that the press corps, not as star-studded as it would have been just three days earlier, had lost its story—and interest. The journalists went through the motions, but their mission had evaporated, in the cornfields of Iowa.

On January 3, three days before the cheesecake delivery, Obama stunned the country by winning the first primary caucuses of the presidential year. The A-list of the national media had moved not to Oklahoma but to New Hampshire, for its presidential primary on January 8.

The bipartisan conference in Oklahoma had become a footnote. Even David Boren, the cosponsor with Sam Nunn, was saying that Obama seemed to be emerging as the very kind of candidate with broad appeal that he and other fans of bipartisanship had hoped for. Some other participants said they hoped whoever won would have a bipartisan "spirit," but they intended to vote for their party's nominee. Nobody said much about a third-party option.

Commentators on the Sunday talk shows had agreed that Obama's emergence left Bloomberg nowhere to go in the race. By the time the bipartisan panel discussion began the morning after Boren's dinner, the air was out of the room. Bloomberg merely bemoaned the state of American politics—"People stopped working together. There is no accountability, no willingness to focus on big ideas"—and he reiterated his non-candidacy.

OBAMA'S SURGE DEFLATES FORUM AND TALK OF A BLOOMBERG RUN, read the *New York Times*'s headline the next day.

By mid-February John McCain, who, like Obama, appealed to independents, had all but clinched the Republican nomination. A few weeks later, Bloomberg consulted with Sheekey, Patti Harris, Ed Skyler and his ad maker, Bill Knapp. Go for it, Sheekey still advised. He had even lined up a presidential campaign staff-in-waiting, putting former Bloomberg workers on the alert in case the mayor gave the nod. Harris and Skyler advised the mayor to stand down. Knapp was said to be in the middle.

Bloomberg pulled the plug: "I listened carefully to those who encouraged me to run, but I am not—and will not be—a candidate for president," he wrote in a *Times* op-ed piece on February 28.

He was too level-headed to run when he knew he could not win. But the temptation had run deep. A couple of weeks before his *Times* piece appeared, Bloomberg emerged almost wistful from a Fifth Avenue party of media heavyweights, including Barbara Walters; Don Hewitt, creator of *60 Minutes,* and his wife, Marilyn Berger, a writer; and Herbert Schlosser, former head of NBC and his wife, Judith, chairwoman of the Martha Graham Center of Contemporary Dance. "I would have carried that crowd," he said, giving scant acknowledgment to the difference between Manhattan's Upper East Side and the nation's heartland.

In his own mind, the presidency was a job not for the glamorous, but for a manager, an administrator.

Yes, McCain or Obama might turn out to be a great president, he acknowledged, "But what the hell do they know about management and dealing with people? Nothing," Bloomberg said to me, a few weeks before he took himself out of contention. "If you look at my company, why, after all the success that we had before I ran for office, would you not think that I couldn't run government? What the hell do I gotta do to prove myself? Or, after the success my company has had and our administration has had, why do you think I wouldn't be qualified to be president of the United States? I mean, for God's sake, I'm not running, but this is not different."

Three weeks after Obama's election, when Bloomberg and I sat down for a postmortem on his dalliance with presidential politics, the mayor reiterated that he never thought he would run. "There was never a time that I really thought it was possible for a third-party candidate to win."

What, then was he doing all that time? "What do you mean what was I doing? Everybody says you would make a great president, you say 'thank you,' what do you say?" In short nothing, as Sharkey had counseled when Bloomberg first asked him how to handle questions about the mayoralty. Sheekey told him, whatever you do, don't say you are *not* running. Keep them guessing while you make up your mind.

And so he finally made his decision and did not run. The moment to realize the fantasy he had harbored since college, to be president—to be the first Jewish president, in fact—had passed.

CHAPTER 13

FINDING ACT III

IN HIS EIGHTH YEAR as mayor of New York, things could hardly have been going much better for Mike Bloomberg. He'd gotten over his presidential fling, he'd figured out what he wanted to do next and he had made it happen. He had a doting paramour, lived in a fine home in a world-class city, his company continued to enrich him and he had built himself a national reputation. Not bad for a kid from Medford, Massachusetts. Not bad, either, for a mogul from Manhattan.

He should have been rejoicing but he was not. Early in his pursuit of a third term, he was cross, even nasty at times, often angry not only in private but in public, especially in his exchanges with reporters, the few unscripted moments in his day. In April 2009, he self-righteously scolded a wheelchair-bound reporter who needed a few extra seconds to silence a tape recorder accidentally triggered during a news conference. In May he called a questioner who asked a pesky but legitimate question "a disgrace" and, refusing to answer the criticism of a possible opponent because he hadn't heard it, snapping at the reporter who offered to quote his critic, "That's nice. Well, that could show you could read."

After "Disgracegate," as it inevitably became known around City Hall, Bloomberg was called upon to explain himself. He used the Popeye defense: "I am what I am," he said, without a hint of a smile.

Crankiness was not a new facet of Mike Bloomberg's personality. He could always be hard to bear when he was unhappy. Why the public dyspepsia at such an opportune time in his life? Because he would not be president? Not likely. Bloomberg does not give himself the luxury of looking back.

No, it was something else and those who knew him well thought they understood. "He's a different guy than he was a year ago," said a friend of many decades. "He breached his own code of ethics. He was deceptive, he did what he criticizes other people for doing—and it bothers him." Either that, or he was bothered that for the first time in his mayoral career, he was being subjected to the kind of scrutiny and criticism that are visited on every mayor. He had pretty much sailed above the fray for a very long time.

Now even supporters who planned to vote for him were disappointed in him, the press was energized—and he had done it to himself.

In trying to fulfill a purely personal ambition, Bloomberg had betrayed his own high standard for political behavior. To hold on to the mayoralty, he had calculated and maneuvered with the skill of an ordinary politician, just like the Albany characters he was always battling, and nothing like the high-minded statesman he held himself to be. To get what he wanted, he had done precisely what he vowed he would never do: go back on his word. The mayor who had prided himself for two terms on raising the standards of New York politics had mortgaged his reputation to the old ways to seek a third. If he didn't like his new identity and the reaction to it, it was for a good reason.

Riding high in his second term, his presidential aspirations blocked, and facing his last year in office under the law, Bloomberg had to decide if he would hear the chorus of counsel saying enough was enough. His closest aides said quit while you're ahead. The desires of the voters were clear—they had twice endorsed a law limiting city officials to two four-year terms. Polls showed the public was adamant: two terms were enough.

Bloomberg knew, every student of New York knew, that twice is blessed, three times cursed; every one of his predecessors who served three terms lived to regret it. But he resolved he would not be miserable like LaGuardia, tired like Wagner or plagued by corruption charges like Koch. He would once again write his own history.

Despite the odds, maybe because of the odds, Bloomberg chose to listen only to an inner voice. It said public life was so much more thrilling than making money, more gratifying than giving it away. It told him he loved the attention, the applause, the deference, the spotlight.

He was also confident that he was "making a difference," and could do more to improve the city if he stayed on as mayor. His inner voice reminded him he had never let others steer his life or make him retreat from risk. It told him to trump history, to discipline his staff, to change the limits of a law that he had previously, and firmly, embraced and to win—or buy—the people's support.

That had not always been his intention. Bloomberg had been adamant about what he would do after City Hall. He would manage his philanthropy. He had bought two town houses a block from his Manhattan home and was renovating them to house the Bloomberg Family Foundation. Said to be worth as much as $20 billion (a guess that fluctuated with the economy), he would concentrate on creatively giving away his money; he would be the Bill Gates of the East Coast.

But after his presidential flirtation ended, he grew restive. Speculation about his future went into overdrive.

Some faculty members at Johns Hopkins circulated a letter asking him to succeed their president, who was retiring. Bloomberg said no. Others figured he could serve in Washington. He denied interest.

Then there was a frisson of rumor about him buying the financially ailing *New York Times.* As Michael Wolff wrote in his biography of Rupert Murdoch, the chairman of News Corporation and the *New York Post,* the rumor seems to have begun when Wolff himself raised the idea in an interview with Murdoch. Bloomberg was not, he insisted to me, interested in being a newspaper publisher. "I don't know anything about it, what do I know about running newspapers?" he said to me. "Murdoch, Mort Zuckerman—you don't like Joyce Purnick, you get an editor in, say write a nasty story about Joyce Purnick, call a reporter, follow her around, make sure you get some dirt on her. I wouldn't do that. My point is, that is the only reason to own a newspaper, so you could do that. But I wouldn't do it at Bloomberg news, I wouldn't do it there."

Friends wondered whether an ego fed by eight years of public attention could retire to the slow and anonymous routine of managing charity. The mayor's mood was well perceived by his friend Michael Steinhardt. "I think he likes hearing himself talk publicly." He was sure the mayor would go batty without his great platform to address the issues of his time.

Other influential friends and business leaders had begun to worry about the city's future. Led by financier Steven Rattner, lawyer Martin Lipton and developer Jerry Speyer, they often spoke to the mayor and to each other about the need for a mayor like Bloomberg to succeed Bloomberg—preferably for *the* Bloomberg to succeed Bloomberg. Sensing a happy nexus between the mayor's unsettled future and a lack of impressive mayoral prospects, they urged him to run for a third term.

As everyone knew, the law stood in the way. So what? His friends thought he could have it changed. They lobbied him in private with the same arguments they then took public: "Two terms is too short," William Rudin, the real estate executive who heads the Association for a Better New York, said to reporters. "I think it is a good thing for us to revisit." Donald Trump pronounced the two-term limit "a terrible idea, an artificial barrier."

Terrible perhaps, but not artificial. Bloomberg actually owed his job to that law, which had forced an obviously reluctant Rudy Giuliani to depart from City Hall. Moreover, Bloomberg had consistently and vehemently supported the limits. "This is an outrage!" he exclaimed in 2005, when the city council toyed with a plan to extend the limit on everyone's service from two terms to three. "There's no organization that I know," Bloomberg had said, "that would put somebody in charge for a long period of time. You always want turnover and change. Eight years is great. You learn for four years. You can do for four years."

Over and over, Bloomberg had buttressed his view with the voice of the people, who had twice voted to ratify the limit. "We cannot ignore their will."

Just a few weeks after Bloomberg abandoned his interest in the White House I asked him about the rumors. It was clear he had given a third term some thought. The mechanics, he noted, would be difficult and, he emphasized, he would need the newspapers' editorial support. Then, just as he was saying he could count on the *Post*'s Rupert Murdoch and the *Daily News*'s Mort Zuckerman, but was uncertain about *Times* publisher Arthur Sulzberger Jr., his press aide intervened to declare the rest of the conversation off the record.

The speculation that Bloomberg wanted a third term was interrupted only by the suggestion that he might be tapped to run for vice president—by either John McCain or Barack Obama. Kevin Sheekey liked the Obama-Bloomberg configuration, chatting up the idea and pairing it with an enticing reminder of Bloomberg's wealth. "Listen, Mike Bloomberg spent $83 [actually $85] million in a reelection simply in New York City," Sheekey said; as a vice presidential candidate, his boss could spend "between zero and a billion."

The mayor predicted that neither presidential candidate would pick him and defensively pronounced himself wrong for the job: he was too old, he said, to work for anyone else. "He'd have to be number one; he always said he wouldn't take it," recalled Rupert Murdoch, slyly adding, "but I think he would have taken either."

It was difficult to envision McCain selecting Bloomberg. The Arizona Republican was already shaky with his party's conservatives and unlikely to tie himself to a pro-choice, pro-immigrant, urban liberal. It was almost as difficult to see Chicago's Obama picking New York's Bloomberg, who was not a big fan of the Democratic nominee. Though neutral in public about the presidential contest, the mayor privately called Obama inexperienced at running things and too willing to make political compromises.

The political grapevine surely carried that disapproving message back to the Obama camp.

Gossip about Bloomberg's future grew feverish after he mingled with media tycoons at their annual July retreat in Sun Valley in 2008. It was in that manicured corner of Idaho that Bloomberg sought out Rupert Murdoch and made the dinner date to talk back in New York. It was there, too, that Bloomberg spent time with friends Martin Lipton, Henry Kravis and Richard Parsons. They had been in touch with other Bloomberg confidants—Mort Zuckerman, Jerry Speyer and Steven Rattner—to encourage the mayor to go for a third term. Particularly enthusiastic was Rattner, who managed Bloomberg's personal fortune. He and his wife, Maureen White, prominent fund-raisers for Democrats, socialized often with the mayor and Diana Taylor, their get-togethers interrupted only briefly when Rattner served as Obama's auto industry czar.

Taylor was convinced Bloomberg would enjoy four more years, and she, too, welcomed the prospect of continuing her glamorous life as the city's unofficial first lady.

"They all came back from Sun Valley loaded for bear, sure he was going to go for it," a business associate recalls. "But there were all those complications."

Complication No. 1 was Ronald Lauder. Art collector and a son of cosmetics tycoon Estée Lauder, he had stumbled around the edges of New York politics for years, never gaining footing. After spending $12 million of his inherited fortune in pursuit of the Republican nomination for mayor in 1989, only to lose big to Rudy Giuliani, he narrowed his sights. Lauder engineered a campaign to limit most elected city officials to two terms totaling eight years, spending $4 million to persuade the public to endorse the idea by referendum in 1993 and again in 1996.

Civic groups, most editorial boards and incumbent politicians opposed the limits as an undemocratic assault on the public's right to elect or reject its leaders. But the voters, encouraged by Lauder's expensive ad campaign, saw the law as a populist tool in a largely one-party city, a way to throw the bums out.

Sensing Bloomberg's change of heart and challenge, Lauder threw down the gantlet. He bankrolled a TV commercial comparing politicians to dirty diapers that "need to be changed regularly." He would fight to protect his pet policy, threatening the mayor with an unseemly wrestling match between two billionaires.

Complication No. 2 was Bloomberg himself. He did not relish the thought of leading the inevitably messy campaign to change a law he once favored.

Complication No. 3 was dissension in the ranks, so rare it was shocking. Bloomberg's closest aides pleaded with him to leave government as scheduled, even appealing to friends, civic leaders and former staff members to help talk the boss out of his apparent resolve.

In a unique breach of staff discipline, deputy mayors Kevin Sheekey, Patti Harris and Ed Skyler failed to deny published reports of their opposition to a third term. They were not only hoping to move on to lucrative private employment, they were also worried about the man whom they had loyally served for many years.

If he persisted, they feared, he risked appearing hypocritical, damaging the political identity he had so diligently nurtured. He was supposed to be the one who stood above conventional politics, who served only the public interest—not party or self. And invoking history, they warned he also risked failure in a third term.

"It's those business friends of his!" said one of the dissenters, still agitated after losing the fight. "What is it to them? They get their friend to stay in City Hall, what do they know about the problem, his reputation, what do they care?"

The summer of 2008 passed without a decision—without a public decision, at least. Bloomberg clearly wanted to run; he may already have decided to run. But waiting helped him in one way he anticipated, and in another way he could not have.

The term-limits law could be amended either through another referendum, or by the city council directly. If Bloomberg had announced his intentions early in the summer, he would have been under pressure to put the question to voters in a referendum. But he would lose that referendum, he knew from a poll he had commissioned in June. The referendum timetable was tight. To get the question on the ballot in November 2008, when the presidential election would insure a large turnout, he would have had to start the time clock with a public announcement in July, no later.

Delay helped him another way. Just as 9/11 had come along to justify an unconventional Bloomberg candidacy in 2001, the tanking economy delivered a rationale in 2008. The financial storm of 2008 struck as the presidential race went into its final lap, hitting Bloomberg's Wall Street hard.

The Treasury Department seized control of mortgage finance giants Fannie Mae and Freddie Mac on September 14. A day later, Lehman Brothers filed for bankruptcy and Merrill Lynch was sold to Bank of America. Two days later, the Federal Reserve took over the shaky American Insurance Group (AIG) with an $85 billion loan, the first of several lifelines. By late September, the country was in turmoil and Bloomberg seized the moment.

He now had the cover of a plausible reason to ram a change

in the law through the city council instead of in a public referendum so that he—and council members—could run for a third term. The city, he explained, needed him to survive the emergency. "I just didn't want to walk away when the going got tough," he said.

His friend and strong supporter, *Daily News* publisher Mort Zuckerman, recognized that reason as mainly pretext. "No, it was not the economic crisis," he remarked. "He wanted to run for a third term. What else was he going to do? He loves being mayor."

Indeed, by the time the economy cratered, the mayor had methodically prepared the ground. He had already canvassed the city's three principal newspapers, and confirmed their support. Murdoch's, never in question, would be the most helpful. The immigrant media baron loved politics, he loved being an influential player and, unlike the more decorous *Times* and somewhat more restrained *Daily News,* his *Post* never hesitated to use the news pages to flog the owner's causes.

In mid-September, about two weeks before Bloomberg confirmed he would go for another term, Murdoch and Bloomberg had their dinner. Meeting at Primavera, the pricey, wood-paneled favorite of the elite on Manhattan's Upper East Side, they talked strategy, joined by Howard Rubenstein, dean of the city's public relations business. Murdoch, who considered the Democrats lining up to succeed the mayor "too horrible, too dangerous" to contemplate, wanted to run an editorial in the *Post* immediately. Wait just a little while, Bloomberg advised. "He said, 'Don't come out for me yet, I don't want to leave you out on a limb,'" Murdoch recalled. The mayor had to take care of more business first.

Bloomberg still needed to secure city council votes, and he had to neutralize Ron Lauder, who could intimidate council members by threatening to bankroll candidates running against them. The mayor promised Lauder that he only wanted the law suspended temporarily, because of the crisis. But when that ploy became legally difficult, Bloomberg offered Lauder a deal: if he permitted an extension of term limits from two to three, the mayor, once reelected, would name Lauder to a commission empowered to restore the two-term rule. It took more pressure from business barons and a tense peace conference with Bloomberg to bring Lauder around. "The words 'crisis' and 'emergency' were used repeatedly," Rubenstein recalled.

Also now on board was the Speaker of the city council, Christine Quinn. She, too, had vowed not to tinker with term limits, but had everything to gain by flip-flopping. A natural politician, Quinn wanted to be the first female and the first openly gay mayor of New York. Having the wealthy Bloomberg indebted to her could be a great boon. Waiting four years to cash in would also overcome an embarrassing scandal over council appropriations going to fictitious community groups.

In all, thirty-five of the council's fifty-one members were completing the permissible two terms. Why not join with the mayor to win a chance at four more years?

An obviously orchestrated rollout began on September 29, when Bloomberg told deputy mayors Harris, Sheekey and Skyler that he was ignoring their counsel. They remained unhappy, but they were loyal, genuinely fond of him, and surely aware that their futures would not be helped by breaking with him.

The next day, a *Post* editorial trumpeted RUN, MIKE, RUN, echoing a prior shout from Zuckerman's *Daily News.* Murdoch's other New York City newspaper, the *Wall Street Journal,* did not editorialize about the matter. The *Times* waited a while; it had to extricate itself from a spring editorial advising the mayor to stand down because "we are wary of changing the rules just to suit the ambition of a particular politician." By autumn, the paper had rediscovered its still earlier opposition to term limits as an infringement on "the voters' right to select their leaders."

On October 2, Bloomberg made it official, announcing his third-term plan while Sheekey and Skyler stood by, their faces revealingly grim. Citing a "crisis of confidence" in the economy, Bloomberg said he would ask the council to amend the law so that he could yet again offer voters his "record of independent leadership."

When a reporter recalled the mayor's flirtation with presidential politics, Bloomberg deflected the implication with a mean shot at Sheekey, his deputy for politics. "Kevin ran for president, I didn't run for president."

The current mayor insisted that he still favored term limits—just three terms instead of two. "If the public doesn't like the process they just have to vote for someone other than Michael Bloomberg," he explained. He did not say what Sheekey had already said—that the mayor would spend at least $80 million to win, again guaranteeing a sharply tilted playing field.

It was all over but the shouting, of which there was a great deal. City Hall shook with populist outrage during council hearings. "Shame on you" and "The city's for sale!" shouted members of the public, who filled the council balcony brandishing signs that read NO KING BLOOMBERG and UGLY WIN! Most were not complaining about the mayor's two-term performance, which, in fact, many praised; they resented his and the council's self-serving change of the rules without letting the public decide the issue.

Bloomberg and his lieutenants summoned support from union leaders, influential ministers and civic leaders, and also the heads of social and cultural groups, a good number of whom had benefited from Bloomberg's philanthropy. Dutifully, the leaders of the Doe Fund, the Harlem Children's Zone, the Public Art Fund, the Alliance of Resident Theaters and the St. Nicholas Neighborhood Preservation Corporation complied. They praised Bloomberg's leadership, insisting that they testified willingly.

The council passed the measure 29 to 22, with the approval of twenty-three of the members facing a service limit. Principle was not widely evident. Even some council members who claimed the high ground by voting no were selfishly interested in retiring the occupants of higher offices to which they aspired.

Bitter complaints about arm-twisting, threats and inducements are traditional in New York politics, but such conventional maneuvering was not the standard Bloomberg had set. Now he risked being unique only in the millions he could commit to such an election battle.

Bloomberg never wanted to talk about why he hadn't let the voters address the third-term issue directly, by a referendum in November 2008. Another option, a referendum in an early 2009 special election, never got traction because it would have forced prospective candidates for city offices to live with uncertainty for too long. But a November plebiscite was certainly possible if Bloomberg had decided soon enough.

He has always been vague about when he made up his mind to run again. A month after the council vote, he recalled making up his mind "during the summer." A month later he told an interviewer it was not until September.

One close friend who had encouraged the mayor's third-term bid feels sure that Bloomberg deliberately ran out the clock because of the poll in June. "His political advisers were telling him he wouldn't win a referendum, his poll showed people would not vote for a third term."

Ironically, once the scope of the financial crisis became clear, the voters would have probably approved a change in the law, but by then it was too late to put the question on the ballot.

Before signing the bill, Bloomberg sat through four hours of public comment, stone-faced and fidgety as he heard an assault of insults, plaints, and words of disappointment. It was a new experience for a mayor accustomed to being treated with deference.

"Please don't let Kevin or ego blind you to the reality of what you are doing," said a man from Bushwick. "To hell with your agenda," shouted a deliveryman. "The creep of totalitarianism starts with a tiptoe of intolerance for the will of the people," complained Michael Rosen, a writer and community organizer. One speaker testified with his back toward Bloomberg, snapping, "I have no desire to look at you." Another accused the mayor of "strong-armed, knuckle-busting tactics."

The law had required Bloomberg to hold the hearing and listen to every minute of it, and so he did. Then, as Michael Barbaro of the *New York Times* wrote, "The left-handed Mr. Bloomberg picked up a black and gold pen and, with a flick of his wrist, rewrote the New York City term limits law."

When I next spoke to Bloomberg, a few weeks later, his approval rating in the polls, though still in the 60s, had dropped 9 points. Admirers were turning on him. The *Times*'s Clyde Haberman called him "The Nullifier" who would have to "convince New Yorkers that they can believe a single thing he says." Wayne Barrett of the *Village Voice,* a fan of the mayor's vaunted independence, wrote a treatise headlined THE TRANSFORMATION OF MIKE BLOOMBERG: HOW THE BENEVOLENT BILLIONAIRE WITH NO POLITICAL DEBTS ENDED UP OWNING US ALL.

The mayor was dismissive. "You don't have to look at columnists who have their own agenda. Just look at facts—what was done in terms of rezoning, improving education, bringing down crime . . ."

The latest polls? He looked annoyed. "What kind of logic is that? I guess I am speechless, I don't know what else to say, I am not gonna govern by polls, I am gonna do what's right."

Did he know that many thought he deliberately delayed revealing his intention to avoid a referendum? His voice rose. "How do they know what I know, what I knew? Why do you even think about it, why do you even read it, or bring it up?"

A sore point. An unwanted scratch in the mirror.

CHAPTER 14

MONEY, MONEY FROM CITY HALL

MEN SO RICH that they are invariably defined by their money need to decide how to wear the cloak of wealth. Warren Buffet likes to boast of his skill at earning it. Bill Gates and George Soros make a worldwide show of giving it away. Mike Bloomberg ranks almost at their level in both respects, but he has obviously decided that neither making money nor giving it away offers enough satisfaction.

Though not uninvolved, he entrusts the day-to-day operations of both his business and his philanthropy to loyal deputies while indulging his ambition for public service and acclaim. Despite his unshakable reputation as a billionaire, he treats his great fortune not as an end but as a means to fulfillment.

Bloomberg's attitudes toward his wealth are hard to discern. Because of his money, his name adorns buildings from midtown Manhattan to Jerusalem, from Baltimore to Cambridge. It labels his computer terminal, his television network, his news division, his radio station, his company's towering headquarters; it dots the campuses of his college and graduate school. It allows him to live large. Yet he dismisses the importance of his wealth even as he boasts of it.

"What's a billionaire got to do with it?" he said in 2001. "I mean, would you rather elect a poor person who didn't succeed? Look, I'm a great American dream," he boasted to the *Times.*

A millionaire in his thirties and a billionaire at fifty-five, Bloomberg has lived lavishly, but not ostentatiously. He has donated generously over the decades to a growing list of charities, becoming one of the largest donors in the country. He has roundly rewarded his most valued business and political associates, and freely supported their own charitable causes. He discreetly helps friends in financial trouble, opens medical doors even to relative strangers with health problems. He has provided handsomely for his mother, ex-wife, sister, daughters and a former companion.

But all his financial giving was arranged with little fanfare—until, late in life, he decided to use his wealth to gain wider recognition in New York and to fuel his campaigns for mayor, to invest yet again in a new career and to use his money as well as his wits to overcome the competition.

Decoding Bloomberg's financial profile is a little like struggling with a jigsaw puzzle that is missing many pieces. The big picture is apparent, but the gaps are great. Though Bloomberg is one of the richest men in the world, no one outside his immediate circle knows how rich. Though he is one of the country's most generous philanthropists, no outsider knows precisely how much he gives away. As founder of a private company that accounts for most of his wealth, he has never had to disclose his assets or his earnings or the full extent of his charities.

At the core of his wealth is the communications behemoth he invented. It was valued at $22.5 billion in 2008, when he bought Merrill Lynch's 20 percent stake. That purchase brought his stake in the company to 92 percent, putting his net worth then at more than $20 billion. But since the company is privately held, there is no continuing market for its stock and the effect of recession or other business turns cannot be measured.

Bloomberg brought a social conscience to his good fortune, always feeling a responsibility for the less privileged. But his great wealth and Wall Street training also narrowed his vision. Try as he occasionally does to be Everyman, he looks upon life through upper-class lenses. Though he made a show as mayor of riding the subways, he insisted during the great recession of 2008–2009 that the failed and irresponsible Wall Street executives deserved their extravagant bonuses. And he could startle a Brooklyn audience of recession-struck Caribbean immigrants by asking, to illustrate a bureaucratic problem, how many of them played golf.

Still, Bloomberg never made an obscene show of his wealth, like Donald Trump, and he let his modest origins tug at his behavior. For years he wore expensive but standard business suits until, well into his mayoralty, a friend introduced him to custom tailoring. He appreciated both the look and the impact on his wallet because he was avoiding the retail markup. "You save money!" he noted. He drinks red wines, but is not precious about vintage, guests at Bloomberg's town house often dine on meatloaf and mashed potatoes, and, revealed his barber, for thirty years, he has scheduled his own appointments for the same $35 haircut.

Determining the breadth of Bloomberg's philanthropy involves guesswork, a melding of public information and confidential records selectively revealed by his staff. Listing the recipients, but without details, his aides reported donations totaling $235 million in 2008, making him one of America's biggest individual donors—the biggest by one calculation. His philanthropy has grown year by year.

He gives to causes large and small, motivated by the same drives that shaped his political and business careers: to be visibly important, to make a difference, to benefit those in need, and to enjoy the resulting acclaim.

At the close of his memoir about making money, Bloomberg describes his standards in giving it away: "After you've gotten used to living like a king, what do you do?" he asks. His advice: stop worrying about taxes, "don't spoil your family" and "buy yourself enormous pleasure" by giving most of the wealth to charity. And, of course, he added, it should be done distinctively: "Having our names on a plaque, on a scholarship, on a research grant . . . rewards us as long as we live. It puts everyone else—our entire community, our country, and even the whole world—in our debt. What greater satisfaction could we possibly get than watching ourselves do great things for humanity?"

Following his own advice, he gives to causes and institutions large and small, with a special focus on public health, education and medical research.

He is exceedingly generous to his alma maters, Johns Hopkins and the Harvard Business School. In his favored field of health, he supports research into malaria, breast cancer, and ALS, and into less conspicuous diseases, including lupus, dystonia and Marfan syndrome.

He gives to Smile Train, a worldwide children's charity that treats facial deformities, and in 2006 began a major worldwide anti-smoking campaign, committing $375 million to it and attracting the support of Bill Gates, who added $125 million to the effort.

Bloomberg also contributes to anti-poverty programs, education ventures, and cultural institutions, including some of their discrete projects, like acoustic guides at the Metropolitan Museum of Art, and has strongly supported Jewish causes, mostly honoring his parents, among them a children's center and an ambulatory care facility in Jerusalem.

A risk taker, as in business and politics, Bloomberg has backed unproven ventures, like a pilot project in Mexico and Vietnam to reduce traffic injuries with bicycle helmets and other measures. And, ever data-driven, he funds studies to track the success of his efforts.

Early in his philanthropic career, Bloomberg directed his biggest gifts not to conspicuous projects in his adopted city of New York, but to places through which he traveled toward success.

By 2009, Bloomberg's cumulative contributions to Johns Hopkins had topped a half billion dollars, according to his adviser, Patti Harris. He has donated scholarships, the astrophysics lab, a renovation of the campus, a children's hospital center, and to an institute that conducts stem cell research.

His central focus at Hopkins is the celebrated School of Public Health that bears his name. He was drawn to public health because others were not. "Mike's a contrarian," says William Brody, the university's president when Bloomberg was its board chairman. "He gives to projects other people don't. He recognized the importance of public health before anyone else did. They don't realize they are living because they didn't get polio or smallpox or whatever. Mike understood that. He thinks in terms of how to move the needle, how to make a difference."

It was while studying at Hopkins that Bloomberg made his first charitable contributions. A friend, Mary Kay Shartle-Galotto, remembers seeing an envelope addressed to the National Association for the Advancement of Colored People in Mike's Baltimore apartment. "I said, 'What are you sending to the NAACP?' He said, 'I always contribute. It's something you have to do.'" It was visible proof of the enduring echo of his father's words to give to the NAACP because "we're all in this together."

Bloomberg used his money to buy into New York's social elite, he spent tactically on promotional literature to win election as mayor, outspending Mark Green by 5 to 1, and the Bloomberg spigot continued to flow once he was in office. The mayor used his own money to help him run the city and to promote his popularity. Unlike any predecessor, he could distribute benefits not only from city funds but also from a parallel structure of giving to cultural and social service organizations throughout the city.

Some of that private giving has come from his own accounts; some has been channeled through grants of the Carnegie Corporation, which does not advertise the officially anonymous source but makes no real secret of it.

Bloomberg's philanthropy in the city is widely known and widely appreciated. It does good. It also does the mayor good. It helps him as surely as doling out government pork helps the less financially endowed politician, maybe more so.

In the wake of the terrorist attack on the World Trade Center in 2001, the Carnegie Corporation distributed $10 million of Bloomberg's money to 137 cultural organizations. Over the years, the Carnegie gifts grew into an institution. In 2008, the Carnegie channel committed to distributing $60 million over two years to 542 New York City groups, benefiting thousands of people active in dance and theater groups, arts organizations, boys and girls clubs, community centers, local zoos, libraries, food pantries, criminal justice organizations, religious nonprofit groups, botanical gardens, programs that help battered women, neighborhood bands and orchestras.

The recipients of what they call "the Bloomberg money" are selected in close consultation with Patti Harris and her staff. Through a process kept strictly confidential, the organizations are vetted for legitimacy. The beneficiaries, many of them removed from politics, well understand the source of the money and are grateful.

The grants can be life-sustaining for small organizations. "Omigod, it's huge, huge for us," said Michael Oakes, managing director of the Paper Bag Players, a theater company for children whose annual budget of $1 million gets $50,000 a year from Bloomberg. "It is a wonderful, wonderful thing to get. It allows us to continue. We love him for it."

As it spreads good will, Bloomberg's generosity also creates an ethical quandary of a sort not faced since Governor Nelson A. Rockefeller used undisclosed private donations to help him govern New York four decades ago. Bloomberg does make some of his donations public and insists that his private philanthropy has no ulterior political purpose, that recipients are selected strictly on the merits, with no quarter given to politics. The mayor emphasizes that he keeps his donations and his governing separate. For many, the lines blur.

"This administration has a right to claim an inherent honesty we hadn't seen in a long time," said David Jones, head of the Community Service Society, a social services organization. "But I think the personal funding has clearly kept the not-for-profit community very pro-Bloomberg. It chills dissent. You are going to watch what you say."

Jones's organization gets $50,000 a year in Bloomberg-Carnegie money. "I got my bribe," he says with a laugh. "I've joked that maybe if I'd gotten more money I wouldn't have done that article"—an op-ed piece he wrote for the *Daily News* criticizing Bloomberg's housing policy. "In fact, I didn't hit as hard as I might."

The Reverend Calvin Butts, pastor of Harlem's influential Abyssinian Baptist Church, says he does not think Bloomberg expects blind loyalty for his donations and would never get it from him. But the pastor readily acknowledges gratitude and admiration for the mayor's largesse, which has been both personal and professional.

Bloomberg attended Butts's son's wedding and dedicated a bench in Central Park to the couple, a gift worth $7,500. Through his own accounts, not through Carnegie, he also gave $1 million to Abyssinian's Development Corporation in 2008—a tenth of its budget. "For any of the organizations he supports it creates enormous good will," says Butts. "For us, it has a great impact because it allows us the freedom to do a number of our development activities." Is it a political asset for the mayor? "It's got to be, at least it is for me."

Just about every public official in New York doles out public money to just about every nonprofit group in New York. Mayors and mayoral aides, legislators, and other local officials routinely distribute so-called discretionary money (a.k.a. pork), and they influence the awarding of contracts and the filling of jobs. Bloomberg has the added advantage of his own largesse: he augments his considerable power as mayor with the influence he achieves as a philanthropist.

That distinguishes him from everyone. So does his ability to practice restraint in using that influence. He does not need to buy support by awarding jobs to the politically connected. He does not have to roll over for wealthy contributors by pushing legislation they seek at the public's expense.

"Instead of giving jobs, and controlling the fiefdoms of a political base, he does it with money," said Richard Emery, a lawyer whose suit led to a democratizing upheaval in the shape of the city's government in the 1980s. "He does it in a high-minded way and it is a great thing. But it has the dual purpose of solidifying a rock-solid political base. It's risky to go against him. His money gives him leverage on everything around him that normal people do not enjoy."

Because of his resources, Bloomberg can serve as mayor with a showboat salary of $1 a year. Joking once with Martha Stewart on television, he said his annual checks come to only 93 cents, because of Social Security deductions, and he frames them, uncashed. He disdains the official residence of mayors, preferring to live in his more luxurious town house.

He has made large private contributions to the state Republican leader to win his support for legislation and to other office-holders despite his proclaimed abhorrence of the polluting role of money in routine politics. He has dazzled congressmen and lawmakers by treating them to trips to Israel, Italy, Greece, Puerto Rico, the Dominican Republic and beyond, flying them to and fro in his company's corporate jet. He has treated politicians and business executives to afternoons of golf at one of his country clubs or weekends in Bermuda.

Bloomberg spent an undisclosed sum on polling and other expenses to explore his chances of running for president, an exercise that bothered few constituents because it was, after all, his money. The public was less tolerant of how his philanthropy was used to smooth his path to a third term, when some top Bloomberg aides leaned on the leaders of groups that received thousands from the mayor's Carnegie money and millions from city contracts, and asked them to testify at the city council in favor of changing the term law, and to lean on recalcitrant council members.

The cooperative beneficiaries, longtime mayoral allies, said they acted out of regard for Bloomberg, not his money. That may be so. But the spectacle of their performance was widely seen as an abuse of mayoral power.

The high-pressure campaign to allow a third Bloomberg term was only the beginning. In short order the mayor's political counsel, Kevin Sheekey, announced that Bloomberg was prepared to spend $85 million on this third campaign—a commitment that most observers figured would grow to $100 million. Bloomberg lined up an army of the best consulting talent to run the campaign with the implied if not actual promise of extra rewards similar to the bonuses of $25,000 to $400,000 showered on aides after his first two campaigns. Expectation of generous donations surely also helped convince the small Independence Party—and the Republican Party the mayor had abandoned during his presidential foray—to endorse him.

Bloomberg's spending for a third term began early in 2009. His television ads began running months before the November election, followed by telephone calls and an onslaught of glossy mailings that began with a twelve-page "Mike Bloomberg Five Borough Economic Opportunity Plan." He grandly promised, as if he had the power of the federal government, "green" jobs and "economic opportunity."

Before Memorial Day he had spent almost $19 million, almost twice what he had spent at the same point four years earlier. His $1.8 million spending on his ad campaign alone equaled the combined expenditures of all three possible Democratic opponents, whose participation in the city's public financing program capped their fund-raising and spending.

Soon, one of them, Congressman Anthony Weiner, dropped out, citing the mayor's fortune. "As a native of Brooklyn, I'd be lying if I said I didn't savor a good scrap," Weiner said. "But I'm disappointed because I'm increasingly convinced a substantive debate simply isn't likely right now." Weiner's decision left William Thompson, the city comptroller, as Bloomberg's likely opponent.

The mayor and close aides seem either puzzled or indignant about dismayed reactions to their spending and bald third-term tactics. They talk as if they were the injured parties, victimized by people who just do not understand a basic reality—that they are different and they are better, that they play by different rules and should be held to a different standard.

Merely raising the subject of his campaign spending risks a mayoral diatribe. When a reporter asked him why, given his proud seven-year record in office, he intended to spend so heavily to win a third term, he snapped, "I don't understand your question, I am not going to talk about the campaign. I think it's one of the most ridiculous things I have ever heard." The reporter pressed on: would he consider capping his spending? "Talk to the campaign."

Another time, he argued that he had to spend heavily because the city was still Democratic and elections were still partisan. "Look at what happened in the last election," he said to me. "We won by not that much—it wasn't 80-20, it was, what, 55-45, about something like that? Let's assume 60-40. Here with him spending a little and me spending an enormous amount and me having a record the public liked—I didn't win going away." The fact is, he did win "going away": 58 percent versus 41 percent is a landslide anywhere.

Bloomberg routinely deplores the corrupting influence of money in other people's politics. When Barack Obama abandoned his commitment to run with only public subsidies and spending limits, Bloomberg privately criticized him for hypocrisy. Another time, before he knew he would be seeking a third term, Bloomberg questioned the money pouring in from real estate interests to the three leading Democrats looking to succeed him as mayor. "Why on earth are the Rudins giving money to these three candidates?" he asked in an interview, referring to principals of a prominent real estate company in New York. "To buy influence! Why are these people taking it? Because they are willing to sell influence. Who is more culpable? I would argue both sides of the transaction."

That is certainly an accurate view of pay-to-play politics. Yet Bloomberg plays, too, making significant contributions to the campaigns of both liberal and conservative politicians, locally and nationally, claiming he makes the contributions not for personal advantage but to benefit New York.

The mayor presents himself as inhabiting a world separate and apart. To listen to him and his entourage, his spending is truly disinterested, not tilted to favor contributors and other sacred cows. The inhabitants of Bloomberg's World see themselves as apolitical and altruistic, virtuous even when they employ the rough tactics of conventional politicians, because they are serving only the public interest. It happens to coincide with Michael Bloomberg's interest, that's all.

If Bloomberg had to solicit contributions like most candidates, wouldn't he compromise, too, rather than risk losing? "I like to think my ethics are more than just the fact that I can afford it," he insists. "People who knew me when I was a young, rich wise-ass as opposed to an old, rich wise-ass, they'd say my ethics have stayed the same."

Perhaps they have. And so has his message. Trust me. I am Bloomberg. I am all you need.

CHAPTER 15

FOOTPRINTS

MIKE BLOOMBERG RAN for a third term by looking to the future, promoting his qualifications to guide the city back from recession to prosperity. The seeds of his legacy as mayor were well established in the eight years of his first two terms. After the tragedy of 9/11 he was at his boldest, stabilizing the city's finances, and reassuring an edgy business community that revival was at hand. As the "Nanny Mayor," he championed public health by waging war on smoking and investing in the public hospital system. He accepted responsibility for revitalizing the public schools, promoted real estate development, calmed race relations, paid attention to the environment and improved even on Giuliani's record in reducing crime.

Though quickly establishing the independence and managerial competence he had promised, the mayor, like the man, was prickly, showing little empathy for ordinary folks. His stubborn insistence on banning the use of cell phones in public schools mystified and angered New Yorkers, more convinced than ever that the mayor, personally BlackBerry-addicted, was out of touch with day-to-day concerns of parents and students.

Despite his idiosyncrasies, he was prudently nonconfrontational, which helped him in the inevitable comparisons to his belligerent predecessor, making it less obvious than it might have been that he shares some of Rudy Giuliani's autocratic attitudes about the news media and civil liberties.

Bloomberg's relationship with the media has been an uneasy one, exemplified by Bloomberg's tendency to address reporters in the City Hall press corps who cover him regularly as "miss" and "sir" at his news conferences.

He often expresses a preference for the business press that covered him in his Wall Street days over aggressive, nosy political reporters. Even after years of experience as mayor, he would obsess about stories that displeased him and accuse the media of caring more about headlines and "gotcha" indiscretions than serious civic issues, never understanding that nearly everything he says or does—or said or did—is fair game.

After the *New Yorker*'s Elizabeth Kolbert mentioned his improper comments to women in one of her articles, "We lost access for a good long while," recalls the magazine's editor, David Remnick. "Finally, I e-mailed him, visited him at the bullpen and, without conceding anything, we returned to normalcy."

Information, if deemed substantive and useful to Bloomberg, is readily provided to journalists by Bloomberg administration officials. Information potentially injurious to him often takes repeated requests, and lengthy delays. The Gotham Gazette, an online newsletter, could not even get acknowledgement of an inquiry about the number of FOIL (Freedom of Information Law) requests submitted to the Bloomberg government, though under that very law, confirmation has to be provided in five days. Other publications have waited months for incomplete information.

Bloomberg's fiscal stewardship benefited from his businessman's acumen, and from his obsession with customer service, the customers now being the people of New York. When the serious budget deficit he inherited from Giuliani was aggravated by the city's loss of commerce and tourism after 9/11 and by a national recession, Bloomberg raised taxes and borrowed heavily, frustrating fiscal conservatives by his refusal to cut services. Prudently, as the city recovered, he put billions aside in the fat years to leave a cushion for his successor—even before he decided to be his own successor.

But Bloomberg's claim to restrained fiscal stewardship, to being a paragon of discipline and independence, with no tolerance for the special interests, does not always hold up. For the most part his fiscal management followed the pattern established by other mayors of New York: they let the national economy set the pace, increasing spending in good times and trimming back or raising taxes—sometimes both—in bad years. And he leads, as they did, with one eye on his reelection prospects.

Bloomberg maintained labor peace and good political relationships with generous union contracts, getting few notable cost savings after a strong start. Early, Bloomberg got the powerful United Federation of Teachers to surrender some prized rules of seniority privilege and to agree to slightly extend the school day. But then politics trumped reform. On the eve of his first bid for reelection, Bloomberg granted the teachers' union a generous contract to discourage its potential political opposition; in his second term he routinely granted all municipal unions increases with no strings attached.

As he approached his third election, he called loudly for reform in the costly pension system, even though Bloomberg's policies deserved a share of the blame for its financial burden. He finally exchanged two days of teacher vacation for a reduction in pensions for newly hired teachers, a deal that won the union leader's enthusiastic welcome. Critics like Nicole Gelinas, of the conservative Manhattan Institute, thought he missed a major opportunity to champion broad pension reform.

In all, Bloomberg's second term was less bold than his first, but he still indulged a yen for the grand gesture. Once again planning ahead for another generation, Bloomberg projected the growth of New York's population and tried to prepare for the resulting insults to the environment and infrastructure. He continued his nationwide struggle to inhibit the sale of guns that invariably found their way to New York.

He sought help for the poorest New Yorkers and tweaked improvements in his call-311 citizen information system. His bent for innovation reached a quirky pinnacle in term two, when he closed a stretch of Broadway to traffic, filled Times Square with lawn chairs and declared the expanse of asphalt an experimental urban park.

Through both terms, except for education reform, nothing got so much mayoral attention as real estate development. The most development-minded mayor in years, Bloomberg made construction and rehabilitation his meat and potatoes, for the most practical of reasons. In land-squeezed New York, development is a proven profit center that mayors can encourage with tax incentives, low-cost financing and other inducements.

Pressing ahead when people were still dubious about New York's future, he made no apologies for pushing through new zoning rules and welcoming most new projects. "How do you think we get the money to pay teachers to help you get a good education?" he asked during a conversation about development.

He was particularly impatient with politically motivated opponents of development, like the combined opposition of labor and city council members who blocked Wal-Mart's expansion into New York. They were afraid the chain's low wages and low prices would undercut other city merchants and workers but Bloomberg could not understand their letting city commerce drift to the suburbs.

"Everybody leaves to go to Nassau County or Westchester," Bloomberg fumed. "Shirley Franklin, the mayor of Atlanta, she laughed at me in the face. They just got the biggest Wal-Mart in Atlanta—she was thrilled. Only *we* can turn victory into shit."

After blocking Giuliani's subsidies to new stadiums for the Mets and Yankees in his first year, judging, in his pragmatic businessman's fashion, that the city could not afford them, Bloomberg later relented. He was lavishly generous to the two teams and their ultraluxurious stadiums, as well as to a new basketball arena in Brooklyn.

The stadiums benefited from tens of millions of dollars in city investments, tax breaks and subsidies, bundled into complex deals whose true cost to the taxpayer may never be clear. The city will gain from economic activity in the long run, the mayor said, as all mayors say about sports stadiums everywhere. Rarely do the predictions meet the promise but the stadiums are built anyway.

Bloomberg also backed incentives for companies to stay in New York, but he approved less "corporate welfare" than Giuliani did.

Overall, Bloomberg oversaw the most massive rezoning in more than forty years, recognizing the city's changing face, especially the diminished role of its once thriving manufacturing base. That left acres of industrial moonscapes to be reclaimed once the city government decreed that housing, office buildings, hotels and stores could rise where factories and plants once stood. The new zoning did not guarantee new building; it only cleared a path for more and more building during and after what had already become the biggest construction boom in thirty years. The cranes worked overtime until the Wall Street meltdown and recession of 2008.

In Bloomberg's first two terms, nearly 18 percent of the city was rezoned, from a ten-acre plot of land on Staten Island to a section of west Harlem where Columbia University is charting a generation of expansion.

The changes made way for luxury towers on a deteriorating stretch of the Brooklyn waterfront in Williamsburg; for the reclamation of a wasteland near the new Mets stadium in Queens; for the upgrading of 125th Street, Harlem's central artery; and for the renewal of Fourth Avenue in Park Slope, where expensive apartments began to replace chop shops and gas stations.

The new rules also restrained some development in congested residential neighborhoods and provided for some manufacturing and affordable housing at various sites, though nowhere near enough to satisfy critics who argue that too many of Bloomberg's plans favor the wealthy.

That tension between eager development and prudent planning is a permanent feature of New York politics. Mayors and other elected officials are inevitably accused of favoring developers who contribute handsomely to their campaigns. Bloomberg's self-financing left him immune to that suspicion, but not to being assailed for favoring friends in his own class of business heavies.

Some architects and city planners bemoan a missed opportunity to chart New York's future more aesthetically and comprehensively—to really lay out communities and to plan in the strictest sense of the word, rarely even attempted in New York. In the judgment of Ada Louise Huxtable, the distinguished architecture critic, Bloomberg "thinks like a developer, not a planner. He knows where the developers are coming from and he understands their numbers, and that seems to be enough. It's not."

Bloomberg's applied his design sensibility to his company's midtown headquarters, not to city planning. The Nets arena planned for central Brooklyn is a case in point. It originally held great promise as a glistening glass wonder designed by architect Frank Gehry. When the developer, bowing to the economy, came up with a less expensive plan by a pedestrian architect and the new design for the Brooklyn stadium looked like nothing so much as a bland, boxy factory, Bloomberg backed that, too. Development is development, good for the city's economy.

In the view, too, of many neighborhood residents, the Bloomberg administration's efforts are preferable to neglect. "The Brooklyn waterfront has been abused, misused and not used," observes Father Joseph Sullivan, retired auxiliary bishop of the Brooklyn diocese. "This man comes in with a very different orientation toward the role of mayor. He's trying to develop the city, not just maintain it."

Development could be the most visible monument to Bloomberg's mayoralty, producing new vistas and reshaped neighborhoods when the economy allows. Less tangible but even more far-reaching would be the success of his education reforms, a subject bearing on his core conviction that American society is doomed if kids don't learn enough to find a place in an ever more complex economy.

"You show me one social problem that wouldn't be obliterated or ameliorated if people had a better education. I don't think you can," he says. The subject triggers a memory of one of the few movies Bloomberg has watched from opening to closing credits—*Charlie Wilson's War,* the 2007 film about a Texas congressman who had covert dealings with Afghanistan. In the last scene, Bloomberg noted, Wilson (played by Tom Hanks) could not persuade his congressional colleagues to appropriate $1 million for Afghani schools, after spending hundreds of millions to rid Afghanistan of the Soviets. "They wouldn't have a million dollars for education. It's a fact. I go to the movies once a year and fall asleep. I didn't fall asleep this time."

Nothing on Bloomberg's agenda has generated as much attention as education, the most politicized and contentious issue in New York City—before Bloomberg, during Bloomberg and surely after Bloomberg. Good public schools and livable neighborhoods are the bedrock of urban America, essential to retaining an energetic middle class and assimilating the constant stream of immigrants.

In New York, the wealthy have always provided for their own safety, luxury and superior private schooling. The poor have always found the city to be an accepting place that mitigates their suffering. But it is the majority in the middle, the city's spine, that can choose to stay or flee and the fate of their children weighs heavily in that decision.

Bloomberg's eagerness, after thirty-three years of dysfunctional community control, to take command and to be held accountable for progress won him acclaim. On that, there is broad consensus, even though he went at the task in his characteristically domineering style.

Patience with elected boards of education and only indirect mayoral influence had begun to wear thin in American cities in the 1990s, when Boston and then Chicago handed control directly to their chief executives. In New York the schools had been run by a virtually independent board of political appointees that supervised thirty-two community school boards, a good number weak and besmirched by patronage and graft.

Mayors ducked responsibility, and even when they tried to exert some influence could only struggle at the margins of a broken system. The clamor for change made mayoral control possible during Giuliani's years, but he never made reform a priority and a hostile state legislature refused even to consider giving him more power than he already had.

Bloomberg campaigned for the right to control the city's educational system and within months of taking office got the legislature's backing. As his agent of change he soon named an all-powerful new schools chancellor, Joel Klein, a star Washington prosecutor with New York roots.

Klein had been an aggressive head of the Justice Department's anti-trust division during Bill Clinton's presidency, but his knowledge of education was scant. Still, Bloomberg wanted a clear break with the past and Klein, a graduate of New York City public schools who went on to graduate magna cum laude from both Columbia College and Harvard Law School, fit the bill.

A wiry man with a bald pate, a fringe of dark hair curling around his neck, and the blunt d's, dem's and do's of the old neighborhood still inflecting his speech, Klein had met Bloomberg socially in Washington in the late 1990s and was recommended for the chancellor's job by mutual friends.

Stubborn, opinionated and not afraid to make enemies, Klein actively recruited a new staff that was stronger on lawyers and statisticians than on educators, and quickly made his quota of admirers and detractors by challenging the status quo and the powerful teachers' union.

Unencumbered by anything like the old Board of Education, Klein gained unparalleled authority. He quickly revamped the hidebound system and battled against what he called the "culture of excuses."

He reorganized staff and procedures not once but repeatedly. There were false starts, errors, redos and fine-tuning as he changed deputies, curriculums and the administrative structure. He even cast Bloomberg in the unusual role of good cop to his own rough bad cop when he feuded with the head of the teachers' union.

Parents groups and local community boards were shunted aside; teachers felt slighted. But Klein and his aides were free to decree innovative policies without worrying about political or community interference. That was a strength of the new system, but it also ran the risk of distancing administrators from communities. Parents in some neighborhoods erupted in fury, for example, when they feared they couldn't get their children into close-by kindergartens because of overcrowding.

Bloomberg and Klein focused on the big picture—on testing, on setting high standards and demanding measurable results. The chancellor created a new "accountability office" and put a Columbia Law School professor in charge. Principals were given more responsibility, weak students were regularly evaluated by special teacher committees, teachers were often judged mainly by test scores and each school was given a report-card grade that confused more than it enlightened.

Klein admitted after several years to having being impolitic and said he wished he had built supportive constituencies at an earlier stage. But he makes no apologies for the direction of the effort he instituted and would press ahead with more reforms if he could, cutting back on teachers' seniority and tenure rights, instituting individual merit pay for teachers, demanding even stricter contract terms than those Bloomberg negotiated.

Crucially, Bloomberg stood steadfastly by Klein through two terms. That has always been his pattern. There has been unusually little turnover in the Bloomberg government and few blatant embarrassments. The most obvious were, in his second term, the departure of a buildings commissioner overwhelmed by construction accidents and of a finance commissioner embroiled in an appearance of conflicts of interest, and his steadfast support for his fire commissioner after the 2007 Deutsche Bank fire had raised doubts about his competence in leading the department.

Even some insiders thought Bloomberg's loyalty went too far, faulting him for his way of sticking by too long, sometimes easing people out by finding them soft landings through his business connections or at his philanthropic foundation.

Notwithstanding the tensions his chancellor generated, Bloomberg liked the way he shook up the system. And in backing Klein, he was deliberately ending the disruptive cycling in and out of school chiefs every two years or so before they had time to make an impact, strengthening the permanent power bloc of the teachers' union as it waited out one chancellor for the next.

Most New Yorkers agree on the value of stability and recognize that Klein's audacity was essential to jolting a mediocre system. But after eight years of Bloomberg's management there was absolutely no consensus on how much the schools had improved, not even any agreement on the facts by which to judge the results. Despite reams of data, reports and analyses that reflect the mayor's business-born dedication to measuring results and settling accounts, the controversies concerning the performance of the city's schoolchildren were sharp and complicated by disagreements about how much progress can be reasonably expected from such a huge urban school system.

New York's school system is on the scale of a small country. It aims to educate 1.1 million students in 1,575 schools. They are taught by 80,000 teachers, all members of the most potent player in New York politics, the United Federation of Teachers. By the end of Bloomberg's second term, the school budget had grown by nearly two-thirds, to $20 billion from $12 billion, driven by a 47 percent increase in teacher salaries (to an average of $72,000 a year) and court-ordered state money from a settled lawsuit. The schools are also much safer and many have been reorganized into smaller units. The number of charter schools has increased as well, from seventeen to seventy-eight, and more are planned.

Encouraging statistics are easier to demonstrate than educational success. Bloomberg and Klein passionately dispute that assertion. Citing progress in graduation rates and state test scores, the mayor and chancellor are convinced that they are turning around an administrative *QE II.* "Keep It Going NYC" exhorted the ads, financed by a nonprofit group Klein controls, as Bloomberg ran for his third term. Klein confidently predicts that the city schools—more than 70 percent black or Hispanic—will be the first urban system to match the performance of students as a whole around the state, though the city, compared with the state, Klein points out, is "three times as black and brown and two and a half times as high-poverty."

Improvement in the schools under Bloomberg and Klein is indisputable. Questions turn on the extent of that improvement—what the numbers mean and whether they are really reliable. Education experts outside the system argue that the state's standardized tests are too easy, or that the questions have been made so predictable that teachers can endlessly drill the marginal students to move them from just below to just above a passing grade.

Critics say Klein takes credit for progress that began under his predecessor, or that city education officials oversimplify and exaggerate. Klein's favorable statistics and claims of success are inevitably encumbered by caveats and challenges. For instance, if the city schools are really better, even weak students should be improving. Are they? In 2008, 74 percent of high school graduates entering the City University of New York's community colleges needed remediation in math or English or both, down from 82 percent in 2002. That means three-quarters of those students were failing in high school, hardly a sign of success in the view of Diane Ravitch, a research professor of education at New York University and Klein's harshest critic. Matthew Goldstein, the City University's chancellor, is more positive: "The arrow is pointed in the right direction, but we still have a long way to go."

Critics of the reformed schools touch on everything from class size to spending on no-bid contracts. The most heated disagreements center on standardized test results. The Bush administration's No Child Left Behind law made testing and accountability a national preoccupation and Bloomberg and Klein eagerly offered New York City as a laboratory. Bloomberg even decided at one point to test kindergarteners and he experimented with privately financed schemes in a pilot program to pay some students for measurable achievement.

Standardized state tests begin in third grade, and the scores of city students in reading and math have risen sharply on Klein's watch. In the mayor's eighth year, 69 percent of elementary and middle school students met state reading standards, while in 2002 fewer than half of fourth graders and only 30 percent of eighth graders had read at grade level. Math scores rose even more impressively, with 85 percent of fourth graders and 71 percent of eighth graders meeting the state standard, compared with 52 percent and 30 percent when Klein took over.

The tests showed the racial gap closing, too, in grades three through eight. In math, black students trailed white students by 17 percentage points compared with 31 percentage points in 2006. In reading, the gap was 22 in 2009 versus 31 in 2006. The most recent scores rose throughout the state, and in other large urban school districts, but they rose more sharply in New York City.

Yet skeptics question the validity of the tests, many suggesting they are too easy, too familiar, or that the pass grade is set too low.

Merryl Tisch, the chancellor of the State Board of Regents, favors more rigorous tests. "I think they will still show improvement, but nothing like the 92 percent pass rate for third graders. How come all these kids need remediation, three-quarters of them? Come on!" She would align the state tests with federal tests, which, in jarring contrast, have registered little improvement in the performance of city students between 2003 and 2007. Klein contends that those exams do not align with what city students are taught.

Another area of gain—and of contention—is the rate of students graduating from city high schools in four years. Klein's department calculates an increase between 2003 and 2008, to 66 percent from 53, after hovering around 50 percent for years before mayoral control. Gains were across the board, and showed a narrowing racial gap. However, critics who have never considered New York's graduation rates reliable continued to question the scope of the improvement, accusing principals of watering down graduation standards, and also of forcing struggling students—called "push-outs"—to quit school.

A typical comment about Bloomberg's achievement is that

of Jennifer Jennings, an analyst at Columbia University. "They are doing better," she said of city students. "The question is how much better. It's the difference between saying there's been improvement and there's been a miracle."

Joseph Viteritti of Hunter College, who edited a book on mayoral control, is convinced there has been improvement. "There is movement, a sense of possibility. But they exaggerate their accomplishments sometimes."

The Bloomberg-Klein publicity juggernaut is a study in energetic persuasion, led by them and promoted by a public relations department at the Department of Education, which one account put at twenty-three employees by 2008. Under Klein's predecessor the PR department had four. State officials say the city routinely reports its statistics late, working overtime to tweak the numbers to its advantage. Tisch worries that Klein and Bloomberg could wind up victims of their own overselling, creating a backlash that could marginalize real gains.

"I think their work is monumental," says Tisch. "They have done some smart, credible forward-thinking things. I just wish along the way they would find a way to be victorious but add a modesty to their victory, emphasize how incredibly hard this has been, how much more we have to do, instead of 'we will show everyone we are the greatest, we are meeting standards'—but no one believes it. The tragic piece of this is if they just played it straight it would show gains and progress."

In Bloomberg's experience, if you want to sell more computer terminals and are convinced of their value, you sell hard. If you want another term as mayor and can spend $80 million or $100 million against weak opposition, you do. If you are confident that education is the key to improving society, you emphasize the positive and promote the hell out of every sign of progress.

Yet as Bloomberg asked New Yorkers to give him a third term, 54 percent were still dissatisfied with the public schools, and most did not clearly associate his leadership with a bright new day in education. Other surveys show appreciation that Bloomberg took on the schools, despite uncertainty about classroom progress.

If Bloomberg's major innovations are to flourish, they will need more time, tending and prosperity. Still, it had been decades since any mayor of New York and school innovation could appear in the same sentence.

CHAPTER 16

MANY A DIFFERENCE

MIKE BLOOMBERG WAS TALKING one afternoon about his early days at Salomon Brothers and a crash that had killed an office rival who was flying his own plane, when suddenly, with no hint of relevance, he advised me, "You should have your own plane by the way, it's a great luxury." Then, without missing a beat, he went back to telling me how he upgraded Salomon's computer on his own time at night—creating, as it happened, an early prototype of the computer terminal that made him a billionaire, and pilot of his own plane.

There it was, Bloomberg on Bloomberg, triggered by the memory of his professional beginnings: *I am successful, I am rich, I even have my own plane, I fly it safely—and what of it? I deserve it, I made my own way, I always have.*

Stubbornly elusive, Bloomberg is also notably consistent. A prideful drive defines his life at every turn, pushing him to make a difference in the world around him and to dominate that world. As his mother recalled, he wanted to run everything even as a boy in Medford, Massachusetts. At college, he headed his fraternity, his senior class and the schoolwide frat organization. And he spoke grandly about a big future: he'd be president of the United States, or head of the United Nations or of the World Bank.

When fate took him to Wall Street instead, he decided he could greatly improve the company's technology and told his bosses he could run the place better than they. And of course he proved his point when they fired him, creating the opportunity that led him to revolutionize the financial information industry.

A millionaire before he devised his eponymous computer and data system, he then became a billionaire many times over, an active social and cultural personage in his adopted city, the owner of extravagant homes and planes and country club memberships. The short, unprepossessing native of suburban New England had diligently plotted his way into the upper echelons of New York, proving that he was as good as members of what he calls the "lucky sperm club"—better in fact, because he didn't inherit his wealth.

A competitive nature marks only one corner of the Bloomberg personality. A conspicuous ego and a fierce self-discipline complete the triangle. He competes not only against others but against himself.

He amassed his Eagle Scout merit badges before he was old enough to claim that lofty rank. As an adult, he kept on laboring to learn Spanish despite an uncooperative ear that renders his accent atrociously gringo. Though not athletic and dismissive of watching others at play, he nonetheless became obsessed with golf, which pits him against himself. "He's always mad at me when I outdrive him, but it's not what are you doing right? it's what am I doing wrong? He will work on it, work on it, work on it," explains John Gambling, the friendly host of Bloomberg's weekly radio broadcast.

One other quality has defined the mature Mike Bloomberg. Whether he is marketing his computer, or exhorting New Yorkers to underwrite a football stadium they did not want or an Olympics bid that bored them, Bloomberg prizes innovation, doing things that others don't do or consider undoable. He is forever eager to experiment, to solve problems and to find new ways of doing things, a pattern that he carried from his business career into his philanthropy and his mayoralty.

He became a patron of the most prominent school of public health in the country, making it his passion, in good part because others had slighted that field. And he has concentrated on making a difference in all of his philanthropy, looking to protect children and not just adults from traffic accidents, or financing research into obscure and not just familiar diseases.

The same impatience with convention appeared in his brash decision to run for mayor without any political experience—and not only to run again, but to manipulate the law so he could run a third time. He is probably the most unusual and perplexing mayor New York has ever seen: diffident, unemotional, hard to like, yet so grounded that he is even harder to disrespect, as he demonstrated in the span of just a few days early in his third campaign.

At the height of a nationwide scare about a swine flu epidemic, Bloomberg's understandable desire to reassure the public came across as callously dismissive. "You've got to remember," he said about the closing of three schools, "we're talking about 4,500 students here in a city of 8.4 million." That was Bloomberg's cold reality talking, even as frightened parents needed something more than the mayor's counsel to move on, get over it, be realistic, like me.

Yet just a day later, Bloomberg's nasal sangfroid set just the right tone as the city learned that four men stood accused of wanting to bomb two synagogues in the Bronx. Bloomberg was calm and substantive as he told a tense city that though we live in intimidating times, everything was under control, the accused had no connection to foreign terrorists and New York was safe. "Sadly," he said, "peace is fragile and democracy is fragile and we have to be vigilant all the time." People felt reassured. A trustworthy adult was in charge.

That has been Bloomberg's style: out of tune one day, on song the next. And what of it? He refuses to find significance in such fluctuations. Allergic to introspection, absurdly coarse, and oddly insensitive, he does not look to self-criticism to propel him to success.

In every realm, his ambition has been to vault higher than others and thus to "make a difference." Unlike the typically empathetic politicians whose self-preservation compels a response to others, Bloomberg listens to himself, relies on his own perceptions and values. Not only in business or in City Hall but even in high school when he dared question the iconic FDR, he stubbornly does as he chooses, resisting dissent even from those near and dear, ever confident he is right.

And often he has been. His business success was all the more notable because he was the upstart who bettered the older, more established companies of Dow Jones and Reuters, leaping ahead when they weren't looking or looking in the wrong direction. He has, over the years, spurned advice to sell and declined attractive offers from business suitors, preferring to expand his computer's content and his company's scope.

He has provided a textbook example of how the flexible risk-taker can outmaneuver the establishment, experience that served as a model for his unorthodox political debut—the 2001 campaign that political pros thought would just be a waste of his money, followed by a uniquely independent performance in his early days as mayor.

It was not all skill and will. Bloomberg's endeavors have been blessed by good fortune. His business success might have been much more modest if he hadn't been fired from Salomon or exiled to the company's tech department, where he tinkered with the technology that became his triumph. Nor did he plan on a Salomon farewell package of $10 million, which seeded his new venture.

In politics, too, Bloomberg was kissed by luck. It was a stunning confluence of circumstances that enabled him to spend his way into the mayor's office in the first place. The skeptical political pros had it right: he could not win, even with his money. Nobody could have anticipated the terrorist attack of 9/11 and his opponent's political frailties and gaffes, the Democratic Party infighting, the support from America's newly reigning hero, Rudy Giuliani.

Many of Bloomberg's mayoral achievements also have their origins in the mood that overcame the city after 9/11. New York desperately needed to be revitalized in 2001 and the public proved willing to put its trust in an unknown businessman, a colorless, postpartisan manager in a City Hall normally ruled by vibrant politicians.

Bloomberg governed not with dramatics, but with ideas. He raised taxes rather than reduce city services. He acknowledged the changing economy of the city and invested in its future with energetic rezoning that would allow growth. He did not create the real estate boom that came with national prosperity a few years into his mayoralty, but unapologetically pro-development, he used taxes and incentives to exploit it and then adjusted as best he could to the subsequent bust.

His successes were not always the ones he initially envisioned. His bold schemes to host the Olympics, to build a state-of-the-art football stadium and city-within-the-city on the Hudson all failed, as did his daring plan to finally control Manhattan traffic and reduce its pollutants. It was with managerial skills in the day-to-day governance of New York, and his conspicuous independence, led by his education agenda, that he made his mark.

The city's public schools received Bloomberg's most sustained attention and they were improved. They did not improve as much as he wished or said they did, but they got better than they had been for many decades. Equally important for the city's long-term future, he made education a direct mayoral responsibility. As long as mayoral control prevails, it is difficult to envision future mayors again shortchanging the schools. In a city of 8 million, 1.1 million of them public school students, mayors will be measured by the performance of the children and that has to go down as Bloomberg's signature accomplishment.

Like other bold mayors before him, Bloomberg was clear from the start about where he wanted to leave his mark. Rudy Giuliani attacked crime and strove to prove the city was governable. Ed Koch repaired the city's damaged books, raised the public's spirit, and built housing for the poor and middle class.

Along with targeting education, Bloomberg decided to teach adults, as well; he got more New Yorkers to stop smoking and to pay attention to their diets and health. And even in failure, he set an important agenda for the future. He did not get his traffic control plan but made it more likely that a future mayor will. He did not attract the Olympics, but he prepared a large stretch of western Manhattan for eventual development and he began a new subway extension. The prospective real estate development could have been better planned, the subway line could have been more user-friendly. But something is primed to happen in areas too long neglected.

In a way, Bloomberg's temperament might have been better suited to another era. The New York of the twenty-first century is too big and complex to let another Olmsted and Vaux create a Central Park, or a new Robert Moses reinvent the metropolis for the automobile.

Contemporary mayors of New York must govern within strict political and fiscal constraints. They are dependent on the national economy in a country less sympathetic to urban America than it was when Fiorello LaGuardia used New Deal resources to lead New York out of the Great Depression. And more than ever, mayors now have to battle against powerful but unsympathetic politicians in the state capital.

Never a natural pol, Bloomberg nonetheless realized that he had to let New York be New York again, which was not inevitable in 2002. The city rediscovered its confidence on his watch. It became the nation's center for speculation and development; it rocked and rolled through one of its economic upswings and was fat and happy until a recession cooled its exuberance.

Bloomberg, like other mayors before him, bowed too low to the powerful, politically important municipal labor unions. And, like them, he did not solve homelessness or poverty or the city's housing crunch.

Mostly, he governed prudently through the flush times and the tough times, and the voters seemed to want him to remain in office even as they disapproved of his manipulation of the law that decreed a limit of two terms—his detour to the dark side. Bloomberg could be one of *them,* they realized, a dreaded selfish pol. He had surrendered to the seduction of politics, the lure of power. But the public was left with no strong alternative, and he was prepared to spend another handsome chunk of his fortune to remind them that when not off on a self-preservational toot, he offered sound and independent leadership.

After eight years in public office, Bloomberg was still a distant character, not well understood even in New York. Yet he had become a national political celebrity, roast-worthy by President Barack Obama. "In the next hundred days, I will meet with a leader who rules over millions with an iron fist, who owns the airwaves and uses his power to crush all who would challenge his authority in the ballot box," Obama told a dinner of White House correspondents and Hollywood celebrities. Then he added after a dramatic pause, "It's good to see you, Mayor Bloomberg."

Nobody laughed harder that night than Bloomberg, the mogul from Medford who sat in the Washington Hilton's ballroom with his glamorous girlfriend, basking in the president's attention and heading for another four years as mayor of New York.

That would not, of course, be enough. Even leading New York through another bad economic patch could not be his last act. After he finally has to leave City Hall, Bloomberg seems destined to write yet another chapter for his biography.

He might spend some of his fortune to stimulate gutsy new educational experiments, or turn to a new media venture. His wistful, protest-too-much inquiries about the *New York Times,* though that company will remain beyond his reach, suggest that significant expansion of Bloomberg News could intrigue him. He might also still dream that he would be forgiven his tardiness in joining the Obama fan club and be allowed to realize his youthful ambition of leading the World Bank.

All that failing, Bloomberg's wealth would still allow him to address governmental problems as if he were a president or promote the commerce of poor nations as if he were his own world bank. Money has never been enough; it is influence that he prizes and is sure to keep pursuing. He has lived out the American dream, written his own Horatio Alger story, and used his power and wealth to upset the conventions of both finance and urban politics and to chart a unique path in giving away money.

He is not warm, beloved, or glib in a profession that demands all three. He learned how to hold his own in public, but could never make a good speech or charm an electorate. And that is okay with him. He is, as he likes to say, what he is. In that, he is like his more vivid predecessors—distinctive, singular characters, none like the other, though all grounded in more traditional politics than New York's 108th mogul-mayor.

And so it is a good bet that there will never be, cannot ever be, another mayor of New York, or triumphant financial engineer, like Bloomberg. He fits no paradigm, sets no precedent. Which, I suspect, suits him just fine.

ACKNOWLEDGMENTS

NO BOOK IS A SOLITARY ENDEAVOR, despite the author's intimate one-on-one relationship with the computer and unfortunate familiarity with tendonitis.

I have many people to thank and hope that I do not miss anyone.

First, always, my thanks to my husband, Max Frankel. His wisdom, patience and love made this book possible, and they make me possible.

I thank Robert Purnick for his unconditional love and support.

Thanks, too, to Peter Osnos, for his encouragement about this project from the beginning and throughout; to Clive Priddle for his caring editing of *Mike Bloomberg* as it honed in on its elusive subject; to Susan Weinberg for her unflagging optimism; and to everyone else I have worked with at PublicAffairs; to Christine Marra for her careful production management and to Gray Cutler for her meticulous copyediting. Jane Gelfman, my agent, could not have been more supportive. All are serious book people, dedicated and professional.

The *New York Times* was long at the core of my professional identity and always will be part of me. I owe gratitude to many people there for their friendship, support and, in some instances, their forbearance. Thanks to Jill Abramson, Fred Conrad, Jim Dao, Alain Delaqueriere, Jim Dwyer, Soma Golden Behr, Clyde Haberman, Floyd Norris, Sam Roberts, Jack Rosenthal, Jeff Roth, William Schmidt, Joe Sexton and Arthur Ochs Sulzberger Jr. A special nod to reporters in the *Times*'s City Hall bureau, always welcoming and generous: David Chen, Fernanda Santos and Michael Barbaro, a soul mate who shares my passion for the circus and possibilities of politics.

Generous, too, was Wayne Barrett of the *Village Voice,* whose tough insights always made me think twice, and Paul Theroux, kind enough to share his memories of Medford, Massachusetts, and a selection from his photo archives.

Judy Rakowsky was of invaluable help reporting on Mike Bloomberg's childhood in Medford; Nate Schweber helped with research and Hilary Costa with transcriptions. I am especially grateful to Ronnie Lowenstein, director of New York City's Independent Budget Office, who could not have been more helpful or patient in decoding fiscal matters for me.

Thank you does not adequately convey my gratitude to the Century Foundation for its hospitality and office space. Richard Leone, Greg Anrig, Carol Starmack, Christy Hicks and many others at the Century made my stay productive and pleasant.

I interviewed more than four hundred people for this book, some "on background," some on the record, some more than once. I could not have written without them. I am especially indebted to several members of the Bloomberg administration, to staff people at Bloomberg L.P., old friends and classmates of Mike Bloomberg, his mother, Charlotte Rubens Bloomberg, his sister, Marjorie Bloomberg Tiven, and younger daughter, Georgina

Bloomberg; I am also indebted to officials at Johns Hopkins University and at the Harvard Graduate School of Business.

A special thanks to two special people: to former mayor Edward Koch, for his candor, openness and inevitably on-point quotes; and to Beverly Solochek, a dear friend, who always listened. Margot and Joel, Jen and David, Erin and Jon showed interest and understanding throughout, accepting my occasional absences and distraction with sensitivity; Julia, Asher, Jake, Phoebe, Ariella and Jemma always made me smile no matter how grumpy my mood.

Now, my subject: I thank Michael Bloomberg, who, with relative tolerance, agreed to talk to me for this book, though he would be the first to admit that he did not welcome the project. He sat for seven interviews in Gracie Mansion, all about an hour long, speaking into my voice recorder and that of his ever-watchful communications director. He was always polite and talkative, sometimes responding to questions not quite asked, but that is his way.

Patti Harris, the mayor's closest adviser, was of critical help. Kevin Sheekey, Bloomberg's political aide, was amusing and told a good story. Edward Skyler, a deputy mayor with a photographic memory, shared useful recollections, Ester Fuchs, a policy adviser, put things in perspective and James Anderson, the mayor's communications director, was always attentive. With admirable good humor and skill, Jim's assistant, Katie Appel, helped me check facts and schedule interviews. Many other members of the city government, especially in the Departments of Law, Education and Health, and at City Hall, helped on matters of policy.

I do not, however, want to leave the impression that I had easy access to the mayor and those around him. I did not, most especially once he embarked on his quest for a third term. After that, he allowed one more interview, cancelled the next and scheduled no more. Almost all of the mayor's friends and associates asked him or a mayoral adviser for permission to talk to me, and if they did were cautious and overflowing with praise. Several spoke in the presence of a mayoral press aide, and access to some people who know Mike Bloomberg best was refused.

Some protectiveness is to be expected, and all mayors of New York inspire caution if not fear because they wield considerable power. But Bloomberg's claims to privacy approach the extreme for someone who chose a public career. A biographer once advised me never even to consider writing about a living public figure and I now know what she meant. But I am glad I pursued the story of Michael Bloomberg—a phenomenon in business, philanthropy and politics. He seems to enjoy making himself difficult to like, yet he is impossible to ignore, and he commands respect for being an original.

Finally, I thank New York, for being New York.

After thirty-five years on the New York beat, I thought first of making the city the subject of this book. I had covered New York's traumas during the fiscal disaster of the 1970s and after 9/11. I had written about six mayors going back to John V. Lindsay, and seen bad times and good, and there was no doubt that the city had finally regained its luster and great promise. But the comeback had been long and slow, stretching over the terms of many mayors. Ed Koch cracked the eggs, Giuliani assembled the ingredients, and then Bloomberg made the omelet.

So Mike Bloomberg became my focus and a biography trumped my plan for a city history. It did so for the simple reason that there had never been a mayor like him and no one had objectively told the remarkable story of his life. A New York life and yet another great New York story.

A NOTE ABOUT ATTRIBUTION

A note about quotations and sourcing. Following my newspaper tradition, I attributed the sources of quotations in the text rather than burden readers with many footnotes.

Unattributed remarks were either widely reported in newspapers or heard by me in interviews or at public events.

INDEX

Abyssinian Baptist Church, Harlem, 86, 198
Affordable housing, 82, 157, 158, 208
AIG (American Insurance Group), 183
Alliance of Resident Corporations, 187
American Insurance Group (AIG), 183
American Museum of Natural History parties, 61–62
American Revolution, 8, 9
Anderson, Jim, 170
Animal House (movie), 25
Anti-Semitism
  Charlotte Bloomberg on, 14
  Focus (movie), 80–81
  Fulani, 114
  Sharpton, 101, 106
  synagogue bombing plans, 222
  William Bloomberg on, 19
Archer, Lord, 63
Armonk farm, 62, 79
Art Commission, New York City, 84
Association for a Better New York, 179

"B-page"/Quotron, 34–35, 42
Badillo, Herman, 92, 95, 98
Bank of America, 183
Barbaro, Michael, 188
Barrett, Wayne, 188
Beame, Abraham, 76, 77, 153
Bell, Sean, 139
Belushi, John, 25
Berenson, Marisa, 63
Berger, Joseph, 93–94
Berger, Marilyn, 172
Berman, Dorothy Sherman, 9, 16
Bermuda home/trips, 68, 69, 79, 129
Biden, Joe, 3
Black, Reverend Richard, 11
Blair, Tony, 159
Blazing Saddles (movie), 81

Bloomberg, Charlotte
on anti-Semitism, 14
background, 9
buying Medford home, 9–10
Judaism, 13
kosher kitchen of, 13
as parent, 13, 14, 15
parents of, 10
personality, 9, 14, 15, 16
relationship with son, 9, 117
on son, 7–8, 14, 220
stillborn child of, 16–17
See also Rubens, Charlotte
Bloomberg, Emma
background/education, 57–58
birth, 57
City Hall position, 133
on parents, 58
Bloomberg, Georgina
birth, 57
education, 58
horses and, 58
on parents, 57, 58–59
personality, 15, 17
Bloomberg, Marjorie
brother's mayoral run and, 81
Medford, 10, 11
See also Tiven, Marjorie Bloomberg
Bloomberg, Mike
Armonk farm, 62, 79
Bermuda home/trips, 68, 69, 79, 129
burial plot, 84
description, 2, 74
diet competition, 65–66
divorce, 58
dream jobs of, 4–5, 73, 79, 173, 220, 226
exclusive clubs, 67–68, 79, 97
on father, 9, 18–19
food favorites, 19, 65
future possibilities, 226–227
godmother of children, 67, 80–81
golf, 39, 65, 66, 68, 69, 79, 131, 193, 199, 220–221
GOP switch, 82–83, 164
home in New York, 1, 57, 58, 68–69
Israel visit, 87–88
Judaism and, 12, 15, 18, 57, 87–88, 97, 168, 195
London apartment, 68, 79
memoir, 25, 37, 49, 56, 63, 73–74, 113, 194
on mother, 9, 13, 15, 18
national recognition of, 158, 161, 162, 168–169, 226
post-mayoralty plans, 177–178
smoking by, 22
surgery, 69
trustworthy friends of, 66–67
as urban liberal, 116, 167, 180
Vail, Colorado home, 79
Vietnam War, 28, 113–114
wedding/marriage, 57–58
See also Mayoralty of Bloomberg; Presidential run/Bloomberg; *specific mayoral races;* Wealth of Bloomberg
Bloomberg, Mike, childhood
about, 7, 8, 10, 11–16, 19–23
birth, 10
Boy Scouts/Eagle Scout, 7, 12, 13, 21–22, 121, 220
college applications, 23
Hebrew training, 15

"ideal of womanhood," 16
Judaism and, 12, 15
Medford, 10, 11–12
New York City, 9
personality, 7, 12, 21
philanthropy ideas, 9
senior thesis, 22–23
smoking by, 22
as student, 11–12, 14, 20–21, 22–23
vacations, 12–13
Bloomberg, Mike, personality
childhood and, 7, 12, 21
crudeness, 61, 70, 74, 79, 82, 109, 110–112
description, 1, 3, 5, 15, 17–18, 27, 68, 70–71, 220, 222
discipline/drive for success, 5–6, 16, 17–18, 219–221, 222–225
innovation, 49, 52, 123, 132, 159, 169, 206, 218, 221
Johns Hopkins and, 25–27
loyalty and, 49, 52, 66, 83, 84, 213
mayoralty and, 17, 128–129, 130, 175–176, 203–204
privacy, 2, 3, 17, 61, 68, 69–70
Bloomberg, Mike, social reinvention
description, 55–56, 59–70
parties, 61–63
philanthropy and, 59
seats on boards, 56, 60, 80
Bloomberg, Susan. *See* Brown, Susan Elizabeth Barbara
"Bloomberg, The" (terminal)
Bloomberg News, 48
e-mail system, 40
foreclosed properties, 52
functions of, 40–42, 44–46, 48, 52
leasing system, 45
Merrill Lynch and, 45–46, 193
Reuters competition with, 43–44
Vatican and, 49
See also Bloomberg L.P.
Bloomberg, William
buying Medford home, 9–10
career, 9, 10, 19–20
Charlotte Rubens and, 10
death, 18, 19–20, 26
on discrimination, 19
during World War II, 19
NAACP and, 19
parents of, 10, 15
personality, 9
relationship with son, 14–15
stillborn child of, 16–17
Bloomberg Family Foundation, 178
Bloomberg L.P./Innovative Market Systems
beginnings, 40, 42–43, 45–46
Bloomberg's wealth and, 49, 192, 193
bond market and, 42–43
business description, 39
Christmas parties, 61–62
class action suit against, 110, 167
company family picnics, 62
decorating scheme, 49–50
discounts and, 45, 49
employee theft from, 109–110
financial information systems before, 41
loyalty and, 49, 52
money to start, 38, 39, 42
offices, 42, 48–49, 50–51
philanthropy and, 84, 86–87
post-Bloomberg character of, 53–54

Bloomberg L.P./Innovative Market Systems (*continued*)
- pregnant employees and, 109, 110
- Salomon experience and, 41–42
- Salomon recruits and, 35, 42
- security/surveillance, 50, 51
- sexual harassment charges, 53, 82, 109–111, 131, 167
- subscribers, 40
- success of, 2, 39, 40, 41, 42–43, 45, 46, 48, 49, 54, 80, 222
- value of, 193
- working conditions, 48–53
- *See also* "Bloomberg, The" (terminal)

Bloomberg Markets (magazine), 46

Bloomberg News
- about, 87, 88
- beginnings, 46, 47–48
- credit lines, 48

Bloomberg on Bloomberg (memoir), 25, 37, 49, 56, 63, 73–74, 113, 194

Bloomberg Radio, 46, 51

Bloomberg School of Public Health, Johns Hopkins, 23, 195, 221

Bloomberg Television, 46, 51

Bloomberg Tower, 50–51

Bond market, 42–43

Boren, David, 170, 171

Boy Scouts/Eagle Scout, 7, 21–22, 220

Bradlee, Ben, 166

Brawley, Tawana, 101

Breaking News: How the Wheels Came Off Reuters (Mooney and Simpson), 43

Breakstone's (National Dairy), 10

Breslin, Jimmy, 2

Brigham's Ice Cream Parlor (Medford, MA), 9

Brock, Bill, 170

Brodsky, Richard, 161

Brody, William R., 107, 195

Brown, Donald W.J., 57

Brown, Susan Elizabeth Barbara
- after divorce, 58–59
- background, 57
- divorce, 58
- on ex-husband, 63–64
- parents, 57
- wedding/marriage to Bloomberg, 33, 37, 57–58

Bruni-Sarkozy, Carla, 65

Bruno, Joseph
- congestion pricing, 160
- Olympics, 143, 148
- state senate, 143

Bruno, Kenneth, 147

Buckley, Thomas, 10, 12

Buffet, Warren, 2

Burden, Amanda, 88

Bush administration, 215

Butts, Calvin, 86, 198

Call-311 system, 40, 133, 164, 206

Capehart, Jonathan, 88, 118, 119

Cardozo, Michael, 125–126, 131

Carnegie Corporation, 196–197, 198, 199

Carter, Dominic, 163

Carter, Jimmy, 166

Central Parks Conservancy board, 60

Charlie Rose Show, 59

Charlie Wilson's War (movie), 210

Cheesecakes, Junior's, 163, 170–171

Chicago Tribune, 130

City Hall description, 123
City University of New York's community colleges, 215
Clinton, Bill
 Bloomberg's views on, 71, 82
 Harlem and, 106
 Klein and, 211
 mayoral race (2001), 106, 117
 mayoral race (2005), 156
 as political celebrity, 3
 presidential campaign/election, 167
 Weinstein meeting, 106, 117
Clinton, Hillary, 111, 166
Collins, Gail, 98
Community Service Society, 197, 198
Comrie, Leroy, 138–139
Congestion pricing
 description, 159
 other cities and, 160
 politics and, 160, 161–162, 224
 Silver and, 160, 161–162
Connelly, Maureen, 88, 118
Corrado, Johnny, 13
Crack epidemic, 94
Crenson, Matthew, 26
Crime in New York City
 in 1970s/1980s, 93–94
 Bloomberg and, 4, 92, 107, 118, 123, 134, 157, 158, 189, 203
 Giuliani and, 78, 81, 82, 93, 94, 118, 123, 203, 224
Cross, Jay, 149
Cudahy, Kathleen, 92
Cunningham, William
 Bloomberg administration, 124, 139, 146, 151
 Bloomberg's 2001 campaign, 88, 108
 property tax rebate, 139
Daily News, 64, 88, 113, 116, 130, 180, 184, 185, 198
D'Amato, Alfonse, 83, 118
Danforth, John, 170
Davis, Susan Carley, 22, 23
De la Renta, Annette, 63
Democratic Leadership Council, 167
DeScherer, Richard, 67
Deutsche Bank building fire, 70, 213
Development
 Bloomberg and, 122–123, 206–209, 223, 224–225
 planners and, 4, 208–209, 224–225
Diallo, Amadou, 155–156
Diamond, Ruth Mofenson, 16
Dinkins, David
 mayoral terms and, 153
 mayoralty, 70, 78, 86, 94, 124
"Disgracegate," 175–176
Doctoroff, Daniel
 Bloomberg administration, 66, 125, 141–143, 145, 146, 149, 150, 151
 Bloomberg L.P., 47, 53, 66
 description/background, 142, 151
 economic revival, 125
 Olympics, 125, 141–143, 145, 146, 149, 150, 151
 PlaNYC 2030 program, 159
 relationship with Bloomberg, 66
Doe Fund, 187
Doherty, John, 125
Dolan family, 147
Dow Jones, 41, 46, 222
Drake, Jamie, 68
Dream jobs of Bloomberg, 4–5, 73, 79, 173, 220, 226
"Drive-by shooting" phrase, 93
Dykstra, Gretchen, 131

Eagle Scout/Boy Scouts, 7, 12, 21–22, 31, 121, 220
Earhart, Amelia, 8
Economic crisis (2008–2009), 183–184, 185, 188, 193, 203, 208
Economist, 66
Education/Bloomberg
- banning cell phones, 203–204
- charter schools, 132, 214
- critics, 213, 214, 215, 216–217, 218
- importance, 209–210, 217
- improvement, 4, 141, 203, 213, 214–217, 218, 224
- mayoral control, 122, 126–127, 144, 154, 161, 211, 224
- paying students, 132, 215
- "push-outs," 216
- racial gap, 216
- school boards and, 126–127
- standardized tests, 214, 215–216
- statistics on school system, 214
- teacher salaries, 214
- teachers' union, 76, 122, 134, 205, 206, 211, 212, 213, 214
- *See also* Klein, Joel

Edwards, John, 166
Eisen, Harvey, 57, 61
Elaine's, 61
Emery, Richard, 199
Exclusive clubs and Bloomberg, 67–68, 79, 97

Fannie Mae, 183
Farmer, Fannie, 8
Federal Equal Employment Opportunity Commission, 53
Federal Reserve, 42–43, 183
Fenster, Steven, 81
Ferdinand, Archduke Franz, 23
Ferer, Christy
- Bloomberg's political ambitions and, 83
- 9/11 families and, 128–129
- relationship with Bloomberg, 60, 83

Ferrer, Fernando
- Diallo case, 155–156
- education, 156–157
- Giuliani and, 99
- Mayor Bloomberg and, 134
- mayoral race (2001), 92, 95, 96, 98, 99, 101–102, 106, 115–116, 117, 155
- mayoral race (2005), 155–157
- Sharpton alliance, 101–102, 115–116

Ferry crash, Staten Island, 141
Financial Times, 41, 66, 81
Focus (movie), 80–81
FOIL (Freedom of Information Law), 204–205
Foley, Kevin, 45
Forbes Magazine, 36, 49, 80
Fordham Road, 96
Fortune Magazine, 48
Forward, 60, 88
Four Seasons peacemaking meeting, 106–107, 117
Freddie Mac, 183
Freedom of Information Law (FOIL), 204–205
Frieden, Thomas
- Bloomberg administration, 125, 127
- Obama administration, 125
- smoking ban, 127

Friedman, Jon, 51
From, Al, 167

Frost, Sir David, 63
Fry, Stephen, 63
Fuchs, Ester, 86, 88, 124
Fulani, Lenora, 114

Galotto, Jack, 20, 25, 26, 27
Gambling, John, 220–221
Garrison, Sekiko Sekai, 109, 111
Garth, David
  Bloomberg's 2001 campaign, 88–89, 117
  description/background, 88–89
Gates, Bill, 178, 191, 195
Gehry, Frank, 209
Gelinas, Nicole, 206
Giuliani, Rudy
  Bloomberg and, 115, 117, 118, 223
  Brooklyn Museum, 126
  crime rates, 78, 81, 82, 93, 94, 118, 123, 203, 224
  elections, 75, 78, 94
  garbage disposal, 133
  mayoral race (2001), 92, 99–101, 117, 118
  mayoralty, 69, 70, 74, 88, 94–95, 105, 123, 126, 128, 133, 204, 207, 211
  9/11 terrorist attacks, 78, 98–99, 100–101, 115, 117
  presidential run, 78
  race relations, 101, 134–135, 138, 156
  Sharpton and, 101, 134–135
  stadiums, 128, 207
  term extension, 99–101
  third term and, 179
Glou, Margie, 11–12
Goldman Sachs, 28, 44–45
Goldstein, Matthew, 215
Gotbaum, Betsy, 60
Gotham Gazette online newsletter, 204–205
Gracie Mansion (mayors' residence), 68, 199
Graham, Bob, 170
Grauer, Peter
  Bloomberg and, 66–67
  Bloomberg L.P., 53, 66–67
Great Depression, 76–77, 225
Green, Mark
  description/personality, 107
  Giuliani and, 99–100, 120
  mayoral race (2001), 92, 95, 97, 98, 99–100, 101–103, 105–106, 111, 114, 115–116, 117, 119, 120, 134, 155, 196
  Weinstein and, 105–107, 117
Green, Stephen, 99
Gridiron dinner, 61
Guardian, 82
Gun control, 4, 158–159, 169, 206
Gutfreund, John, 31, 32, 34, 36, 37
Gypsy moths, 8

Haberman, Clyde, 188
Hagel, Chuck, 170
Hanks, Tom, 210
Harlem Children's Zone, 187
Harris, Patti
  background, 84, 85
  Bloomberg's 2001 campaign, 84–85, 87, 89, 118
  Bloomberg's philanthropy, 84, 195, 197
  Bloomberg's presidential run, 167, 168, 170, 172
  as Mayor Bloomberg's advisor, 112, 123–124, 182, 185

Harris, Patti (*continued*)
relationship with Bloomberg, 66, 84–85, 88
third term plans, 182, 185
Hart, Gary, 170
Harvard Business School/Bloomberg
acceptance, 16
contributions to, 194
mother and, 16
views on, 27–28
Hass, Nancy, 60, 66
Hayek, Salma, 70
Hayt, Elizabeth, 65
Herbert, Bob, 2
Hevesi, Alan, 95
Hewitt, Don, 172
Hill, Janine, 33
Home Depot, 131
Horwitz, Gedale, 35, 38
Huckabee, Mike, 166
Hunt, Al, 46

Independence Party
Bloomberg contributions, 133, 200
mayoral race (2001), 114
mayoral race (2005), 158
Innovative Market Systems. *See* Bloomberg L.P./Innovative Market Systems
International Best Dressed List, *Vanity Fair*, 65

Jacob Javits Convention Center, 143, 150
Jennings, Jennifer, 216–217
Jennings, Peter, 1
Jerusalem Report, 87–88
Jets football team, 143, 149
"Jingle Bells" (song), 8–9
Johns Hopkins/Bloomberg
acceptance, 23
Bloomberg School of Public Health, 23, 195, 221
contributions to, 23–24, 80, 194, 195, 221
father's death and, 20, 26
fraternities, 25–27, 220
personality/activities at, 25–27
presidential position of, 178
Johnson, Magic, 157
Jokes (Bloomberg's) compendium, 110
Jones, David, 197–198
Junior's cheesecakes, 163, 170–171

Kaufman, Henry, 31, 37
Kelly, Mrs. (teacher), 21
Kelly, Raymond, 85, 124, 138
Kennedy, Edward (Ted)
mayoral race (2001), 106
presidential aspirations, 107
Klein, Joel
description/background, 127, 211
as education chancellor, 126–127, 212–216, 217
Knapp, Bill, 88, 172
Koch, Ed
Bloomberg and, 118, 135
mayoralty, 69, 70, 75, 77–78, 80, 84, 88, 89, 91, 123, 127, 177, 224
run for governor, 78
Kravis, Henry, 181

La Côte Basque, 56
Lack, Andrew, 47

LaGuardia, Fiorello
Great Depression and, 76–77, 225
as mayor, 76–77, 82, 177, 225
Office of Civilian Defense, 77
retirement, 77
Lalley, Mr. (teacher), 23
Langone, Ken, 131
Lattimore, Owen, 26–27
Lauder, Estée, 181
Lauder, Ronald
background, 75, 181
run for mayor, 75, 114
term limits and, 181–182, 184–185
Lehman Brothers, 183
Letterman, David, 99
Leventhal, Nathan, 81, 124, 126
Lewinsky, Monica, 71
Lewis, Michael, 30
Liar's Poker (Lewis), 30
Liberal Party, 158
Lieberman, Joseph, 169
Lincoln Center for the Performing Arts board, 60, 80
Lindsay, John V., 77, 82, 89
Lipper, Kenneth, 33, 80, 81
Lipton, Martin, 179, 181
Lo, Andrew, 42
Loeser, Stu, 170
London apartment, 68, 79
London Daily Mail, 58, 64
"Lucky sperm club," 60, 220
Ludsin, Steven, 52
Lynch, Patricia, 147, 160

Macchiarola, Frank, 85
MacMillan, Duncan, 42
Madison Square Garden, 147
Madonia, Peter, 132
MarketWatch, 51
Martha Graham Center of Contemporary Dance, 172
Mayoral control of education
Bloomberg, 122, 126–127, 144, 154, 161, 211, 224
in Boston/Chicago, 210–211
Mayoral race (2001)
Badillo, 92, 95, 98
Democrat divisions, 105–107, 115–116, 117
economic recovery and, 108
election day, 117–119
Ferrer, 92, 95, 96, 98, 99, 101–102, 106, 115–116, 117, 155
Giuliani's term extension request and, 99–101
Green, 92, 95, 97, 98, 99–100, 101–103, 105–106, 111, 114, 115–116, 117, 119, 120, 134, 155, 196
Hevesi, 95
9/11 terrorist attacks and, 91, 98, 99–101, 108, 110, 111, 114, 223
polls, 92, 107–108, 116, 117
results, 118–120
Vallone, 95
Weinstein, 105–107, 117
Mayoral race (2001) Bloomberg
ad campaign, 108, 115, 117–118
announcement of candidacy, 96
as candidate, 95, 96–97, 103
city problems and, 82
crudeness and, 109, 110–112
Democratic policies of, 116
Democrats and, 114, 116

Mayoral race (2001) Bloomberg (*continued*)
exclusive clubs and, 67–68, 97
financing, 2, 4, 74, 83–84, 97–98, 114–115, 117–118, 120, 196
focus group, 92
Giuliani's endorsement, 117, 118, 223
Giuliani's term extension request and, 99
GOP switch, 82–83, 164
Independence Party, 114
media and, 96, 112–113
9/11 aftermath and, 108, 223
philanthropy and, 84, 86–87
preparations, 81–82, 83–89, 92–93
reasons for running, 78–79, 80, 107
recognition and, 1, 2, 92
"robo-calls," 117–118
sexual discrimination charges (Bloomberg L.P.) and, 109–111
targeted mailings, 115
websites and, 98
Weinstein endorsement, 106
See also specific staff/advisors
Mayoral race (2005)
campaign spending, 157
conditions of city, 153–154
endorsements, 157
Ferrer, 155–157
polls, 155, 156
results, 158
Mayoral race (2005) Bloomberg
ads/negative research, 156–157
class-action suit (Bloomberg L.P.) and, 110
condition of city, 153–154, 157
financing, 157
Independence Party, 158
Liberal Party, 158
philanthropy and, 157
reelection mandate, 158
targeted mailings, 157
tax rebate and, 154
Mayoral race (2009)
Bloomberg's campaign/spending, 200–201
Bloomberg's opponents, 139, 200–201
Mayoralty of Bloomberg
absences, 69–70, 129
all-male off-the-record dinner, 111–112
approval ratings, 130, 141
bicycle for transportation, 135
call-311 system, 40, 133, 164, 206
commissioners, 124–125
congestion pricing, 159, 160, 161–162, 224
crime rates, 4, 92, 107, 118, 123, 134, 157, 158, 189, 203
development/rezoning, 122–123, 142, 143, 146, 149–151, 206–209, 223, 224–225
economy, 4, 140, 205
failures summary, 4, 224
garbage disposal, 128, 133
government turnover and, 213
Gracie Mansion and, 68, 199
"green" programs, 159
gun control, 4, 158–159, 169, 206
inauguration first term, 121–122
leadership vs. management, 134–135, 137, 139

micromanagement and, 131–132
national recognition and, 158, 161, 162, 168–169
New York City conditions and, 121, 205
patronage and, 132–134
pension system reform, 205–206
personality and, 17, 128–129, 130, 203–204
planners on development, 4, 208–209, 224–225
PlaNYC 2030 program, 159–160, 162
police tactics and, 4, 123, 138, 139
political independence and, 128, 131, 135
property taxes/rebates, 129–130, 139–140, 154, 223
public health, 4, 22, 65, 122, 127, 128, 141, 154, 203, 224
race relations, 4, 123, 133–135, 138–139, 203
reelection mandate, 158
salary, 68, 133, 199
smoking ban, 4, 22, 127, 128, 141, 154, 203, 224
social services, 128
stadiums for Yankees/Mets, 154, 207
successes summary, 3–4, 153–154, 203
summary, 221–226, 227
traffic control, 4, 128, 131
women's issues/rights, 112, 131
See also Education/Bloomberg; Olympics/New York City (2012)

Mayoralty of Bloomberg/third term plans
advisors objections to, 67, 177, 182, 185
announcement of, 186
Bloomberg's anger and, 175–176
Bloomberg's standards and, 176–177
city council and, 184–185, 187
Democratic opponents, 200–201
economic crisis (2008-2009) and, 183–184, 185, 188, 203
Lauder deal, 185
legislation on, 5
money and, 199–201, 202
objections to, 186, 187, 188–189
philanthropy and, 187, 225
polls, 183, 187–188, 189
public hearing on, 188–189
reasons for, 177, 178, 183–184
referendum timing and, 183, 187, 189
rollout of, 185–186
supporters of, 179, 180, 181, 183, 186–187, 225–226
See also Term limits

Mayoralty of New York City
city council and, 75
difficulties with, 74, 75–76
New Yorkers on, 74, 75
overview of mayors, 76–78
power of, 75
runs for governor/president and, 75, 77, 78
See also Mayoralty of Bloomberg; *specific mayors*

Mayors Against Illegal Guns, 169

McCain, John
  Bloomberg as running mate, 180
  presidential campaign, 84, 168, 172, 180
McCarthy, Joseph, 27
McFadden, Mary, 63
McGuire, Robert, 85
McLaughlin, George, 11
McNamara, Robert, 81
Medford, Massachusetts
  Bloomberg family, 7, 9–11
  description, 8
  history, 8–9
  Jews and, 10–12
Media and Bloomberg, 96, 112–113, 175–176, 204–205
Meehan, Michael "Mungo," 66, 67
Memoir (*Bloomberg on Bloomberg*), 25, 37, 49, 56, 63, 73–74, 113, 194
Merrill Lynch
  "Bloomberg, The" (terminal) and, 45–46, 193
  economic crisis (2008-2009) and, 183
Metropolitan Museum of Art/ Bloomberg
  board, 60, 80
  donations, 195
Meyer, Charles Henry, 57
Milbank, Dana, 165
Miller, Arthur, 80–81
Miranda, Luis, 156
Molinari, Guy, 84
Mooney, Brian, 43
Morgan Stanley, 28, 44–45
Morris, Annette E., 57
Moss, Mitchell, 88
Movies/Bloomberg
  financial backing of, 67, 80–81
  watching, 39, 81, 210
Moynihan, Daniel Patrick, 85, 88
Mucha, Zenia, 83–84
Mudd, Roger, 107
Murdoch, Rupert
  biography, 178
  Bloomberg as newspaper publisher and, 178
  Bloomberg as presidential running mate, 180
  Bloomberg's third term plans, 180, 181, 184, 185
  mayoral race (2001), 102, 116
Museum of the City of New York, 128

NAACP (National Association for the Advancement of Colored People)
  Mike Bloomberg and, 196
  William Bloomberg and, 19
National Dairy (Breakstone's), 10
National Rifle Association, 159
Netanyahu, Benjamin, 88
Nets arena, 209
New Deal, 77, 225
New York Magazine, 63, 110
New York Post, 41, 61, 69, 94, 102, 116, 127, 130, 132, 134, 180, 184, 185
New York Public Library board, 60
New York state legislature
  pace of, 160–161
  See also specific individuals
New York Times, 43, 48, 93, 97, 98, 116, 135, 172, 178, 180, 184, 185–186, 188, 226

New Yorker, 79, 204
Newsweek, 69, 164, 168
9/11 terrorist attacks
Bloomberg's philanthropy and, 196–197
description, 98
families and, 17, 128–129
Giuliani and, 78, 98–99, 100–101, 115, 117
ground zero site, 145–146
mayoral race (2001) and, 91, 98, 99–101, 108, 110, 111, 114, 223
No Child Left Behind law, 215
Norris, Floyd, 43, 48
Nunn, Sam, 170, 171

Oakes, Michael, 197
Obama, Barack/administration
Bloomberg and, 67, 180–181, 201–202, 226
Frieden, 125
as political celebrity, 3
presidential run/election, 67, 164, 166, 168, 171, 172, 173, 180–181, 201–202
roasting Bloomberg, 226
Obama, Michelle, 65
Offit, Morris, 31
Ohabei Shalom, 15
Oliver, Katherine, 112
Olmstead, 225
Olympics/New York City (2012)
Albany triumvirate and, 143, 145
Bloomberg's dream of, 137, 141, 142, 145, 147–148, 149, 150, 151
Bloomberg's reelection and, 151, 153, 154
Bruno and, 143, 148
defeat of, 4
as development catalyst, 142, 143, 146, 149–151
Doctoroff and, 125, 141–143, 145, 146, 149, 150, 151
Dolan family and, 147
Jets football team and, 143, 149
locations for, 142–143
NYC 2012 campaign, 125, 142
Pataki and, 143
public and, 141, 146–147, 151
Silver and, 143, 145, 146, 147–149, 151, 160
stadium defeat, 4, 148–149, 151
stadium plans, 143, 147
Westway underground highway and, 146
Outsell Inc., 41

Page, Mark, 124
Paper Bag Players, 197
Parsons, Richard, 181
Pataki, George
downtown rebuilding, 145
mayoral race and, 83, 84, 97, 118
stadium and, 143
Pearl Harbor attack, 23
Pearlstine, Norman, 47
Pelli, Cesar, 50
Pension system reform, 205–206
Pentagram, 51
Perot, H. Ross, 164, 165
Perry, Jay, 32, 33
Peyton-Jones, Julia, 63
Phi Kappa Psi fraternity, Johns Hopkins, 27
Phibro Corporation, 36, 37

Philanthropy of Bloomberg
amounts (2008), 194
anti-smoking (global) campaign, 195
Bloomberg L.P. and, 84, 86–87
childhood and, 9
description, 2, 5, 79–80, 192, 194–197
Harris and, 84, 195, 197
Johns Hopkins and, 23–24, 80, 194, 195, 221
knowledge of, 192–193
mayoral race (2001) and, 84, 86–87
mayoral race (2005) and, 157
mayoralty and, 196–200
memoir discussion, 194
plans after mayoralty, 177–178
public health, 194–195, 221
social reinvention and, 59
third term plans and, 187, 225
through Carnegie Corporation, 196–197, 198, 199
PlaNYC 2030 program, 159–160, 162
Polygraph test, 109
Posner, Rabbi David, 57
Presidential run/Bloomberg
bipartisan conference, 163, 169–172
end of, 4–5, 172–173
foreign policy and, 167–168
as independent, 164–165
mother on, 14
non-campaign of, 163–172
polls, 165, 199
religion and, 168
sexual discrimination lawsuits and, 167
Sheekey and, 163
spending, 165
"spoiler" position and, 166
travels and, 169
Unity '08 and, 166
Pressman, Gabe, 108
Primavera, 184
Public Art Fund, 187
Public Authorities Control Board, 143
Public health/Bloomberg
anti-smoking (global) campaign, 195
mayoralty, 4, 22, 65, 122, 127, 128, 141, 154, 203, 224
philanthropy and, 194–195, 221
smoking ban, 4, 22, 127, 128, 141, 154, 203, 224

Quatorze Bis, 65
Quinn, Christine, 185
Quinnipiac University polling, 155
Quotron/"B-page," 34–35, 42

Race relations
Bloomberg, 4, 123, 133–135, 138–139, 203
Giuliani, 101, 134, 138, 156
police tactics and, 4, 123, 138, 139, 155–156
Sharpton and, 119, 134–135, 138, 139
Rafshoon, Gerald, 166
Ramirez, Roberto, 106, 116, 119
Rangel, Charles, 85, 116
Rather, Dan, 1
Rattner, Steven, 67, 179, 181
Ravitch, Diane, 215
Reinking, Ann, 64
Remnick, David, 204
Republican National Convention
Bloomberg and, 154, 155
protestors/lawsuits, 154–155

Republican Party
Bloomberg contributions, 133, 200
See also specific individuals
Resolution Trust Corporation, 52
Reuters
financial information and, 41, 43–44, 47
Thomson Corporation merger, 54
Revere, Paul, 9
Ridgewood Senior Center, Queens, 96
Rivera, Dennis, 116, 134
Rockefeller, Nelson, 2, 114, 161, 197
Roosevelt, Franklin Delano, 23, 77
Rose, Charlie, 59
Rosen, Michael, 188
Rosenthal, Richard, 32–33, 37
Ross, Diana, 63
Rubens, Charlotte
childhood/parents, 10
education/career, 9, 10
William Bloomberg and, 10
See also Bloomberg, Charlotte
Rubenstein, Howard, 184, 185
Rudin, William, 179
Rudins, 202

Sacco, 23
Salk, Lee, 64
Salk, Mary Jane, 64
Salomon, Ferdinand, 30
Salomon, William R.
Bloomberg and, 29–30, 31
career of, 30
description/character of, 30
Salomon Brothers & Hutzler
description, 28–29, 30–31
history, 30
Phibro Corporation and, 36, 37
Salomon Brothers & Hutzler/Bloomberg
change and, 31, 35–36, 38
ethics and, 29, 37
interview, 29–30
leaving, 36–38, 220
money and, 32, 37–38, 39, 223
personal life, 56–57
personality and, 31, 32, 33, 36, 37
Tech Support/Quotron, 33–35, 42, 219, 223
views on, 28–29
work at, 31–36
Salt, 65
Schepps, Dorothy Rubin, 22
Schlein, Stanley, 118
Schlosser, Herbert/Judith, 172
Schoen, Douglas
Bloomberg's 2001 campaign, 88, 115, 117, 118
Bloomberg's presidential run, 164
Schrader, Richard, 100
Schwarzenegger, Arnold, 159
Scoppetta, Nicholas, 124–125, 132
Secunda, Thomas, 35, 42, 48
Serpentine Gallery, Kensington Gardens, 63
"Seven Deadly Sins" party, 63
Sexual discrimination charges
Bloomberg L.P., 53, 82, 109–111, 131, 167
Bloomberg's presidential run and, 167
Sharkey, Kathleen, 23
Sharpton, Reverend Al
anti-Semitism and, 101, 106

Sharpton, Reverend Al (*continued*)
  description, 76, 101
  Mayor Bloomberg and, 119, 134–135, 138, 139
  mayoral race (2001), 92, 101–102, 106, 115–116, 117, 119, 120
  Tawana Brawley case, 101
Shartle-Galotto, Mary Kay, 20, 26, 196
Shaw, Marc
  Bloomberg administration, 124, 126, 129, 139, 146
  property tax rebate, 139
Sheekey, Kevin
  Bloomberg administration, 124, 161, 180
  Bloomberg's 2001 campaign, 85, 89, 117, 118, 119
  Bloomberg's 2005 win, 158
  Bloomberg's presidential run, 163–164, 165, 166, 170, 172
  relationship with Bloomberg, 66, 173
  third term plans, 182, 185, 186, 200
Sheinkopf, Hank, 100
Siegel, Fred, 94–95
Sills, Beverly, 60
Silver, Sheldon
  Bloomberg relationship, 126, 144, 145, 146, 147–148
  congestion pricing, 160, 161–162
  Democrat Party importance, 144–145
  description/background, 144–145
  Giuliani and, 100–101
  Manhattan and, 145–146, 148–149, 161
  mayoral control of schools, 126, 144
  Olympics, 143, 145, 146, 147–149, 151, 160
  political power, 143–145, 161–162
  West Side development, 146–147
Simon, William, 30, 31
Simpson, Barry, 43
60 Minutes, 172
Skyler, Edward
  Bloomberg administration, 124, 127, 128
  Bloomberg's 2001 campaign, 88, 106
  Bloomberg's presidential run, 167, 168, 172, 186
  relationship with Bloomberg, 66
  third term plans, 182, 185, 186
Slavin, Neal, 81
Smile Train, 194
Smith, Liz, 96
Smoking
  anti-smoking (global) campaign, 195
  New York City ban, 4, 22, 127, 128, 141, 154, 203, 224
Snoddy, Raymond, 81
Soros, George, 191
Spago, 61
Speyer, Jerry, 179, 181
Spitzer, Eliot, 160
Spruill, Alberta, 138
St. Nicholas Neighborhood Preservation Corporation, 187
Stadlen, Michael, 12, 21
State Board of Regents, 216
Staten Island ferry crash, 141
Steinberg, Michael, 67
Steinhardt, Michael, 67, 167, 178
Steinhauer, Jennifer, 135

Stewart, Martha, 199
Stone, Sharon, 59, 109
Streisand, Barbra, 106
Studios Architecture, 51
Sullivan, Father Joseph, 209
Sulzberger Jr., Arthur, 180
Sunday Times, 63
Sunshine, Kenneth, 106
Swine flu epidemic, 221
Symposia Group, 165
Synagogue bombing plans, 222

Taylor, Diana
  background/description, 64–65
  as Bloomberg's companion, 58, 64, 70, 181, 226
Taylor, Douglas, 44
Teachers
  salaries, 214
  union of, 76, 122, 134, 205, 206, 211, 212, 213, 214
  See also Education/Bloomberg
Term limits
  Bloomberg's support of, 5, 179
  change complications, 181–183
  history on, 177, 182
  public endorsements, 177, 181
  See also Mayoralty of Bloomberg/third term plans
"Terminal Man," 54
Theroux, Paul, 8, 21–22
Third term. *See* Mayoralty of Bloomberg/third term plans; Term limits
Thompson, William, 201
Thomson Financial Corporation, 41, 44, 54
Thomson Reuters, 54
Times of London, 101
Times Square as urban park, 206
Tisch, Merryl, 216, 217
Tiven, Marjorie Bloomberg
  on brother, 14
  City Hall position, 133
  on Medford, 11
  on mother, 14
  See also Bloomberg, Marjorie
Traffic control
  Bloomberg mayoralty, 128, 131
  congestion pricing and, 159, 160, 161–162, 224
Treasury Department (U.S.), 183
Truman, Harry, 19
Trump, Donald, 61, 179, 193
Trump, Ivanka, 65
Tufts University, 8
Turner, Kathleen, 157
Tweed Courthouse, 128

Ullmann, Liv, 63
United Federation of Teachers, 205
Unity '08 reform group, 166
USA Today, 49, 54

Vail, Colorado home, 79
Vallone, Peter, 95
Vanity Fair, 65
Vanzetti, 23
Vaux, 225
Vietnam War, 28, 113–114
View, The, 59–60
Village Voice, 110–111, 188
Viteritti, Joseph, 217
Volcker, Paul, 42, 43

Wagner, Mayor, 177

Wal-Mart, 207
Walcott, Dennis, 125, 138
Walker, Jimmy "Beau James," 70
Wall Street Journal, 34, 36, 46, 47, 127, 185
Walters, Barbara
  Bloomberg and, 55, 59–60, 61, 172
  View, The, 59–60
Washington Post, 165
Wealth of Bloomberg
  "Everyman" and, 135, 193
  financing mayoral race (2001), 2, 4, 74, 83–84, 97–98, 114–115, 117–118, 120, 196
  financing mayoral race (2005), 157
  lifestyle and, 5, 79, 97, 192, 193, 219, 220
  mayoralty and, 196, 197–200, 202
  net worth, 178, 192, 193
  presidential run, 165
  recognition and, 191–192
  third term plans, 199–201, 202
  See also Bloomberg L.P.; Philanthropy of Bloomberg
Weiner, Anthony, 201
Weingarten, Randi, 76
Weinshall, Iris, 131
Weinstein, Harvey
  background, 105
  mayoral race (2001), 105–107, 117
Westway underground highway, 146
White, Maureen, 181
Whitman, Christine Todd, 170
Wilmot, Paul, 59
Winkler, Matthew, 34, 46, 47
Wintour, Anna, 65
Wolfensohn, James, 31
Wolff, Michael, 110, 178
Women's National Republican Club, 96–97
Worlock, David, 41
Wrightsman, Jayne, 63

Zegar, Chuck, 42
Zuckerman, Mort
  Bloomberg's third term plans, 180, 181, 184, 185
  mayoral race (2001), 116

© Fred R. Conrad

ABOUT THE AUTHOR

JOYCE PURNICK, a veteran New York reporter and editor, wrote the award-winning "Metro Matters" column at the *New York Times* for ten years. She joined the paper in 1979, after writing at the *New York Post* and *New York Magazine,* becoming the first woman to head the *Times*'s City Hall bureau and Metro department. She has, so far, covered six mayors of New York. Ms. Purnick, a Barnard College graduate, lives in Manhattan with her husband and is the admiring stepmother of three and grandmother of six.

PUBLICAFFAIRS is a publishing house founded in 1997. It is a tribute to the standards, values, and flair of three persons who have served as mentors to countless reporters, writers, editors, and book people of all kinds, including me.

I. F. STONE, proprietor of *I. F. Stone's Weekly,* combined a commitment to the First Amendment with entrepreneurial zeal and reporting skill and became one of the great independent journalists in American history. At the age of eighty, Izzy published *The Trial of Socrates,* which was a national bestseller. He wrote the book after he taught himself ancient Greek.

BENJAMIN C. BRADLEE was for nearly thirty years the charismatic editorial leader of *The Washington Post.* It was Ben who gave the *Post* the range and courage to pursue such historic issues as Watergate. He supported his reporters with a tenacity that made them fearless, and it is no accident that so many became authors of influential, best-selling books.

ROBERT L. BERNSTEIN, the chief executive of Random House for more than a quarter century, guided one of the nation's premier publishing houses. Bob was personally responsible for many books of political dissent and argument that challenged tyranny around the globe. He is also the founder and was the longtime chair of Human Rights Watch, one of the most respected human rights organizations in the world.

. . .

For fifty years, the banner of Public Affairs Press was carried by its owner, Morris B. Schnapper, who published Gandhi, Nasser, Toynbee, Truman, and about 1,500 other authors. In 1983 Schnapper was described by *The Washington Post* as "a redoubtable gadfly." His legacy will endure in the books to come.

Peter Osnos, *Founder and Editor-at-Large*